Jane's Story

Biography of
Heeni Te Kirikaramu / Pore (Jane Foley)
Woman of Profound Purpose

By
Alfred D. Foley

14 Vipond Road, Whangaparaoa,
Auckland 1463, NEW ZEALAND.
Phone: +64 9 424 8689.

ISBN 0-476-00522-1

Copyright © A.D.Foley 2003

Original Manuscript

All rights of copyright at law and in equity including legislation in New Zealand, Australia and all other jurisdictions of the world which recognise the law of copyright are reserved.

No part of this manuscript may be reproduced or transmitted in any form or by any means, electronic or mechanical, including photocopying, recording or storage in any information retrieval system or otherwise without the prior written permission of the author Alfred Denis Foley of 14 Vipond Road, Whangaparaoa, Auckland 1463, New Zealand.

Cover design by © Vadim Boussenko 2004-05-13
Printed and bound by Repro Graphics Limited
15 Auburn Street, Takapuna, Auckland.

*This book is respectfully dedicated
to the memory of Jane and her own special Aria*

The Tirairaka

Foreword

I was just eight years old when my grandmother, Jane Foley died in the Rotorua Hospital on 24th June 1933 at the age of 96 years. I can even remember them taking her away to the hospital some few days beforehand. I was one of a family of five, one big sister, one older brother and two younger, the family of Jane's eldest (Foley) son Jimmy and our mother Margaret (Maggie) whose maiden name was Clayton. There was our uncle Harry also and we all lived together in the house in Whaka Road.

Although our grandmother was confined to her bed during the years that I knew her, she still possessed most of her faculties especially her keen eyesight and hearing. I can remember her being interviewed by the historian James Cowan and other eminent visitors mostly from the Anglican Church, who would sit with her for hours. I also remember seeing her war-chest which she kept at the foot of her bed. It was a long black box lined with green felt and it contained her stripped down rifle, a box of bright copper percussion caps, a lead mould and some cartridges.

Her bedroom was the first on the left down the passage from the front door and one day when I heard voices coming from her room, I peeped in to see who Granny was talking to. There, hopping about on the rail at the end of the bed was a little fantail. "Oh its you Mar" I heard Granny say, then I watched as the bird flew up over her head and higher still until it disappeared through the opening above the window. That wasn't my only memory of strange happenings at Granny's house. Once I heard a loud knock coming from her bedroom and I heard her say "If you're a friend, knock again" and, sure enough, the knock did come again.

Perhaps all this was just a small boy's fantasy but, for my part, it has lived with me for all of my life and marvellously now seventy years later, I find myself writing her biography.

Parts of her story have been narrated before and most particularly her exploits during the Waikato Wars and her heroic act of bravery by insisting on remaining at the Gate Pa to fight alongside the men and also of her magnificent compassion in carrying water to the dying British officer in complete disregard of her own safety. This particular episode was also featured in the recent television documentary *"The New Zealand Wars"* by Professor James Belich of the University of Auckland and also by Greenstone Pictures in their *"Epitaph"* series. But there was much more to Jane than that which had never before been told. The greatest among them being her unwavering faith in Christianity and the doctrine of equality of the sexes and the ability of women to rise with men to meet any occasion. She always said that her proudest moment arrived when New Zealand became the first country in the world to have granted all adult women the right to vote knowing that she had been privileged to have played her part towards its achievement. Her story is chronologically correct and the events as recorded are as factual as she and other witnesses have been able to describe whether by written account or spoken word. An attempt has also been made to fathom her innermost reasoning. Where did she find the inspiration and the courage to do what she did and what divine influence guided her?

It was never my intention to remain strictly within the confines of historical documentation nor to create an altogether formal chronological record of her life, but rather I wished to unveil an intimate human interest story which would not only incorporate all of these things but also probe the depths of inherent ancestral influence, divine inspiration, human emotion, steadfast principle and unshakeable conviction, all of which virtues were present in abundance within this most remarkable woman, born of two vastly different civilisations and upholding the finest traditions of both.

It was Professor Belich who urged me as one of the few remaining descendants who could remember Jane, to write her full biography as he was first to acknowledge that there was much more to her story than just her involvement in the New Zealand wars particularly during her later life amongst the Irish settlers of KatiKati, also as an advocate and first grade interpreter in the Native Land Court and as a staunch feminist who broke through the restraints placed on women of both races.

If there was a message I would leave for those of the family to follow, it would be to all of her descendants that they should study Jane's genealogy (**whakapapa**) that is included here with her story as it springs from the two canoes of greatest ancestral connection. They should now make their own additions to follow on from whichever member of Jane's two families they succeed and let it serve as a permanent record of where they come from.

Lastly, to the female descendants among whom are my own three daughters and four grand-daughters. I would urge them to remember Jane's words as she rested under that certain *hinau* tree on **Mokoia** Island: *"As long as you, the **tirairaka** remain on this earth, our female line shall flourish"*.

A.D.Foley
April 2003.

14 Vipond Road, Whangaparaoa,
AUCKLAND 1463, New Zealand.

Jane Foley
Circa 1870 (33 years old and living at KatiKati).

Contents

Foreword i
Contents v
The Canoe Genealogy xi
Maps Map of the Waikato War Zone xii
        Plan of Attack on the Gate Pa (29th April 1864) 100
        Operations at Matata and TeTeko (1865) 171
Plates Jane Foley circa 1870 .... iv and 195
        Heeni Te Kirikaramu (Jane Foley) circa 1900 x
Bibliography, Acknowledgements and Literature Cited x

Chapter .... **Page**

1   Jane 1
    Flashback into the past

2   Birth of Maraea 6
    The birth of the baby Maraea on Mokoia Island in 1820

3   Impending peril for Te Arawa 12
    The threat of retribution from Ngapuhi

4   Battle lines are drawn 16
    Te Arawa prepares for war against Hongi Hika and his Ngapuhi

5   The battle of Mokoia 23
    Defeat of Te Arawa and the abduction of Maraea to Tai Tokarau

6   A flower grows in Tai Tokarau 31
    Maraea is nurtured as a Puhi Maiden

7   Betrayal of the innocent 36
    Maraea is traded by Hongi Hika for guns

8   To an image born 42
    Birth of Jane and the Treaty of Waitangi

v

Chapter		Page
9	Tale of family, flag-staffs and fear	46
	The family finds a mentor and Hone Heke cuts down a flag-staff	
10	A forced evacuation	52
	The sacking of Kororareka and a flight to safety	
11	Return to Te Arawa	58
	The family is reclaimed by Te Arawa and taken home	
12	Journey through to adulthood	65
	Jane returns to Auckland, grows up, meets and marries, then divorces	
13	War comes to the Waikato	71
	Jane decides to take up the cause of the Maori King	
14	A family at war	76
	Jane, her mother and her four children go to war with Wi Koka and his Koheriki	
15	Flight into the hinterland	83
	The Koheriki narrowly escape capture in the Hunua Ranges	
16	The great escape	89
	Wi Koka leads the fugitives through enemy lines and out to safety	
17	A parting of the ways	94
	Jane sends Maraea and the children to Te Arawa while she and Neri stay to fight on	
18	A woman of passion	101
	Koheriki joins Ngai-te-Rangi to defend Gate Pa and Jane insists on staying to fight	
19	A woman of compassion	109
	The battle of Gate Pa and Jane's heroic act of clemency towards the fallen enemy	

Chapter		Page
20	A last call to arms	117
	Ngai-te-Rangi's last stand at Te Ranga and the devastating costs of war	
21	Champions for the return home	124
	Ngai-te-Rangi sues for peace, Koheriki goes home, Jane and Neri return to Te Arawa	
22	Wars end and losers weep	130
	The victors divide the spoils of war but flames of new resentment flare in Taranaki	
23	Seeds of an ill-conceived insurgence	137
	The rise of Pai-marire in Taranaki and its spread to the Bay of Plenty	
24	A battle of minds and divine intervention	147
	Jane matches her faith in Christianity against the evils of Hauhauism	
25	A new war, a new cause	156
	The capture of Hori Tupaea by Jane and the Uenukukopako at Rotoiti	
26	Hauhau venom broaches the surface	162
	The murder of the Reverend Carl Volkner and James Fulloon in the Bay of Plenty	
27	End of an era for Jane	172
	Te Arawa goes to war against the Hauhau and Jane fights her last battle	
28	A momentous change of direction	181
	Jane meets Denis Foley and travels to Auckland to visit her ailing father	
29	A new door opens	189
	First the courtship and marriage to Denis, then the move to KatiKati to live	

Chapter	Page
30	Shamrock amongst the fern 196

George Vesey Stewart's Ulster settlers arrive in KatiKati and become new neighbours for Denis and Jane

31	Of good times and bad 205

More settlers pour in, the district prospers but then depression strikes New Zealand

32	Another time, another crisis 213

Denis succumbs to an Irish over-indulgence and Jane nearly loses her life

33	A spiritual healing process 221

Jane starts Denis on the road to recovery and they visit the Pink and White Terraces

34	Eruption 230

The devastating Tarawera Eruption and how Jane survives it on Mokoia

35	Aftermath and after-thoughts 239

Rescue parties break through to Te Wairoa and Jimmy Foley takes a hand

36	A family re-established 248

The district returns to normality and Jane finds a new interest

37	Death and the dream sequence 257

The death of Maraea and Jane follows her on her journey to the spirit world

38	Tangi 263

Mourners from all Te Arawa and beyond come to pay their respects to Maraea

Chapter		Page
39	Death and a defining moment	273

Denis drowns in the Uretara River and a distraught Jane decides to leave KatiKati forever

| 40 | The house in Whaka Road | 280 |

Jane and Margaretha-May go to live in Rotorua but tragedy strikes again

| 41 | March of time, grief and war | 287 |

The region develops, another untimely death and the family again goes to war

| 42 | Mokoia heritage | 296 |

Jane recounts the history of Mokoia and works to establish hereditary ownership

| 43 | Journey's end | 306 |

The colours of her rainbow grow pale as Jane turns towards Te Rerenga Wairua

Bibliography, Acknowledgements and Literature Cited

Buck Sir Peter:	*The Coming of the Maori*
(Early Maori ritual and mythology)

Cowan James:	*The New Zealand Wars Vols. 1 and 2*
(Oficial records of Hone Heke's war 1845-46,
the Northern Waikato war 1863-1864,
the campaign against Te Kooti 1868-72)

Gray Arthur J, MA.	*An Ulster Plantation*
(The KatiKati settlement)

Orange Claudia:	*The Story of a Treaty*
(Kawanatanga and Rangatiratanga)

Stafford D.M.	*The Founding Years of Rotorua*
The New Century in Rotorua
(Early Te Arawa history, The Tarawera
eruption and other local events)

Miscellaneous Data:	(Foley family papers including Native Land
Court Minutes and some of Jane's own
writings)

Heeni Te Kirikaramu (Jane Foley)

*Circa 1900 at age 63 years
Reunited with her flag after it was captured by a British patrol in the Hunua
Ranges in 1863.*

The Canoe Genealogy

Te Arawa

Mataatua

Te Arawa		Mataatua	Year
Tamatekapua — Hei — Tia — Ngatoroirangi		Toroa	1300
Kahumatamomoe	Tuhotoariki	Wairaka	
Tawakemoetahanga	Rangitauira	Tamateakitehuatahi	1350
	Tukahua		1400
Rangitihi	Tumaihi	Uaimua — Uenuku rau	1450
Tuhourangi	Tumakoha		
Uenukukopako	Tarawhai	Kato o Tawhaki — Rangiteaorere	1500
Whakaue	Ahiahiotahu	Rutunga — Kaiure 1	1550
Tutanekai	Tutahingakiao		
Whatumairangi	Rangimamao	Te Ungakiuta — Te Atuaotepo	1600
Ariariterangi	Tawari — Uruwaea	Tumanawa pohatu — Te Auhuakira	
Kainuku = Waihirere	Marua — Korokaihau	1650
Te Tawha	Ngariritaua		
Whakatauihu	Nukuroa = Hinera	Whakawai	1700
Ngorengore	Whakanana	Te Umu	
Kirinui	Te Koriwai = Horo	Whakamarurangi	1750
Te Ngahoa — Rangitauninihi		TeAwekotuku	1800
Kelly = Maraea			
(Taane Tuarua)	(Taane Tuatahi)		
Foley = Jane = — TeKirikaramu			1850
James John Sophia Henry	Sophia Rangiteaorere Atutahi		
Isobella Margaretha	Rangitauninihi TeNgahoa		1900
			1950

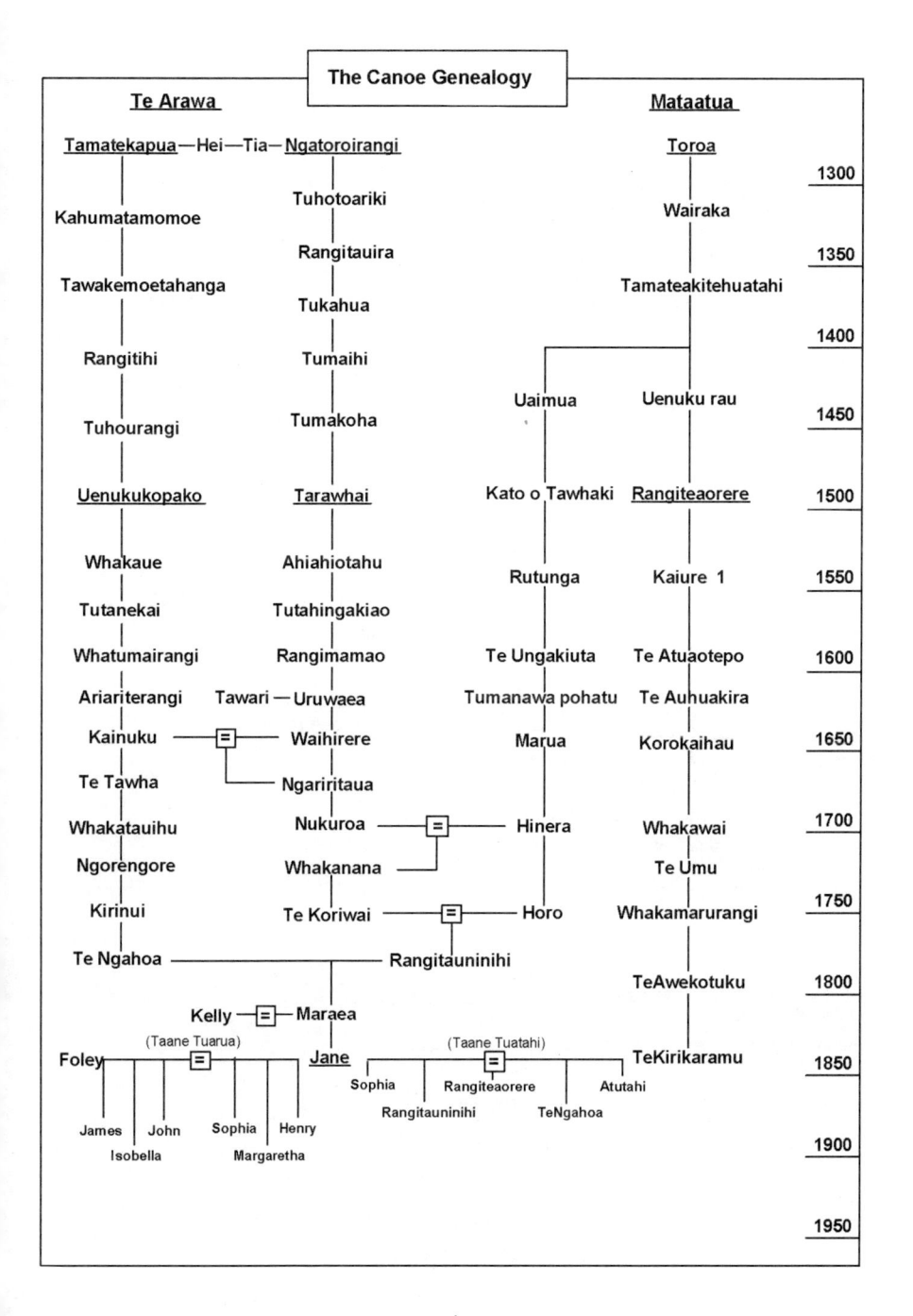

xi

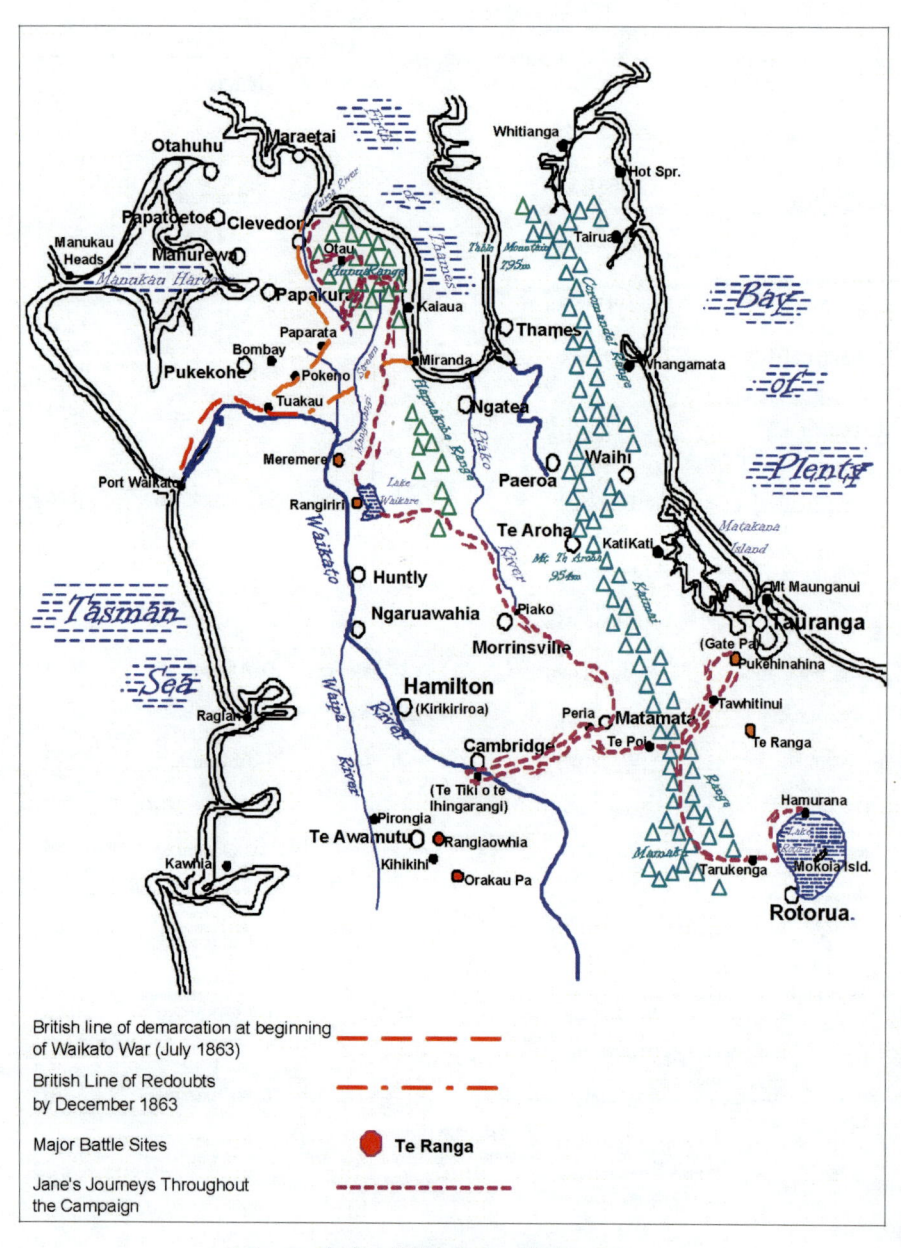

Map of the Waikato War Zone
(1863–1864)

Jane's Story Chapter 1

Jane

The horses had slowed to a walk, their puffs of breath like spurts of steam blowing brightly in the crisp early morning air.

The hill stretched long and high above them and away at the top there was sunlight flooding across the road bright and sparkling with the promise of another warm and fresh new day.

But to Jane sitting huddled under the heavy traveling rug, her frail body snuggled closely up against her son Jimmy for extra warmth, there were nothing but shadows thrown by the line of tall fir trees growing along the roadside, blocking out the sunlight and plunging everything into bleak and melancholy gloom.

Frost crystals glittering white, reaching far up into the branches of the trees to hang there in delicate flight and, down on the roadsides the hoar frost encrusting the light pumice soil, a myriad glassy needles cascading down the embankment now held in motionless suspension, a sculptured diorama of ice.

Small puddles long since frozen over and an icy mat spreading all across the road to be crunched under the hooves of the horses and carried around on the wheels of the buggy as they draw slowly up the steep incline.

And out to the left where there are no tall trees, only gently rolling slopes running all the way down to the lake, the sun has already spread its bright and warming rays to dispel the cold that had come with the night and arouse the host of living things that dwelt in this small corner of the world.

But how long, Jane wondered, must we wait before we too might emerge from the shadows and savour again the joyousness that only a warm and sunny day could bring?

Jimmy sat tall and assertive in the driving seat of the buggy. He was fully aware of the discomfort his old mother was suffering as she sat next to him clasping the rug closely around her and burying her head against his side. It was quite a nippy morning to be sure and in the shadow of these trees, where the frost had not even begun to melt, the very air itself seemed laden with ice.

However, the road to the top of the hill before them was long and steep and the horses could not be pushed any harder for they would still have to face a long day ahead if they were to complete the journey before nightfall.

In polite society, a smartly turned out four wheeled buggy, drawn by a pair of high stepping horses was always a delight to behold, something broadly accepted as the elite of private transport of the time.

But here in this isolated setting, where land settlement remained very much in its infancy and good all-weather roads were few and far between, perhaps a more practical vehicle would have been a block dray or even a bullock wagon. The horses however were willing enough and though being of light utility stock, were coping well with the heavy going and the unfamiliar conditions.

Beautiful animals both. "Black Bess" on the left and "Jack Johnston" on the right, glossy black all over save for a slender white blaze on the forehead of each. Black Bess ("Bessy") was Jimmy's favourite as she would not only go into harness as a draught animal in any position, but would also serve as an excellent saddle horse when required. Jack Johnston ("Jack") was named after a world champion

American Negro boxer of that name who visited Australasia and, it was rumoured, even paid a quick visit to Rotorua at about the same time that "Jack" was born.

"Hup Bessy", "Hup Jack" called Jimmy to his charges and so the long climb up through the frigid shadows dragged slowly onwards. Her hat pulled hard down almost over her eyes, Jane ventured to peer wistfully out to the sunny side of the road that overlooked the lake. Her fingers and toes were still freezing but it helped just to look to where the sun was shining even though she knew that it would always remain beyond her reach until such time as the trees and their shadows would at last be left behind.

Through half bemused eyes, she noticed that part way down the slope there was a row of tall wooden poles, three in particular standing out as they appeared to be the tallest. Of course, she surmised, they would be part of the power line that carried the electricity from the new power station at Okere Falls to the township of Rotorua.

It must have been upon one of those taller poles that, as reported in the *Rotorua Morning Post*, a small Maori boy was electrocuted when he climbed up to see if he could get a view of his father who had been taken away to hospital in Rotorua. It was true that from such vantage point the whole of the Rotorua township including Pukeroa Hill where the hospital was situated, could be seen clearly across on the other side of the lake. How would a small boy know that to touch the wires on any power line would be fatal? "That's true Mama" Jimmy offered, "a live wire would look just the same as a dead one". Jane shuddered at the thought.

Her mind still dwelling on that tragic event, Jane gazed pensively out over the lake, and it was only then that she came to realise that she too had cause to ponder and reflect deeply upon the tableau that now rolled out below her. The scatter of small villages and settlements strewn along its shores, the smoke from their morning fires drifting hazily above, and there in the distance the township of Rotorua with its broad cluster of buildings arrayed along the waterfront and the reflection from their many windows glinting in the sunlight. Plumes of billowing steam from Whakarewarewa on the one side and Ohinemutu on the other providing not only a fitting backdrop to complete an idylic setting but also to serve as a reminder that this was the centre of a very active thermal region.

So much to witness the ongoing stirring of pastoral and urban life that busied itself in the demands of a new day dawned, but all the while Jane was conscious of a foreboding presence that drew her eyes ever outwards towards the centre of the lake. For out there loomed the imperious figure of Mokoia Island rising up out of the water like the reaching prow of some monstrous phantom canoe (***waka atua***) and assuming the personification of a guardian (***kai tiaki***) to watch over all who would come within his domain. His flanks draped in a mantle of primordial forest, his head bedorned with the "***Hutu Totara***" head dress of the legendary ***Hatupatu***, ever vigilant and protective of the ancient treasures (***taonga***) of Te Arawa entrusted to his keeping by generations of the past.

For it was there, concealed somewhere on his slopes, that the giant chief ***Tuhourangi*** lay buried as were the remains of other Arawa chiefs some of whom had lived out their lives in peace and others, like her own grandfather ***Te Ngahoa***, had fallen in battle. The imposing presence of Mokoia standing in mute abeyance to the demands of his calling brought back to Jane her own precious memories of her beloved mother Maraea who had herself in death been committed to the care and safe keeping of this eternal ***kai tiaki***.

Mere mortal custody of the island was however entrusted to the four subtribes of Te Arawa whose generations had occupied and tended the cultivations (***maara***) from time immemorial. These were ***Ngati***

Rangiteaorere and *Ngati Uenukukopako* in the North and East, *Ngati Whakaue* in the South and *Ngati Rangiwewehi* in the West. Jane herself, through her mother Maraea, could claim descent from all four of those ancestors.

In deep reflection Jane allowed her mind to travel back through time to that dreadful day when, dressed all in black as was the custom, she accompanied the funeral cortege to the graveside in the burial ground (*urupa*) known as *Tokanui* and watched as her mother was lowered to rest amidst her relatives (*whanaunga*) who had gone before her. For Maraea this was where life began and, as destined by her guiding force (*Atua*), this was where in this world it would end. Again Jane felt that surge of overwhelming grief that had brought her to her knees beside the open grave to offer up her lament of yearning (*tangi aro*) for her beautiful mother who had nurtured and defended her through her tender years and remained faithfully by her side throughout that epic period of hardship, sacrifice and battle that was to follow until at last together they came home to the sanctuary of their own people of the land (*tangata whenua*).

At last they had reached the top of the hill and Jimmy had reined in his charges to rest awhile before pressing on with the journey. "Here we are Mama, you can come out from under that blanket now. The sun is shining brightly, the birds are singing in the trees and all the world is fain to play. It will be mostly all down hill from now on and we should reach the coast well before this day is ended". But even though Jane was relieved that they had at last drawn free of the shadows and she had begun to feel the warmth of the sun again, her mind remained transfixed in Mokoia and the events that had taken place those many years ago. It was as if some benign spiritual power was calling her to linger awhile amongst her ancestors (*Tipuna*) in due deference to their authority (*mana*) before she might return to the real world where her own life story was about to unfold.

Jane's Story Chapter 2

Birth of Maraea.

In accordance with olden day Maori cultural tradition, when the wife of one of chiefly rank (*tino rangitira*) or of the priesthood (*tohunga*), was about to deliver a child, certain intrinsic preparations had to be made in strict observance of the spiritual reverence (*tapu*) that attached to such hallowed event.

A maternity house (*whare kohanga*) was to be built in some secluded spot away from the village and its floor spread with the finest of mats especially made for the occasion. A suite of female attendants (*tapuhi*), normally headed by an experienced relative, was to be appointed to wait on the mother-to-be within the whare kohanga whilst other servants would be delegated the duties of preparing and delivering food and water to the door as and when called upon. Entrance to the whare kohanga itself however would remain forbidden (*tapu)* to all but the expectant mother and her chosen tapuhi only. The tribal priest (*tohunga)* would be called upon to pay appropriate homage to the goddess of child birth (*Hine te iwaiwa*) and pray that a normal delivery be made without complication.

Such was the case when *Rangitauninihi*, wife of the young fighting chief *Te Ngahoa* of Ngati Rangiteaorere announced that her own time was drawing near and, on the island of Mokoia in the centre of lake Rotorua, the village of *Hauanu* became alive with activity as the news of the imminent blessed event was announced.

The whare kohanga had been built on the fringe of the heavy bush where the ground began to rise steeply above the more gentle slopes occupied by the village and the cultivations running up from the edge of the lake on the Eastern side of the island. With the tapuhi now assembled and the other servants alerted, Rangitauninihi was escorted to the whare kohanga there to begin her labour. In strict observance with tapu, her husband Te Ngahoa was permitted only to accompany her as far as the entrance where he would yield all authority to the senior tapuhi and thence depart to await the outcome.

At the commencement of labour, the young expectant mother was induced to assume a squatting position in the centre of the room and support herself by holding on to hand posts erected for that purpose. The senior tapuhi then assisted from behind by passing her arms around the abdomen and applying gentle rhythmic downward pressure to aid expulsion.

The cutting of the umbilical cord (*iho*) at completion of the delivery, was entrusted to the senior tapuhi who gently massaged the attached end towards the abdomen where it was tied securely with fine flaxen fibre. The cord was then cut to a length as measured from the tip of the thumb (*konui*) to the nearest joint after which the cut end was smeared with oil from the seeds of the N.Z. Ash tree (*titoki*) and wrapped in a dressing of the inner bark of the lacewood (*houhere*).

The afterbirth (*whenua*) was placed in a small flax basket, taken up into the bush and buried in a secluded place where it could not be disturbed or walked over.

Tradition would demand however that the dried cord (*iho*), after it was separated from the navel (*pito*), would be ceremoniously placed in the cleft of, or buried at the foot of, a selected tree (often a *hinau*) which would thereafter be referred to as "The cord of- (*Te-Iho-o* —)the name of the new born child.

After giving birth to her first-born child, Rangitauninihi was ceremoniously escorted down to the sacred pool at the lake's edge named Waikimihia (the historical pool where Hinemoa rested after her epic swim to the arms of her lover Tutanekai four generations beforehand). There she bathed in the warm and soothing waters to be cleansed not only physically but also spiritually for she as yet remained under tapu and it was only after that ritual was consummated that she could become reunited with her husband Te Ngahoa and be made ready to receive a ceremonial visit from other members of her extended family (*whanau*) and well wishers who had gathered to welcome the new addition to the tribe

The ceremony of welcome, known as *koroingo*, was particularly observed on the birth of a first-born child and announced with the sounding of the shell trumpet (*putatara*). The young mother with her child in her arms would sit in the doorway of the whare kohanga as the relatives of both mother and father placed gifts in the open space before her. Elders (*kaumatua*) from either side would each address speeches of welcome to the family of the other and then directly to the child itself.

Ancient chants and songs (*waiata*) recounting the mythological creation of mankind, the development of the child within the womb and the final emergence into the world of the living would be interspersed as appropriate amongst the speeches until at length the formal visit to welcome and honour the new arrival was brought to an end.

Soon after the ceremonial visit, the mother would prepare to return to the village and resume her normal duties and immediately she and the baby had vacated the whare kohanga, that structure together with all materials and contents associated with it, because they remained tapu, had to be destroyed by burning to prevent them from becoming a source of danger to others. The village priest (*tohunga*) would later be called upon to conduct a tapu-lifting ceremony over the site itself so that it might also be rendered free of any lingering clandestine danger.

By natural progression, the next important event in the development of the child was the baptismal (*tohi*) rite when members of the extended family (*whanau*) accompanied the parents and their newborn to a special stream (or pool) where the officiating priest (*tohunga*) would sprinkle the child with water from a sprig of the *karamu* shrub dipped in the stream. Ritual incantations would then be recited to invoke the many qualities of skill in the domestic crafts (if the child is female) and, by prior arrangement with the parents, the child would be dedicated to a particular god (usually Rongo the god of peace and agriculture).

At the completion of the tohi ceremony for little Maraea however, the procession made its way slowly back to the village and on the way they paused to rest beneath a certain hinau tree and as Rangitauninihi stood in its welcome shade and gently rocked her baby in her arms, there appeared a little female fantail (*tirairaka*). At first the little bird darted to and fro above the heads of the small assembly and then suddenly, perhaps impetuously, she flew down to alight upon the head shawl (*kahu kohanga*) of the baby where for a few brief moments she held still to twitter a happy song before returning to the branches overhead where she continued to flit from limb to limb as all fantails are wont to do.

To those who observed this delightful little interlude, it was recognised as a good omen and the tohunga at once acclaimed the visitation and called upon the assembly to witness the messenger in the form of the tirairaka who was sent by the Te Arawa tribal goddess and guardian of all birds and forest creatures (**Kura Ngaituku**) to whom the baby would now be dedicated and whose spiritual symbol (*aria*) should henceforth and forever remain for her and all of her female descendants, the tirairaka.

Following the babtism (*tohi*) rite where the child was rendered tapu by the sprinkling of water, came the return to normal (*pure*) ceremony which was usually conducted at the parents' dwelling house where the family wealth, comprising the finest mats and cloaks upon which were placed highly prized articles (*taonga*) of greenstone (*pounamu*) and whalebone (*paraoa*) ranging from war clubs to hair, ear and breast ornaments, would be spread out in the front porch. The people would gather to greet the returning tohi procession with ceremonial weeping and the priest would recite ritual chants invoking the gods to inculcate the child with the foundation of knowledge and skills to accompany her in her journey through life.

The gathering would then move closer to the porch to greet the child with more weeping of welcome and when the speeches were ended, a feast would be held on the open courtyard (*marae*) and thus the child would be formally received into the society of her family and her tribe.

And so, according to the Christian almanac, it was in the year 1820 that the baby Maraea (full name Maraea Taunakiwehe) was born to Rangitauninihi and Te Ngahoa on the island of Mokoia in Lake Rotorua. That memorable occasion was to mark the convergence of two absolute blood-lines that had continued unbroken for an assumed 18 generations, the one stemming from *Ngatoroirangi* the omnipotent high priest who accompanied *Tamatekapua* and the Te Arawa canoe from Hawaiki, through Ngati Uenukukopako to Rangitauninihi, and the other from *Toroa* the captain of the Mataatua canoe through Ngati Rangiteaorere to Te Ngahoa.

It will be acknowledged however that at that time, the inhabitants of the greater Rotorua region had not yet encountered the white man or his culture and continued to live under the traditional authority of a feudal fiefdom controlled by the ruling aristocracy (**Rangatiratanga**) and the priesthood (*Tohunga ahurewa*), a system that had prevailed without challenge from the time of the third migration from Hawaiki at the beginning of the fourteenth century AD. The ceremonial customs and procedures as described in the foregoing account of the birth of Maraea are therefore authentic and remain truly representative of that particular era.

Jane's Story Chapter 3

Impending Peril for Te Arawa

Village life on the island continued to thrive in peace and harmony just as it had done since the arrival of the Te Arawa settlers those many hundreds of years ago. Cultivations of kumara, taro and gourd (*hue*) required constant attention, the preparation and preservation of food supplies including birds and seafood and the general upkeep of the dwelling houses (*whare kainga*) kept the elderly, and the female inhabitants in particular, fully occupied whilst the younger males were encouraged to indulge in the more adventurous pursuits such as battle training, canoe (*waka*) skills, hunting and fishing.

Firstly as a babe wrapped snuggly in a shoulder rug (*pikau*) and later as a toddler holding the hand of her mother, little Maraea was to accompany the field party sometimes down to the lake to take the small freshwater crayfish (*koura*) and more often to the cultivations to tend the crops. But now she is nearly four years old and quite able to run on ahead with the other children and even stop and explore mysterious places on the way.

One such mysterious place was the tiny house with the carved posts and pointed roof that sat on the edge of the kumara plantations and housed a strange stone image in the shape of a squatting man who looked angry and forbidding especially to little children. This was of course the ancient kumara god **Rakeiora** who was brought to Mokoia from Taranaki and renamed **Matua-o-tonga** and was there not to frighten little children but rather to preside over all of the Mokoia cultivations to perpetuate fertility and protect against plague and pestilence that might be visited upon them by some evilly disposed outside force.

It was late in the evening when their war canoe (*Waka taua*) glided silently up to the mooring place marked by the totara tree named *Atuahu* below the village and Te Ngahoa and his war party came ashore to rejoin their families after an absence of several days. Quietly they had arrived and quietly they had been received by their loved ones as a sense of grim foreboding had accompanied their return. Te Ngahoa drew his wife and child towards him and after a prolonged silence in which he had gazed upon them in deep meditation, he decided that he would reveal the cause of his profound consternation.

Their recent excursion to the mainland had taken them on a fraternal visit to *Tuhourangi*, the subtribe that occupied the *Tarawera - Rerewhakaitu* region to the South and East of Rotorua. There they were summoned before the tribal chiefs who had called together the fighting columns (*taua*) from throughout the region for a council of war (*runanga pakanga*). The chief *Te Horo* was first to address the assembled war parties and began by recounting a recent incident of disquieting significance that had taken place at the Green Lake (*Rotokakahi*).

The people living on the fortified island of *Motutawa* in Lake Rotokakahi were aroused one morning by a clarion call (*karanga*) emanating from a party of strangers that had assembled on the far shores of the lake. A request was made for canoes to be sent across to collect them as they wished to visit and pay homage to the Tuhourangi people. However, the inhabitants of the island became apprehensive and alarmed at the presence of so many armed warriors amongst those who would visit them and, on closer observation they were recognised as the vanguard of a *Ngapuhi* war party returning from a raid on tribes of the lower North Island and that their leader was none other than *Te Pai-o-terangi*, the nephew of the firebrand Ngapuhi chief *Hongi Hika*.

Being fully aware of the treacherous nature of the Ngapuhi as experienced by many unsuspecting tribes in the past, Te Horo who at the time was in command of the island fortification, had then to decide whether to accept the offer of peace (*rongo*) as extended and despatch the canoes to collect the visitors, or to refuse the offer and thus deliver an insult which could have future grave repercussions. With some trepidation therefore, he made a decision to send only one canoe to bring not more than ten passengers to the island at a time and, upon the arrival of the first party, his worst misgivings were confirmed when ten heavily armed warriors were seen to alight and that their leader Te Pai-o-terangi was not among them.

Not to arouse suspicion however, the traditional ceremony of welcome (*mihi*) was performed by the host party and suitably acknowledged by the guests (*manuhiri*) who were then invited to pass through the palisades and advance onto the inner courtyard (*marae*). But just as the visitors became lost to view from their compatriots on the far shore, Te Horo signaled to his own warriors to swiftly disarm their unsuspecting quarry and confine them to the prison compound.

The ruse was repeated four more times without being discovered until a total of fifty Ngapuhi had been disarmed and rendered harmless but it was just as the last group was being taken to the enclosure that one man broke away and fled down to the lake and into the water where he struck out for the distant shore. At once the canoe was sent after him but by then he had reached the middle of the lake and although he was overtaken and quickly despatched, he had managed to alert the main Ngapuhi party and warn them of the subterfuge.

A tumultuous uproar surged across the lake from the remnants of the Ngapuhi assembled on the shore as they became aware of the deception that had taken them so completely by surprise. Their enraged leader Te Pai-o-terangi called across to Te Horo and charged that he would return with an army and avenge the insult that

Tuhourangi had dared to flaunt before the might of Ngapuhi and that recompense (*utu*) would be exacted with the shedding of much blood.

Te Horo in reply called upon his adversary to withdraw from the whole of the Te Arawa territory through which safe passage would now be granted. "And as for your threat to return with your armies, **E kore te kokopu e hoki ano ki tona puehu** (A kokopu would not go back to the mud it has just stirred up)."

So the depleted war party of Ngapuhi returned to the North and the people of Tuhourangi resumed their everyday activities and as the time elapsed, memories of the incident began to fade.

It was with grave concern however, that word had reached Te Arawa that Ngapuhi, under Hongi Hika, was now on the rampage and moving South. Already some of the coastal tribes had been attacked and plundered leaving death and destruction in the wake. A personal challenge was relayed from Te Pai-o-terangi to Te Arawa that the time had now come for utu to be exacted in revenge for the insult inflicted on him and his party by Tuhourangi at Rotokakahi. "For soon the many waters of Te Arawa will run red with their own blood".

The message was therefore made very clear to the council of chiefs assembled that day at Rotokakahi. Te Arawa must prepare for war. This also was the message that Te Ngahoa and his followers had brought home to Mokoia and the people of Ngati Rangiteaorere: *"ka mate te hapu tahi, ka ora te hapu wene"* (the man that has only one family might be killed; the man that has many families might live).

Jane's Story Chapter 4

Battle lines are drawn

The year is 1823 and the paramount Ngapuhi chief Hongi Hika and his flotilla of war canoes have anchored in Tauranga Harbour. Not the slightest resistance was offered by ***Ngai te rangi***, the domiciled inhabitants (***tangatawhenua***) on his arrival, probably because they would have been made well aware of the likely consequences of any show of defiance against the powerful Ngapuhi. Besides, they had already been informed that the main purpose of Hongi's incursion into the Bay of Plenty was to attack Te Arawa in their own territory and avenge the defeat inflicted on a Ngapuhi war party at Rotokakahi and also, with their own devastating defeat at the hands of Te Arawa when they had been driven from their lands East of the Kaituna River still weighing heavily on the minds of Ngaiterangi, the prospect of a strategic alliance was a distinct possibility.

It didn't matter to Hongi that it would take almost another year before he would be ready to move against Te Arawa, he was fully aware of the magnitude of the task and the meticulous preparation that had to be made before embarking on such a formidable engagement. Strategy was a word he had learned from the white man (***Pakeha***) who had come to the Bay of Islands (***Te Taitokarau***) as whalers and traders and befriended the Ngapuhi people.

It was on one of their tall sailing ships that Hongi, in the year 1819, was taken to England for an audience with King George III when he attracted wide interest and salutation as the first indigenous native dignitary from New Zealand to be received by the royal court of Great Britain. During the visit, he was invested in many personal and communal gifts ranging from suits of armour, ceremonial swords and also ploughs and other agricultural implements to take back to his people ostensibly for the "betterment of their subsistence". But the wily Hongi had other ideas, for when the ship called at Port Jackson (Sydney), Australia on its return to New Zealand, Hongi traded the entire shipload (with the exception of his suits of armour and the swords) to local merchants in exchange for muskets, gunpowder and lead.

At home in the land-locked and safe anchorage of Taitokarau, shared exclusively by itinerant seafaring Europeans and the incumbent and extremely adaptable Ngapuhi, Hongi set about reinforcing the power of his war gods with his newly acquired weapons of destruction. This placed him at an iniquitous advantage over all of the other tribes who had not yet come under the influence of the Pakeha and knew nothing of their advanced weaponry. It was inevitable therefore that the warlike Ngapuhi under the unscrupulous Hongi Hika should soon embark on a devastating rampage over the length and breadth of the North Island.

Back in Rotorua, word had been received that the Ngapuhi had landed at Tauranga and was preparing to march on Te Arawa. A council of war (*runanga pakanga*) had been called on Mokoia where fighting chiefs representing the subtribes of Ngati Whakaue (Te Moko), Tuhourangi (Te Horo), Ngati Rangiteaorere (Kirinui), Ngati Uenukukopako (Te Umanui), Ngati Rangiwehewehi (Te Tawha) and Ngati Pikiao (Te Tuhi) were in attendance.

The strategic plan unanimously adopted by the assembled council was one that had been traditionally employed by Te Arawa with unqualified success in the past. A defensive stand would be made on Mokoia by amassing the resources of all of the subtribes sufficient to withstand a long and protracted siege should that become necessary. All canoes would be withdrawn to the island thus denying the invader the means of crossing in any great number.

Marauding forays and rearguard action against the advancing enemy would of course be carried out but all such encounters would be kept brief with the home parties retiring intact and always remaining free to rejoin the main defensive body on the island.

Immediately therefore the plan was put into action and canoes began to arrive in numbers bringing loads of materials to strengthen the defensive palisades, food supplies to fill the store houses and kumara pits (*rua*), women and servants (*mokai*) to gather firewood and prepare the food and lastly, the warriors in their distinctive formations to practice the defensive manoeuvre known as *toka tu moana* (the rock that stands in the ocean).

However this grand plan relied altogether on the presumption that Ngapuhi was bound to make an overland attack as there was no direct navigable waterway linking Lake Rotorua with the sea by which they could launch a canoe-borne offensive (*waka taua*). The prognosis was therefore that Ngapuhi would leave their war canoes at *Maketu* and march inland from there. The deployment of the Te Arawa advance guard along that route would be made accordingly.

But alas Te Arawa with all this strategic planning had lamentably under-estimated the sheer sagacity of one Hongi Hika.

True perhaps to form, the Ngai te rangi of Tauranga, in a gesture of appeasement to Ngapuhi, had provided an experienced guide to mark a possible alternative route by which their war canoes could be navigated by way of the Little *Waihi* estuary (a few miles East of Maketu), up the *Pongakawa* Stream and selected tributaries and thence by portage over wetlands to Lake *Rotoehu*. Further portage would be necessary to transfer from Rotoehu into Lake *Rotoiti* and from there it would be plain sailing into Lake Rotorua by way of the *Ohau* channel at *Mourea*.

Hongi contemplated the difficulties involved in using such a devious route and in particular the length of overland portage between Lakes Rotoehu and Rotoiti but the element of surprise combined with the advantage of having his canoes available for a mass attack on Mokoia would far outweigh the disadvantages and so he made his decision. The alternative route would be adopted.

Thus by this one stroke of military genius, Hongi Hika set about to explode the myth of the impregnability of Te Arawa in their island fortress of Mokoia.

In a large scale raid such as that made by Hongi Hika when he descended from Taitokarau to rampage down the East coast of the North Island through *Tamaki Makaurau* (Auckland), *Ngati Paoa* (*Hauraki*) and into Ngaiterangi and Te Arawa Territory (Bay of Plenty) as far South as *Matata*, his expedition would have been traditionally made up of several compact forces of one hundred and forty warriors known as *hokowhitu* which means twenty times seven. Each hokowhitu would be composed of a number of closely related men who would obey their chief implicitly and die to the last man if called upon. It is estimated therefore that at least ten hokowhitu comprising a total force (*ope*) of 1400 fighting men in perhaps 20 war canoes (*waka taua*) of various capacities left Taitokarau on that expedition and whilst the number selected for the raid on Te Arawa on the island of Mokoia has not been reliably recorded, the most popular estimate as concurred amongst descendants of the sub tribes that were involved in the engagement, was ten war canoes. This would give an approximate total of 700 fighting men (five hokowhitu).

The incursion up the Pongakawa River from Little Waihi and into Lake Rotoehu was uneventful. The crews (*waka taua*) of each canoe had been split into two groups, one on each side of the stream to control the hauling ropes and keep their lengthy but shallow draft vessels towards the centre where the water was deepest. It was not until they had arrived at the lake and had begun to re-launch their canoes that their presence was detected by Ngati Pikiao and the alarm was sounded and relayed to Mokoia.

The success of this manoeuvre was brought about by yet another example of the inimitable generalship of Hongi Hika. Having first overcome the small garrison left by Te Arawa at Maketu and completely annihilating the ancient fortress (*pa*) at ***Pukemaire***, Hongi despatched an armed raiding party in a direct overland route towards Rotorua. At once the waiting Te Arawa advance guard challenged them and, as planned, proceeded to engage in brief running skirmishes which were to continue deep into Te Arawa territory. This was of course a clever diversion by Hongi to keep Te Arawa occupied whilst leaving him free to concentrate on getting his canoes into Lake Rotoehu without distraction.

The lake district to the East of Rotorua was dominated by the subtribe of Ngati Pikiao who had, throughout history, assumed the sovereign guardianship (***kaitiaki***) *of* that region. Upon the sudden and totally unexpected arrival of the main Ngapuhi war party at Rotoehu therefore, it befell Ngati Pikiao in honour (***mana***) bound to seek the first encounter. But here as in all of the other outlying regions, only a small strike force was to be deployed with instructions to engage in brief delaying combat only in accordance with the grand Te Arawa defensive plan.

This small force comprising not more than twenty men under the command of the young chief ***Te Rakataha*** prepared to lay an ambush on the Eastern side of the narrow isthmus separating lakes Rotoehu and Rotoiti. By then the first of the Ngapuhi war canoes had arrived in ***Pohue*** Bay at the head of Lake Rotoehu and was preparing to land and it was only then that Te Rakataha came to realise that an attempt was about to be made to transport the canoes overland across the isthmus into Lake Rotoiti. He ordered his men to remain concealed until the enemy canoe had run aground and its crew had put down their weapons and manned the hauling ropes to commence the long overland portage.

A short, sharp flank attack was then launched with such ferocity that the enemy broke in disarray and those who were not struck down immediately, raced back to the landing place with their attackers in hot pursuit. But when Te Rakataha and his followers burst into the clearing, they were astounded at the sheer measure of the Ngapuhi "armada" that had now filled the bay. Reluctantly therefore they were obliged to break off the engagement and retreat into the bush.

The portage of the canoes was resumed along the track known as The path of Hinehopu (*Te Ara-o-Hinehopu*) and despite the determined efforts of Te Rakataha and his brave band of fighters who stood in defiance until the very last man had fallen, the task was completed and all ten *waka taua* were re-launched and made ready for war at *Tapuaeharuru* at the Eastern end of Lake Rotoiti.

However, the supreme sacrifice paid by Te Rakataha and his men was not altogether in vain as they did succeed in holding up the advancing Ngapuhi long enough to enable the Ngati Pikiao people living around the shores of the lake to retreat to the hills taking their families and possessions with them, thus avoiding direct confrontation with an invader that would show them no mercy.

And so the unrelenting Hongi Hika pressed on with his vainglorious crusade to exact vengeance (*utu*) from Te Arawa for daring to humiliate the prime of Ngapuhi at Rotokakahi in that historic incident when subterfuge duelled with subterfuge and that of Tuhourangi triumphed.

It only remained for the flotilla to sail totally unchallenged down the length of Rotoiti to the now abandoned village of Mourea and thence through the Ohau channel into Lake Rotorua, there to behold before them like some sleeping amphibian monster (*taniwha*), the bush-draped island of Mokoia and the awaiting hokowhitu of Te Arawa.

Jane's Story Chapter 5

The Battle of Mokoia and the Flight of the Tirairaka

The following is a translated account of the battle of Mokoia as narrated by *Harete Hiria* of Ngati Pikiao to her grand-daughter *Riritawhai* (Nellie), daughter of *Hikapuhi Poihipi* and Alfred Clayton of Lincolnshire, England and aunt of the present author. (Harete was one of the original *Tapuhi* who attended Rangitauninihi at the birth of little Maraea on Mokoia).

"Early on that morning as we of the village of *Hauanu* on Mokoia looked towards the East to greet the sunrise with the ancient Ngati Pikiao clarion call (*karanga*) *"Te rakataha itua o nga hiwi o Matawhaura"* (the sun rises from behind the hills of Matawhaura), we caught the glint of flashing paddles (*hoea*) as a great war canoe loomed large before us from out of the shining sun. At once the alarm was sounded and all of the fighting men raced to take up their appointed positions in accordance with the main defensive plan and we women gathered together the children and retired to the furthest end of the open ground away from the waters' edge and up close to the fringe of the dense bush.

Te Ngahoa with Ngati Rangiteaorere and Uenukukopako took up the central position along the waterfront near the totara tree named *Atua ahu* and they were flanked by Tuhourangi, Ngati Rangitihi and Whakaue in the West and Ngati Pikiao and Rangiwewehi in the East. A reserve party (*taua*) made up of volunteers from other smaller subtribes, our older men and even some of our own fighting women (*wahine toa*) was positioned between us and the forward guard.

Placed at intervals along the waters' edge, were stockpiles of wooden missiles made from short lengths of *manuka* and limbs of other trees that were about as thick as a man's wrist and as long as his forearm, and each piece sharpened at each end. So the island defences were prepared and all was made ready to repel the Ngapuhi invaders

Out on the lake, Hongi by now had marshalled his canoes in a vee formation placing his own vessel at the van and there in the prow he stood resplendent in his suit of armour complete with plumed helmet and clutching a great ceremonial sword. The sight of this fearsome warrior chief arrayed in such strange garb as had never been seen in Te Arawa before could not fail to strike an element of awe into the hearts of all that were aligned against him.

He did not launch his attack immediately but elected to make two complete circuits around the island, feigning landings at several places and all the time keeping up an incessant war chant (*tutu ngarahu*) challenging the enemy to battle to which those on the shore most vociferously responded in kind.

When at last the Ngapuhi formation stopped opposite the village, our high priest (*tohunga*) ran down to the waters' edge and produced from beneath his cloak the symbol (*aria*) of the god *Ihungaru* consisting of a lock of human hair braided with mulberry (*aute*) bark which he dipped into the lake to call upon the waves to rise and swamp the advancing canoes. Although the lake responded and created great waves which dashed against the canoes causing not a little panic amongst the occupants, this action was short lived and quickly subdued as it became apparent that the Ngapuhi gods were proving the more powerful and so the invasion drew closer.

Te Ngahoa and his party, now armed with their throwing sticks, waited until the first canoe came within range and then, on his command, the first broadside of missiles was launched. This caused absolute mayhem amongst the invaders who, in their frantic attempts to evade the shower of missiles, caused the canoe to capsize and spill them along with their weapons into the water. The first to scramble ashore were quickly despatched whilst the others following, seeing the disastrous fate of their comrades, turned and struck out for the other canoes. Hongi's canoe, although standing further off shore, did not entirely escape the onslaught and during the commotion in trying to pull back out of range, a stray missile was seen to strike his plumed helmet and send it toppling into the water where it sank out of sight never to be seen again.

The invaders continued to probe the defences along the shoreline looking for the weakest point that would offer the least resistance. Upon selecting the most vulnerable spot, Hongi decided to bring to bear his newly acquired musket (*ngutu parera*) assault which would be certain to strike terror into the hearts of the unsuspecting defenders. He therefore ordered his most heavily manned canoe to thrust headlong through the defensive barrage of missiles until it ran aground. There the men were to immediately fan out, take cover and train their muskets upon the exposed enemy. Thus a bridge-head was successfully gained and the battle of Mokoia moved into its final phase.

In effect, the gallant defenders of Mokoia, armed only with their traditional Maori weapons, were no match for the musket armed Ngapuhi who showed no compassion and did not hesitate to exploit that ruthless, devastating advantage to the full.

With his full compliment of musketeers now landed and dug-in along the shoreline, Hongi employed an ancient military manoeuvre known as ***kokoti*** in which he ordered his regularly armed fighters to make a feint attack into the heart of the enemy formations and then retire with sufficient loss to tempt their pursuers down to within range of his muskets. There they were to throw themselves flat against the ground to allow the muskets to be fired over their heads and directly into the line of the pursuers. Wave after wave of Te Arawa were brought down by this deception before they came to understand and respect the devastating firepower of these deadly new weapons.

All that day the battle raged with terrible casualties being inflicted on both sides but with neither yielding ground nor conceding defeat. As night fell the fighting was halted and time was taken to collect and dispose of the dead and attend the wounded. Hongi who had suffered considerable casualties despite his superior firepower, took advantage of the lull in the fighting to send some of his canoes back to Mourea to collect reinforcements which had arrived there overland from Maketu as part of the raiding force that he had dispatched earlier. It is said that had he not been able to call on those reinforcements, his attack on Te Arawa would surely have ended in defeat."

In the same darkness, Rangitauninihi searched among the dying and wounded on the battlefield until at last she came to her husband Te Ngahoa lying mortally wounded, a gaping bullet wound in his chest. She cradled his head in her lap and called to him to be strong that she would try to save him. He looked up into her eyes, smiled and spoke "It is too late for me now, my life is over and I must go to the place from whence spirits depart (*Te Rerenga wairua*) there to await my departure to join my ancestors (*Tipuna*) in **Hawaiki.** What of our little girl Maraea ?" "She is safe and with her aunt Mango" Rangitauninihi replied. "Then you must take her and go at once to the mainland" urged Te Ngahoa. "There is a small canoe hidden on the other side of the island. You must take it and cross to Te Awahou".

Rangitauninihi gazed resolutely into his eyes and spoke " I shall never leave your side. Wherever you go, I shall go also. If you must die here on this battlefield, then I shall take up your arms and stand over your body until I too shall be struck down. For then we shall go to

Te Rerenga wairua together".

As the new day dawned, Hongi with his freshly reinforced army prepared to deliver the 'coup de grace'. The Te Arawa forces had been so depleted that they were no longer able to man the perimeter defences and were compelled to withdraw into a smaller defensive formation around the besieged village. Hongi boasted that he would emulate the crayfish (*koura*) and clasp the remnants of Te Arawa between its claws and slowly crush them together until the last sign of life had been extinguished.

So the remaining defenders of Mokoia, men, women and children were herded together in the centre of the battlefield defiant to the end with attempts still being made to break out of the net but inexorably diminishing in number as one by one they were to succumb.

At this desperate stage when all seemed lost, a woman appeared from the ranks of Ngapuhi, ran up to Hongi and cast herself upon the ground before him. "Oh great chief of Ngapuhi" she cried, "Know me for who I am for I am *Te Aokapurangi* myself of Te Arawa and given in wedlock to one of your most noble warrior chiefs. I beg of you now to spare the lives of the young, the women and the children that they might live in sorrow of this day".

Whether out of some perverted sense of humour or sheer sadistic pleasure, Hongi replied "Woman of Te Arawa I hear you and I charge you thus: You look to be a generous woman as I am a generous man. I will therefore spare the lives of as many of your people as can pass between your generous thighs".

Te Aokapurangi stood aghast at the cruelty of this cynical, leering man who towered above her and then, as if in response to some divine guidance, she ran across the marae to *Tamatekapua* the great meeting house (*wharenui*) and climbed up onto the roof where she frantically hauled herself up to the carved head (*koruru*) atop the front barge boards (*maihi*) and sat astride the gable end with her legs stretching down either slope. With a shrill cry she called to the people huddled together on the courtyard (*marae*) "*Ka tuwhera te tawaha o tahu; kiatere hei tangatarau ki muri tata kino*" ("the gates of mercy are open; hurry let all of the people rush in behind").

Only a few remaining warriors and the older men who preferred not to surrender and become slaves but to die on their own land chose not to enter but remain and fight to the death "*He toa taua, mate taua; he kura whenua ke rokohanga*" (A warrior dies in battle; not so the land which remains forever).

A profoundly amused Hongi, who had stood watching all the while, called to Te Aokapurangi astride the roof, *"He wahine, he whenua e ngaro i te tangata"* ("by women and land men are lost"). "You have truly outwitted me and by that I shall keep my word".

And thus was a total massacre avoided and the legend of "the lady astride the koruru" was born and, although the prime of Te Arawa now lay dead on the battlefield, it was due only to the single-minded resourcefulness of Te Aokapurangi that some of the people, however so pitifully few, would now survive to rekindle the fires of tribal unity and live mayhap to fight another day.

Scooped up in the huddled mass that crammed into the great house of Tametekapua on that day, was little Maraea with her aunt Mango who was now her only surviving close relative (*whanaunga*).

In the days that followed, Hongi sailed triumphantly around the villages bordering the shores of both lakes Rotorua and Rotoiti where the depleted numbers of inhabitants could offer little or no resistance to his demands of submission and servility. Ohinemutu, the ancestral home of Ngati Whakaue, was to come in for special attention as its steaming ovens were to provide the means of preserving the tattoed (*ta moko*) heads of the fallen Arawa chiefs to be borne in triumph by the returning Ngapuhi to their home base (*kainga*) in Taitokarau. Slaves and servants (*mokai*) were also selected and taken away in bewildered groups not knowing what their fates might be.

The crowning glory of any such conquering legions upon their return to their home bases was the taking under the care of the clan chieftan (*aho ariki*), a bevy of young girls carefully chosen in accordance with their high ranking bloodlines (*rangatiratanga*). These little hostages were never to be treated as slaves however but rather nurtured as virgin (*puhi*) maidens to be watched over by female attendants charged with preserving their virginities until such time, for example, that a desirable alliance was to be formed with chiefs of other tribes or that the cementing of peace between two warring tribes in a ceremony called binding peace (*hohou rongo*), was to be inaugurated.

It was inevitable therefore that little Maraea, because of her impeccable bloodlines running directly to both the Arawa and Mataatua canoes, should become a natural selection duly to be taken by Hongi to his stronghold at *Tahuna* (near Kaikohe) in Taitokarau. Her aunt Mango was to accompany her and become one of her female attendants.

On an autumn day when a brooding silence hangs in a shroud over the island, after the dead have either been taken home for grieving (*tangi*) on their own marae or laid to rest in the urupa of Mokoia upon whose fields they had fallen, when all of the people have gone away and the village left deserted, it is early morning and the rays of the sun are playing through the rising mists (*the tears of Papatuanuku*) as they lift towards the sky and from a certain hinau tree on the fringe of the shadowy bush, there appears a little fantail (*tirairaka*) which flies out over the now desolate and trampled plantations.

Inquisitively she darts from place to place alighting onto the wreckage of the kumara huts, the flattened fences, the mounds of earth thrown up by the fighting forces, even the house of **matua o tonga** the kumara god, anxiously searching for something that seems continually to elude her. Nervously she circles the fields again flying higher and higher until she reaches such height that she can see the whole island spread out beneath her and she becomes afraid.

But high in the celestial home of his sky father (**Ranginui**), the god of the winds (*Tawhirimatea*) looks down on the little bird and takes pity. He orders up the south wind (**Te hau ma tonga**) to swoop down across the island, gather up the little bird and whisk her away in a flash to the North.

Jane's Story Chapter 6

A flower grows in Taitokarau

When the time came for Hongi Hika and his war party to depart Te Arawa, the exaction of his vengeance (*utu*) well and truly satisfied, little Maraea and her aunt Mango were taken from Mokoia across the lake and down through the Ohau channel to **Taheke** (on the North-western end of Lake Rotoiti) where all of his spoils of war along with its luckless human content of captive slaves and servants (*mokai*) had been marshalled and divided into separate bearer units, each under the command of a warrior chief, in preparation for the long overland journey to the coast at Maketu.

Mango wrapped her little charge in a warm and comfortable shoulder cloak (*pikau*) and hoisted her high up onto her back to hold her firmly whilst allowing her freedom to look about her as the long walk continued. Along the way, Maraea would cry at times and complain of being sore and Mango would put her down and let her walk alongside until she grew tired and wanted to return to the pikau. All that day they marched until darkness forced them to stop and bed down for the night and on the next day they reached Maketu where they were made to prepare food and attend to the demands of their new masters until such time as the great canoes were made ready for their voyage North to Taitokarau.

Boisterous were the sounds of welcome for the return of Hongi and his victorious army (*hokowhitu a tu*) as his canoes hove into view off the shores of **Paihia** in Taitokarau. High chiefs and tribal elders (*kaumatua*), visiting dignitaries (*manuhiri*), performing parties (*kapa haka*) and warrior bands (*toa taua*) had assembled along the shoreline to chorus their welcome with chants, action songs and displays of physical prowess whilst those in the canoes responded with war chants that echoed their recent exploits and victories.

As the parties moved up from the shore and onto the *marae* for the formal ceremony of welcome (*powhiri*) for the return home of their champions, it was ominously significant to note that the warriors of both the welcoming party and those returning, were performing their war dances (*haka*) brandishing not the traditional long (*taiaha*) or short (*patu*) weapons but the flintlock muskets (*ngutu parera*) of the Pakeha. They that gave Ngapuhi an overwhelming advantage over all of the other tribes of Aotearoa and they that would change the course of and drastically increase the death toll of inter-tribal warfare forever more.

And herded together in the centre of the marae, in full display for all to feast their eyes upon, stood a pitiful segment of a once proud Te Arawa people, fearful of an eventual outcome at the hands of a feckless captor in a strange new and unfriendly land. And in their midst, huddled in her pikau on Mango's back, was a wide eyed Maraea not understanding what all the noise was about but feeling secure nevertheless because Mango was there.

Snug in her perch, she could gaze about her and see the tall trees and the hills beyond the marae and suddenly out of the sky, darting and frisking above them came a special little bird, not to settle but to circle and twitter a happy greeting and then to disappear back into the sunlight.

Maraea looked up in instant recognition and delight and as her very own friendly little messenger the tirairaka faded from her view, she snuggled back down into her pikau to fall into a deep and happy sleep. It had truly been a long and tiring day for one very little girl.

A year had passed and life in the fortified stronghold of Tahuna had settled to a regular routine for Mango and Maraea and the longing in their hearts for Mokoia and their loved ones had at last begun to ease.

At home amongst his family (*whanau*), it appeared to Mango that Hongi had put aside his fearsome belligerence as he had his weapons of war and that now he had assumed the role of a benign and kindly father. Visitors were received and entertained with frequent regularity and among them, being welcomed with the highest esteem, were dignitaries of the Christian Church of England. Missionaries who had become established in the Bay of Islands under the leadership of the Reverend Samuel Marsden and whom were dedicated to spreading the gospel throughout Taitokarau and eventually all of Aotearoa.

It had in fact become one of Mango's daily duties to accompany little Maraea to the school conducted by the Reverend Mathews who had come to live at Tahuna and was provided with a dwelling house by Hongi. Despite their age differences therefore, both Mango and Maraea were to be introduced to Christianity and an English education together.

A life destined to combine the teachings of two widely diversified cultures was thereafter to be conferred upon Maraea in the years that followed.

As a Puhi maiden, held under strict containment (*tapu*) in the household of Hongi Hika the paramount fighting chief of Ngapuhi, Maraea came to learn of the prestige of her position, the accompanying mana that it inherited, the veneration of tribal genealogy (*whakapapa*) and the wise administration that it demanded. She also learned the highest crafts and skills among women such as the weaving of fine cloaks, mats and baskets, techniques of pattern making, colouring and dyeing and the preparation of the finest foods.

Absolute obeisance to the high chief was to be observed at all times and her presence before him was to be immediate upon his summons.   Her female attendants were charged never to leave her side.

These things that made her so different from the other children of the village were all very confusing to Maraea as she was much too young to understand the significance of her specially appointed position.

As she grew older however, there were occasions when she would be summoned before the high chief to be presented to visiting chiefs and dignitaries (*rangatira*) of other tribes to be afforded the solemn respect befitting of her rank, there to remain at their pleasure until dismissed to retire with her attendants.   Some of those visitors being entertained by Hongi, she observed were white men from the tall ships that lay at anchor down in the bay.

As a pupil of the Reverend Mathew's little school in the village, which she attended every day, she was introduced to a whole new culture that came from another world far away over the great sea of Kiwa (*Te moananui a kiwa*).

She learned of a great new god who reigned supreme over all other gods and of how he had sent down his own son to teach the people how to live together in peace without war.   She learned the ten commandments and that she must strive to live by them always.

In the classroom she learned to read and write and was thereby elevated to a world of new knowledge that had opened up before her. Books to be read, pictures of new people and places to be studied, dress fashion and exotic new materials to be worn, civil and social behaviour and deportment to be practiced.

All of these things conferred upon her as a child growing up in an exciting new environment that had never before come to the shores of this land of Aotearoa.

And as the enlightening years unfolded, Maraea was also seen to blossom into a beautiful young woman. She grew tall and stately, long and slender of limb, head held high in attestation of her proud Te Arawa heritage and an impeccable genealogy. The fact that she was a Puhi maiden under the prohibition of the high chief made such restrictions in her social intercourse the more desirable and her fame had spread to surrounding tribes from which ardent aspiring suitors were never to be found wanting.

Jane's Story Chapter 7

Betrayal of the Innocent

There were times when Hongi would gird again his cloak of war and rally his war parties around him to hear his inflammatory speeches against an enemy that had delivered insult or other cause for retribution and, after further speeches by leading warriors and displays of agility and skills in the handling of their weapons, the entire party would form up and march out of the pa on their errand of castigation of whichever hapless clan (*hapu*) that had dared to challenge the might of Ngapuhi.

Noticeable to the folk of the village assembled to farewell their fighting heroes (*toa taua*) and bid them overpowering success and triumph over the enemy in the battles to come, were two of Hongi's most trusted generals, his cousin **Kawiti** of the *Ngati hine* hapu and his nephew **Hone Heke** both doughty warriors who had each gained fearsome reputations on the battlefield and each of whom were destined later to share the mantle of supreme power over all of Ngapuhi from an ageing Hongi Hika.

To Mango and Maraea, their own early fear of the terrifying Hongi Hika had slowly begun to settle as they came to know him as the benign patron head of his extended family (*whanau*) in which, by virtue of their own fate, therein they were obliged to share. However in the ultimate, as history would relate, that deeply ingrained despotic, bestial belligerence that had impelled him to embark on his merciless rampages of atrocity and massacre throughout the country was never to be quelled and would continue to fuel his lust for bloodletting until the day he died "*E kore e ngaro, he pono hinengara te manawa*" (The true desire of the heart cannot be hidden).

Foremost on his mind was the retention of the vast superiority of firepower he had attained over all of the other tribes by his early acquisition of the musket (*ngutu parera*). His arsenal however was not large and needed to be replenished and extended with not only more muskets in reserve and to compensate for those that had been lost during his campaigns but also gun powder and the lead with which to mould the bullets. The ill-gotten advantage that he had gained with this new age weaponry had to be maintained at all costs.

He was aware that muskets and powder had now become available in limited quantities from the captains of some of the tall whaling ships that had since made the Bay of Islands their Southern port of call and had already established a trading post at **Kororareka** (Russell). The musket trade however demanded vast quantities of goods such as salted pork (from a now established pig flock descended from those first liberated by Captain Cook in 1770), fresh vegetables and scraped flax fibre (to be made into rope and sacking) to be used as barter.

Hongi was aware also that some of these ships had called at the fledgling settlements of Auckland, Tauranga and Maketu and had therefore made contact and opened up trading links with the Ngati Whatua, Ngaiterangi and Te Arawa tribes all of which would be seeking to purchase the *ngutu parera* and thereby win back fighting parity with Ngapuhi. Also of concern to him was the fact that supplies of produce to be bartered were far more plentiful in those Southern regions than they were in Taitokarau.

It became clear to Hongi therefore that some further inducement to trade with Ngapuhi would have to be conceived.

And so there came a day when Maraea was summoned before the high chief to be presented to a handsome young pakeha man who had been welcomed by Hongi as a very special guest. Maraea recognised him by his uniform as a captain from one of the newly arrived ships in the Bay.

He seemed to be delighted that she was able to converse with him in English and display a surprising appreciation of social etiquette. For her part, she became enchanted with the warm and gentle manner in which he greeted her, his tall and commanding bearing, his smiling blue eyes and his shock of unruly auburn hair. This stranger alone had awakened an emotion within her that she had never before experienced and her own eyes became wide in wonderment.

This man was Captain Thomas William Kelly, originally from County Kerry in Southern Ireland and now master of the American whaleship "*Kiowa*" out of New Bedford, Massachusetts, USA.

On the voyage down to New Zealand, his ship had called at Port Jackson (Sydney), Australia to deliver a cargo of agricultural implements, tools and building materials to meet an ever growing demand from the new settlers of that country and in return, he was able to refill his holds with merchandise for the on-going voyage to the Bay of Islands in New Zealand. Predominant in that merchandise was a large quantity of muskets and gunpowder to be traded with the natives in exchange for fresh food and provisions for the whaling expedition into the Southern Ocean.

Back in America, such action would have been prohibited as "gun-running" but in this remote outpost of Kororareka in the Bay of Islands, where reformation under the influence of the British flag had not yet been asserted, such unconscionable practice was allowed to pass quite without dissent.

It was inevitable therefore that the ever alert Hongi, through his agents among the merchants of Kororareka should be informed of the imminent arrival of this highly covetous cargo and that he would make immediate advances to the ship's captain to visit him in his retreat at Tahuna there to partake of his hospitality as they discussed the exchange of their merchandise.

In the cut and thrust of barter and exchange that was to ensue, the unscrupulous Hongi introduced a timely master stroke. The age old lure of romance, the awakening desire of the heart, the way of all flesh. The extra inducement that he had looked for to secure an advantage over all other rivals.

It mattered not to him that he would be flaunting before this alien pakeha a flower of aristocratic descent. One who was entrusted to him under sacred care (*tapu*) to be nurtured as a *puhi* maiden strictly for the perpetuation of the pure chiefly (**Rangatiratanga**) bloodline.

When it came down to a choice between the preservation of tribal dignity (*mana*) and gaining a military advantage over his enemies, the supremacy of power that the shipment of guns would bring him became paramount. The sacrifice would be made and Maraea would be gifted to the pakeha Kelly.

In due course Maraea was again summoned before the high chief to be told that she would henceforth be placed in the care of Captain Kelly who would take her to live on board his ship in the bay at Kororareka. Mango would however no longer accompany her and she must prepare to go alone.

Later that day, when the Captain came to collect his prize, Maraea's heart became heavy with grief. She despairingly clung to her beloved Mango and cried out in vain that she wanted never to leave her.

But Mango gently took her by the hand and delivered her up to the tall stranger and watched him place his arms reassuringly about her and smile down into her wistful, tear-filled eyes and, as he led her along the path that ran down to the shore and the awaiting longboat that would carry them out to his ship laying at anchor in the bay, she turned and looked back appealingly to the small group of villagers who had gathered to bid her farewell. And there in their midst stood a heart-stricken Mango, trying desperately not to betray her feelings yet gripped in suffocating grief as she watched her baby of all those tender years being carried off in the arms of this stranger from a different world far over the sea. She watched until they faded from her view and then as she turned to make her lonely way back to the village, herself now reduced to an ordinary slave, the tears would be contained no longer.

As the days passed and her bewilderment slowly gave way to intrigue and fascination with her new surroundings, Maraea found that life on board this ship with the handsome captain, towards whom she had already felt a strong attraction from the day she had first set eyes on him in the house of the high chief, could be quite charming and exciting. And as they shared their company together there developed a warm and intimate relationship that was to inevitably lead to surrender with tender and consummate love.

There would be days when he would take her ashore to explore together the straggling seaside township of Kororareka with its scatter of stores and public houses, its surrounding thatch-roofed dwellings (*whare*) of the native inhabitants, its colourful jumble of strangers from all nautical corners of the earth. There were also the short sailing excursions up and down the coast for the interchange and conveyance of merchandise extending in diversity from blankets, prints and iron cooking pots, to fresh fruit and vegetables, timber and bales of prepared flax fibre.

But all the while Maraea was to observe that the ship was steadily being provisioned for a much longer voyage the destination of which she could not possibly imagine. The empty oil casks being stored in the hold, the lean and hard working sailors, harpooners, fledgers and oarsmen for the chase-boats being recalled to the forecastle, the songs that they sang as they went about their work, the atmosphere of expectation that pervaded the air.

There shortly followed an evening when her captain came to tell her that he was about to leave on a voyage that would keep him at sea for some considerable time and that she must prepare to be taken ashore to live without him until he could return. He had arranged with the Reverend Henry Williams for her to be cared for at the mission station at *Paihia* where she would be encouraged to continue her education and also assist in the teaching of the younger children during her stay.

For a long time he held her in his arms and pledged his deep and undying love and gave his solemn promise that he would come for her as soon as his whale hunting expedition into the Southern Ocean was completed. He begged that she uphold her faith and trust in him that soon he would return to be by her side again. And she believed implicitly with a faith that was not to die throughout the years that were to follow.

Jane's Story Chapter 8

To an Image Born

It was the ever devoted Reverend Mathews who was first to greet Maraea when she was brought to the mission station at Paihia. He had come over from Tahuna only that day to learn from his fellow missioners of the arrangements that had been made for her reception and when she arrived escorted by her captain, her heart leapt with joy and delight as she recognised her old and endearing mentor.

It was the Reverend Mathews also who persuaded Hongi to release Mango to him so that she could be reunited with Maraea. And great was the joy of that reunion when they clung to each other amidst tears of ecstasy and relief as each poured out her heart to the other and prayed that never again would the time come when they should be made to part.

Maraea related all that had happened in the time that she had been away and of the love and devotion that had developed between her and her gallant captain and how she could barely wait for the day to come when he would return to carry her off to his home far away over the sea. She quite happily busied herself with her work at the mission and felt sublimely secure in the knowledge that her beloved Mango would always be there.

But as the days ran into weeks, Maraea came to experience the natural physical changes within her that signalled the approach of gestation and upon confiding with Mango, she was to learn that she was indeed with child and that soon she must prepare for her confinement. The news at first brought alarm and dismay, not knowing what to do or where she could go. She could not return to Tahuna as by now she had lost the sanctity of her birthright (*tapu*) and would be disowned by the faithless Hongi and his disciples.

The ever protective Mango however, knowing well that the time was fast approaching when a safe and secluded haven would need to be found for her confused and mystified young charge, she sought the wise counsel of the Reverend Mathews and, as it transpired, a solution came immediately to hand.

The good Reverend had just been commissioned to take charge of a new mission station at **Kaitaia** that had recently been established at the invitation of the **Ngati Hao** and **Te Rarawa** tribes of the Hokianga and along the North-western coastline, and where the leaders of which, **Tamati Waka Nene** and **Nopera Panakereao**, being far less warlike than their Eastern neighbours had expressed their preference for the peaceful doctrine as espoused by the Christian Ministry. (These two chiefs were among the first to pledge their allegiance to Queen Victoria at the signing of the Treaty of Waitangi). Mango and Maraea were offered safe refuge as guests of the Reverend Mathews and his family and would be well looked after as preparations were being made for the arrival of the baby.

And so the remaining weeks passed by in quiet contentment but as her time drew nearer, Maraea became more and more fearful. She felt imperilled and afraid and missed her gallant and masterful captain and his lordly commanding presence. She sought the reassuring comfort of Mango's arms and she spoke of her absolute faith in her captain that he would come back to her soon, take her in his arms and pledge again his undying love. She looked up to Mango with large and appealing eyes and cried "He will come back to me Mango, I know he will". The older woman hugged her closer to her breast, caressed her lovely shining black hair and said nothing.

In joy it came to pass that on the 28th day of January in the year 1837, with Mango and Mrs Mathews in attendance, Maraea gave birth to a beautiful baby girl who was to be named Jane (*Heeni*) after the wife of the Reverend Mathews as a token of the high esteem in which both Maraea and Mango held that family.

There was to be no ancient baptismal rite (*tohi*) for Jane as was observed at the birth of her mother on the island of Mokoia just seventeen years beforehand but rather would she be initiated into the Christian Church in a ceremony conducted by the Reverend Henry Williams and called to witness by Mango, the Mathews family and other resident clergy of the Church of England.

And in the early evening of the baptismal service, Mango walked with Maraea and the tiny baby Jane in the garden of the mission station and as they neared the end of their walk there appeared from out of the trees at the fringe of the surrounding bush, a little *tirairaka* darting and flitting as she came, alighting briefly onto the garden wall and pausing to sing a happy little song before swooping over the young mother and child thence to depart as swiftly as she had come. Mango and Maraea looked at each other and cried out in delight. Their guiding force (*atua*) had not forsaken them and had sent her symbol (*aria*) the tirairaka with a message of welcome to the newest addition to their principal female line (*ariki tapairu*) and reassurance that all would bode well for them in the future.

The little group was to remain at the Kaitaia mission station until shortly after Jane had become 2 years old when they were sent for by the Reverend (now Archdeacon) Henry Williams to return to Paihia where they would assist with a reception for a large number of guests who had begun to gather on a very important and historic occasion. There would be visitors representing the Anglican, Wesleyan and Catholic churches, members of the newly inaugurated Crown Colonial Government and newly arrived European settlers from Great Britain, France and America.

Maori tribal leaders (**rangatira**) from all around the region were congregating on the beaches, their great war canoes presenting an awesome sight as they intermingled with the deep sea trading vessels and men-o'-war of the British Navy as they lay at anchor in the bay

To little Jane, standing with her mother on the shore of the bay, the sight of the great canoes and their painted, loud chanting, paddle thrusting warriors emerging from the water and forging up onto the beach was to remain indelibly imprinted in her infant mind to be relived on occasion throughout her long and eventful life to come.

The occasion was the signing of the Treaty of Waitangi by the assembled leading chiefs and Captain William Hobson R.N. first Governor of New Zealand on February 6th 1840 when New Zealand became part of the British Empire. The Treaty which was drawn up by James Busby, British Resident in New Zealand who was domiciled at Waitangi, and witnessed by Bishop Selwyn and Archdeacon Williams of the Church of England, Bishop Pompallier of the Roman Catholic Church and other dignitaries of the Government, Clergy and the Queen's Services, provided for cession by the chiefs of their sovereignty over their respective territories to Queen Victoria, and promised the Maori people the Queen's protection and "all rights and privileges of British subjects." The Treaty also guaranteed the Maori undisturbed possession of their lands, and gave the Queen the sole rights of purchasing these lands.

And as for Maraea, on each new day she searched wistfully among the many visiting gentry for a familiar face and out over the bay for a glimpse of a certain tall ship, but all to no avail. What had become of her gallant captain? Was he still hunting whales in the forbidding Southern ocean? Had he become shipwrecked on some lonely desolate shore? Or had he really on that day sailed out of her life forever? She was never to accept the latter and would cling to her faith for as long as she lived.

Jane's Story Chapter 9

Tale of Family, Flagstaffs and Fear

A regular visitor to the mission station at Paihia was one Richard Russell a Ships Chandler from Sunderland in England who had arrived in Kororareka to set up a now thriving business in the maritime trade servicing the numerous merchantmen, whalers and visiting warships that sailed under the flags of Great Britain, France and the United States of America that had made the Bay of Islands their regular port of call. He had become one of a mixed bag of merchants who plied their trade in this busy outpost that had by now become the hub of the South Pacific.

Like many of the early British settlers' and merchants that accompanied the missionaries to New Zealand, Richard Russell was a religious man who was always ready to assist in setting up the mission stations and also to devote his services towards the introduction to and the conversion of the Maori people to Christianity and in that pursuit, his contribution was to merit the highest recognition.

Through his contact with the Church Mission, he became fully acquainted with the plight of the many dispossessed slaves who had become caught up amongst the spoils of intertribal war and carried off into hostile territory to remain forever in deprivation of their ancestral birthright. Many of these unfortunates were to find themselves abandoned later by their captors who had tired of them and cast them out to fend for themselves amongst the flotsam and jetsam of humanity that frequented the new settlement of Kororareka. Others were given refuge in the mission stations where they would be better cared for in exchange for their labour in the kitchens, gardens and in the fields of the newly established mission farm at Waimate.

It was through his concern for the welfare of these unfortunate exiles that Richard Russell was to discover a very special little family group with whom, it was so destined, he would share a close and intimate future. There developed an impulsive, warm and mutual feeling amongst them which would soon lead to a flourishing relationship with Mango and Maraea happily sharing their time between the mission station and the chandlery at Kororareka and little Jane in no time developing a strong attraction to her new found friend who in turn was delighted that she had taken upon herself to call him Papa.

In the early years following the signing of the Treaty of Waitangi, Hone Heke, who was the nephew of Hongi Hika and married to Hariata Rongo the daughter of that chief, had inherited the mantle of paramount chieftaincy (*aho ariki*) of the Ngapuhi tribe together with the *tapu* observances which had been founded and perpetuated by his forebears.

However, the character of Hone Heke was curiously complex. History would show that whilst he had indeed inherited much of the warlike belligerence of his despotic uncle, he would also display passion and patriotism together with a shrewdness sharpened by his early encounters and dealings with the foreign (*pakeha*) traders who had come to Taitokarau.

He was able to foresee the possible far reaching consequences of colonisation with an indiscriminate flooding of the land with a dominant alien population which could soon subjugate the original native inhabitants (*tangata whenua*) and rob them of their sovereign authority. He pictured a giant wave of pakeha humanity sweeping in from the sea to swallow up the Maori canoe (*waka tangata*) and disgorge its contents onto the rocky foreshore.

To aggravate the situation further, he was forced to accept that the seat of Government had already been transferred to Auckland.

Such wide scale immigration as he had envisaged would likely not display the sympathy and high regard for his people as was brought by the early missionaries, traders and settlers who had come amongst them bringing true devotion and understanding and certainly not to exploit or dispossess them of their lands. The Ngapuhi, like most other tribes throughout *Aotearoa* cherished feelings of the highest esteem and regard (*aroha*) for the missionaries who were afforded total immunity to move without molestation among the people, even on the battle fields, to minister their Christian charity to all who were in need whether friend or foe.

The young Heke had lived for a short time at Paihia in the mission station established by the Reverend (later Archdeacon) Henry Williams who became beloved throughout Ngapuhi as *"Karu Wha"* (four eyes) because of his habit of wearing his spectacles low down on his nose which gave the impression of two pairs of eyes. The respect he had formed for the missionaries through their devotion towards the welfare of his people was to remain with Heke throughout his mostly wild and turbulent life. It was during his period at the mission station that he learned something of the ways of the pakeha and the history of their civilisation which he turned to good account in his later dealings with a horde of self-interested speculators, land seekers, traders and also Government administrators that came to Taitokarau after the signing of the Treaty of Waitangi in 1840.

Prior to 1840, Heke in collusion with other influential chiefs namely *Pomare, Titore* and (to a lesser extent) *Kawiti* , had established a kind of customs enforcement agency in which they levied anchorage and landing charges on all ships that entered the Bay. The dues so collected, together with returns from the sale of food supplies and other commodities, had provided them with a sustainable and lucrative income.

In 1841 however, the New Zealand Government under Governor Fitzroy introduced an Ordinance where all customs duties and taxes were payable exclusively to the Crown. This led Heke to suspect that the Treaty that he and other chiefs had signed on behalf of the tribes of Aotearoa, was merely a ruse of the pakeha to usurp the authority of the Chieftaincy (***Rangatiratanga***) and that in reality, it had all along been the secret intention of the Government to seize upon the lands of all Maori as soon as it became militarily strong enough to do so.

It was in 1844 that Heke decided to take action that would test the true intention of the Pakeha once and for all. He decided to challenge the authority of the Governor to set up the colours of the Union Jack (*te kara*) on Maiki Hill and also his right to restrict access to the Bay of visiting whaling and trading ships of other nations.

He assembled a strong war party (*taua muru*) and began by plundering and looting the stores and public houses of Kororareka. For three days he remained in the town allowing his young bloods to ransack stores and private houses alike, seizing whatever they fancied and, on the third day the flagstaff on Maiki Hill was cut down.

When the news of the raid reached Governor Fitzroy, he decided that the situation demanded immediate punitive action and he sent an urgent appeal to the Sydney Colonial Office for troops to assist in putting down the uprising and, in due course the barque "Sydney" with a company of 180 officers and men arrived in the Bay. Two weeks later the Governor arrived in the frigate HMS "Hazard" accompanied by the Government brig "Victoria" with a detachment of the 96th Regiment under Lieutenant-Colonel Hulme.

The Governor and Hulme were all for immediate hostilities but due to the efforts of Archdeacon Henry Williams and the moderating influence of the Hokianga chief Tamati Waka Nene, Fitzroy was persuaded to withdraw the troops and redress the Maori grievances.

He finally agreed to abolish the customs duties and substitute a property tax only and also to order the troops back to their headquarters. For his part, Heke offered to erect another flagstaff.

However, just five months later the flagstaff was cut down for a second time. It has been recorded that on that occasion, Heke had been greatly influenced in his action by the Acting-Consul of the United States when he was reminded by the mischievous Consul of a similar revolt against the imposition of custom duties in his own country which culminated in the infamous "Boston Tea Party". Heke was hugely impressed and he burned to do likewise.

Fear and apprehension now gripped the settlers around the Bay and in response to an urgent appeal, the Government brig "Victoria" was despatched to Kororareka with a small detachment of thirty men led by a subaltern to re-erect the flagstaff. Archdeacon Williams had earlier unsuccessfully appealed to the Colonial Secretary and the Magistrate not to again flaunt the *kara* in the face of the natives at least not until it could be guarded efficiently for otherwise, it was likely to be cut down again.

Next morning the township awoke to find that the hill at Maiki had again been rendered flagless. The top mast had been carried away but the flag itself remained in the possession of a few friendly Maori who lived at the station. Heke and his taua fired a triumphant volley from the beach and launched into a frenzied haka of defiance.

Thoroughly frustrated with Heke's insolence, Governor Fitzroy wrote to the Governor of New South Wales making an urgent appeal for further military assistance and, in compliance with his request, two companies of the 58th Regiment numbering 207 men of all ranks received orders to embark for New Zealand but, by the time they had reached the Bay of Islands, the flagstaff was down for the fourth time and Kororareka was in ashes. The Heke wars had begun.

Tribal folklore recounts that after the flagstaff on Maiki Hill was cut down for the fourth time, a replacement pole was brought in from the forests of Hokianga and laid at the stump of its predecessor. But when the military detachment arrived to erect it next morning, they found that it had been spirited away in the night, It so transpired that an old chief of a neighbouring tribe had ordered its recovery as his guardian spirit (*atua*) had come to him in the night and reminded him that when that pole (*rakau*) was a living tree, he had been born under it. It would therefore be an omen (*aitua*) of disaster bringing trouble, even death, should Heke carry out his threat to cut it down again.

There followed a frantic hunt for a mast to which no Maori could lay similar claim and ultimately the mizzen mast of an American vessel was purchased by a Government official who felt "morally certain" that no Maori could possibly have been born anywhere near it.

This mast, the fifth, stood for nearly two months before Heke's axe laid it low and a bereaved Kororareka was obliged to wait another eight years before the *kara* would again adorn Maiki Hill.

Standing in witness of all these events was the bemused little family group of Mango, Maraea and little Jane with their mentor and protector Richard Russell. They were to experience fear of the raiding war parties that rampaged through the township, the British soldiers who had arrived by ship in the Bay to come ashore, depart and then come back again, and lastly the impending threat of all out war away from which there would be nowhere to run.

Jane's Story Chapter 10

A Forced Evacuation

Immediately upon the arrival of the men of the 96th Regiment under the young subaltern Ensign J. Campbell, they were put to work improving the defences on Signal Hill (*Maiki*) against another attempt by Hone Heke to attack the flagstaff. A wooden blockhouse capable of holding 20 men was built around the foot of the mast which was sheathed in iron to a height of ten feet (3 metres) as protection against the tomahawk. A deep trench was dug around the blockhouse to permit its only access by way of a plank which could be drawn up when not in use.

Down on the flat a timber stockade was built around the Polack family home near the beach at the Northern entrance to the township and a smaller blockhouse was built on a mound at the rear and close to the track leading up to Maiki Hill. It was on an earth mound at the rear of the blockhouse that three ship's guns were mounted whilst a fourth gun had been taken to the other end of the town above *Matauhi* Bay to guard against any likely attack from the South.

In all, the regular garrison amounted to about 50 men under the command of Lieutenant E. Barclay and Ensign Campbell neither of whom was an experienced soldier. In addition there was a detachment of marines from HMS "Hazard" and also a small section of volunteer civilians and old soldiers who manned the battery of ship's guns outside the lower blockhouse.

During the night of 10 March 1845, an estimated 200 warriors under Hone Heke and *Te Pokai* landed at *Oneroa* at the rear of Kororareka and stealthily worked their way up to the foot of Maiki Hill and, in the grey dawn of the new day, they watched from their concealment until the door of the little blockhouse was swung open, the plank lowered across the ditch and half a dozen men under Ensign Campbell had emerged from the morning mist to march off down the hill on a work assignment.

Scarcely had the men begun their march when the morning silence was shattered by the crackle of rifle fire from the direction of Matauhi Bay and the resounding boom of a cannon in reply. Ensign Campbell at once called out the full garrison and ordered them to take up a defensive position outside the trench and overlooking the town whilst he would take a small detachment to investigate the cause of the gun shots.

This was Heke's chance and with a yell from their leader, the warriors were up and firing at the soldiers outside the blockhouse while others dashed inside to quickly subdue the few remaining occupants. The surviving soldiers on the outside were forced to retreat down the hill to join up with Ensign Campbell and fall back on the lower blockhouse having completely lost their own. And in this time, the triumphant Heke, having first to overcome the problem presented by the iron sheathing, succeeded in cutting down the flagstaff for a fourth time.

Meanwhile, a force of 45 marines from the "Hazard" under Acting Commander David Robertson had marched to the heights overlooking Matauhi Bay for the purpose of establishing a defence line against any attack from the South. They had just reached the top of the hill when they heard rifle fire and the boom of the one-gun battery on their own side of the valley. It was a war party commanded by ***Kawiti*** whose role was merely to create a diversion to keep the pakeha soldiers occupied while Heke completed the main task of assaulting the flagstaff on Maiki Hill. A heated battle then took place in which severe casualties were sustained by both sides before Robertson and his men were forced to fall back towards the township.

Down on the beach the detachment under Lieutenant Barclay, quartered in Polack's stockade between the beach and the lower blockhouse, entered the battle. Their first shots were directed against the Ngapuhi who had appeared on the hills above Oneroa Bay but then the *Kapotai* tribe from *Waikare*, the third division of assailants entered the fray to close up a half circle that now completely rimmed the township.

Heke, on his hilltop station stood watching the proceedings below. He had achieved his objective and indeed that was all that he had intended.

There was no proper co-ordination for the defence of the township among the naval authority, the military and the Police Magistrate with each giving their own independent orders as they thought fit which resulted only in the whole situation falling into total disarray. Such was the disorderly mess when a message was sent to the besieged township ordering the women and children to take shelter in Polack's stockade and for all able-bodied men to report to the lower blockhouse to man the ship's guns.

Thus Mango, Maraea and little Jane were to find themselves caught up amongst a throng of agitated mothers, frightened children, confused elderly and disabled folk and herded into the stockade to be told to take cover behind the protective timber palisades and keep their heads down. Richard Russell, after leaving his charges within the relative safety of the stockade, went to report to Mr C. Hector, a civilian of much resolution who had been given charge of the lower blockhouse battery.

As by then all that Heke had come for had been accomplished, he had no intention of attacking the civilian population and he was surprised that a kind of panic seemed now to have overtaken those in authority. He had sent down the wife and daughter of the signalman Tapper under the protection of a white flag to advise of his intention to cease all hostilities but by then a mass evacuation had already been put into action. Lieutenant Phillpotts, the senior combatant officer, after consulting with Mr Beckham, the Police Magistrate, determined the complete evacuation of the place. He gave orders that the troops and the civilian population should go aboard all of the available ships in the Bay. These were HMS "Hazard", the United States warship "St. Louis", the English whaleship "Matilda", the Government brig "Victoria" and Bishop Selwyn's schooner "Flying Fish".

By that time however, the battery of guns outside the lower blockhouse at the rear of the stockade manned by Mr Hector and his civilian volunteers, had kept up a steady bombardment which at least prevented the Kapotai from entering the town. Their only casualty was Tapper, the signalman whose wife and daughter had earlier been sent down by Heke, who was wounded while serving one of the guns. When the order came to abandon the guns and clear the area, Hector's disgust was extreme and he swore that he could have retaken the flagstaff hill if he were given 50 volunteers.

So began the total evacuation of the entire exotic (*tauiwi*) population of Kororareka. Firstly the women, children, aged and disabled were ferried out to the awaiting ships in the Bay. Mango, Maraea and Jane were put safely aboard the schooner "Flying Fish" of Bishop Selwyn, there to anxiously await news of Richard Russell whom they had feared for during the firing of the heavy guns and the sharp crackle of return fire from the Ngapuhi.

Next came the soldiers and civilian volunteers who continued to fight a rearguard action under the covering fire from the "Hazard" standing off the shore. During the evacuation, some of the unarmed small boats were to come under heavy fire as they pulled in to take off the people huddled in groups on the beach.

One of the last of the civilians to make his escape was Richard Russell who had, under grave risk of fire from either side, had returned to his chandlery to collect several items of personal value that he did not wish to fall into hostile hands. He, along with others who were forced to evacuate, was resigned to accept that should he ever be allowed to return to Kororareka, he would find little evidence of his storehouse or its contents but charred remains. His future must therefore lie elsewhere but for now, his immediate responsibility was to return to his adopted family aboard the "Flying Fish" and reassure them that all would be well.

So the heavy day ended with the Ngapuhi, since finding the township totally abandoned, happy to break off the engagement to become absorbed in looting and drinking grog, seizing blankets, clothing, tobacco and various other stock from the unattended stores. There was the occasional shot fired from the frigate that fell amongst them but little regarded by the marauders who were busy loading their canoes with loot to be carried off to their villages.

Next morning those on board the boats at anchor in the Bay, watched as one building after another in the settlement was set on fire until all but the Anglican and Roman Catholic churches and mission houses including the house of Bishop Pompallier (all of which were scrupulously protected from harm), were ablaze and a huge mass of black smoke hung high and unmoving over the Bay. The funeral pyre of Kororareka.

Recounting the action many years after the war, **Riwhitete Pokai** of **Kaikohe** described the annoyance of the Ngapuhi at the indiscriminate shelling from the "Hazard". "We treated the women and children kindly and took those who remained late off to the ships in our canoes, but as soon as they were all put safely aboard, even before that, the man-o-war opened fire on our people on the beach. That was an act of treachery to shell us after the town had been given up by the military and some of us were angry that we had not tomahawked all of the pakeha we could find".

Early on the following day, 13 March 1845, the fleet of five sailed for Auckland and, for little Jane, standing with her mother on the after deck of the "Flying Fish" and looking back over the Bay, the sight of the whole township burning and the towering cloud of smoke reaching up to the sky, would remain forever in her memory as the last days of Kororareka. She was just eight years old.

As for the completely engrossed Maraea, her large and lucid eyes now troubled and bewildered, she searched beyond this scene of chaos and destruction and allowed her mind to drift back in time to the days when all about her was new and exciting. A host of tall ships under the flags of many nations anchored in the Bay, the hustle and bustle of the traders and the townsfolk as they plied their wares twixt ship and shore. And where once at anchor rode the tall ship of her blonde captain who had come to her with tender adoration and she in turn had rendered up to him her heart.

Yet now as she looks back over an empty Bay, the morning sun clouded by the smoke from the burning township, she becomes fearful that like the waves that are gliding gently beneath her, so the dream she had long cherished was slowly slipping away. What if he should return to find her gone? Would he be angry that she had gone away? Would he come and find her wherever she might be?

Together they stood looking back in silence at the gradually diminishing scene. Little Jane with her head snuggled into her mother's side and the proud Maraea, with her head held high and her arm clasped protectively around her little daughter and each of them immersed in individual thought.

Jane's Story Chapter 11

Return to Te Arawa

Fears of invasion by Ngapuhi spread like wildfire throughout the settlement of Auckland after the five shiploads of refugees landed and the distressed people from Kororareka related their experiences. The defences of the town were hastily strengthened and all able-bodied civilian reserves were called up and placed under the command of the regular military. However, with the arrival of warships from Sydney which by mid-April 1845 had brought a further 470 officers and men to compliment the resident garrison made up of the 58th and 96th Regiments, the threat of invasion could be safely dismissed and all efforts directed towards preparing a task force to retake Kororareka and, on 27 April an expeditionary force sailed North from Auckland.

In October the Secretary of State for the Colonies, Lord Stanley, announced that Captain Fitzroy had been recalled and that Captain George Grey, who was then Governor of South Australia, had been appointed as the new Governor of New Zealand. Captain Grey arrived in Auckland on 14 November 1845 and he sailed to the Bay of Islands a few days later to re-establish the authority of the Crown.

After hoisting the flag on the beach at Kororareka on 30 April 1845, the Government forces under Lieutenant-Colonel Hulme marched on Pomare's pa at *Otuihu* and from thence there began the resumption of the conflict with *Heke* and *Kawiti* and their Ngapuhi legions which would extend into the hinterland and meet with defeat in the battles of Omapere and Ohaewai before emerging victorious for the colonial troops with the fall of the fortress of *Ruapekapeka* (the bat's nest) in January 1846 and so the *Heke Wars* of the North came to an end.

The final (victorious) assault on Ruapekapeka was given under the command of the Maori-despising Lieutenant- Colonel Henry Despard who had come to this colony harbouring the presumptuous maxim that one British soldier was the equal of at least half a dozen savages. However, by the time the campaign had ended, he was forced to admit that the originality and skill of the Maori in battle and in fort-building "far exceeded any idea that could have previously been formed of it".

The total force placed under his command during this engagement was 68 officers and 1100 men comprising seamen, Royal Marines, HEIC Artillery, soldiers of the 58th and 99th Regiments and 50 civilian volunteers led by the redoubtable Mr Hector. Ordnance comprised three naval 32-pounders, one 18-pounder, two 12-pounder howitzers, one 6-pounder, four mortars and two rocket tubes. In addition, there were 450 Maori warrior allies under the friendly chief **Tamati Waka Nene.**

The combined force in opposition under Heke and Kawiti totalled 500 fighters equipped with muskets and tomahawks only.

In 1848, at a meeting of agreement (*hui whakaae*) at Pomare's pa at Otuihu, a proclamation, issued by Governor Grey permitting those who had been concerned in the war to return peacefully to their homes, was received with relief by the Ngapuhi and their allies. The proclamation raised the blockade of the East Coast from Whangarei to Mangonui and also relieved the Bay of Islands district within a radius of 60 miles in any direction from Kororareka, from martial law. And so peace returned to the North un-embittered by punitive land confiscation or by vendettas provocative of future wars.

At the meeting (*hui*), the dauntless old Kawiti, whilst confessing that he had had enough of war and only wanted to make peace, stated "I did not commence the war but I have borne the whole brunt of the fighting. Hear me however, it is not from fear for I felt no fear when the shot and shell burst all around me, I intend making peace but not from fear. Whatever happens to me hereafter, I have one consolation, I am not in irons nor am I in an Auckland gaol. I have stood against the soldiers of the greatest white nation of the world but I am satisfied they are men not gods (*atua*), and had they nothing but the musket (*ngutu parera*) as we had, the bat (*pekapeka*) would still be in his nest".

Heke had lost the war but carried his point. At the hui he charged Governor Grey that the corpse (*tupapaku*) of the flagstaff at Kororareka should not be "roused to life as those who had died in cutting it down could not be roused to life". This was a major dictate and it was to the Governor's credit that he did not insist upon the restoration of the tupapaku for as long as his two old adversaries had lived and it was not until 1853 that **Maihi Paraone Kawiti**, the son of old Kawiti, and his kinsmen set up a new mast on Maiki Hill in token of the binding peace (*houhou rongo*) that had since grown between the two races.

One further proclamation to be read out at that hui and to have far reaching significance was for the liberation and return to their home tribes of all slaves and descendents therefrom that had been abducted by Ngapuhi during the inter-tribal (musket) wars of the 1820's and 30's which rampaged down through the North Island as far South as Cook Straight. The Government would hereinafter arrange transport and assistance to ensure that all of these displaced persons should be returned safely to their hereditary homelands.

Meanwhile back in Auckland, Richard Russell, under the auspices of the Church Mission, had set up a refuge for the bereft and dispossessed evacuees from Kororareka who had found themselves stranded amongst strange surroundings without any means of sustenance and support. These people were to require proper housing, food for the table and assistance in finding new employment until such time as they were able to become fully integrated into the new society of Auckland. The continued education of the young was also demanding of timely attention.

Providing a secure home for the disinherited victims of war, slavery and family abandonment among the younger refugees was to become the dedicated preoccupation of Richard Russell in that particular time of need but, history would record that this concept would grow throughout the Eastern seaboard with similar safe havens being established in Tauranga, Maketu, Whakatane and Opotiki. This was on account of the developing trade between the Bay of Plenty, which was fast becoming a major source of food supply, and the rapidly expanding settlement of Auckland.

In that period it shall be appreciated that the only means of access to those regions was by sea and already a sizeable fleet of merchant craft operated by Pakeha and Maori alike had been kept busily engaged in the transhipment of both produce and people. Among the people who commonly used these waterfront refuges were itinerant families on their way to settle new territories, traders on buying missions, older established settlers and mission workers on return visits to Auckland and children from the more remote settlements being sent to the established schools in Auckland to receive a proper education. Chief among the users of these stopovers, were Maori families who would bring their own food, do their own cooking and, by tradition share it with anyone caring to partake.

It was to the education of the young that Richard Russell was to devote most of his time and it was not long before he had enlisted the aid of the more enlightened of the refugees to become teachers whilst the Church was prevailed upon to provide the classrooms and equipment. There were some among his newly found charges however that had been left totally abandoned after their flight from

Kororareka and were now perceived to be orphans. These were the descendants of slaves of Ngapuhi.

In consultation with the Bishop and other authoritative parties, he therefore arranged to have all of these waifs and strays taken in as wards of the Church and it is to their credit that some of these forgotten children were later to aspire to become teachers themselves and go amongst the Maori people to spread the Christian word.

Richard had already assumed total responsibility for Mango, Maraea and little Jane to the extent that he had given them his name. Mango and Maraea were content to work at the mission school as housekeeper and part-time teacher while little Jane was happy to continue with her education along with the other children all of whom had now become members of one close-knit family.

Shortly after word had come through of the Government proclamation that all captive slaves were to be returned to their homelands, there arrived one day on the doorstep of the Auckland mission school, a small delegation from Te Arawa and, in particular a trio representing the sub-tribes of Ngati Rangiteaorere and Ngati Uenukukopako. They were Arona, Nini and Pokai and they informed Richard that they had come to take their descendants (*mokopuna*) home. There were four children of Arawa descent attending the school one of whom was Jane and, although she now bore the name of Russell and could legally have remained with her foster father, it was the decision of Mango and Maraea that they should all return to their roots (*turangawaewae*) together.

And so it was that in the year 1848, Mango, Maraea and Jane along with the other descendants of Te Arawa were escorted by Arona and his delegation to the land of their ancestors there to be welcomed by their tribal kinfolk (*hapu*) with tears of both joy and profound relief that at last the gods had heard their prayers and returned their mokopuna to their rightful home. It had been just twenty-four years since Mango and the baby Maraea had been taken by Hongi Hika.

Mango was to discover that in her absence, vast and far-reaching changes had come about amongst her people and homeland. The village and community on Mokoia Island had been rejuvenated and restored to its normal busy and industrious lifestyle with extended cultivations, new dwelling and communal housing and even the addition of a church and mission station. The people themselves had become almost entirely converted to Christianity and already there were pakeha families living amongst them.

At *TeNgae* on the Eastern side of the lake and about eight miles from Ohinemutu, the Reverend Thomas Chapman had established a mission station and Church and had also opened a school which had attracted children from all around the Eastern Rotorua, Rotoiti and Okere districts. All of the arable land around the mission station had been tilled and planted in maize and wheat and a water driven flour mill had been installed above the TeNgae Stream. Produce from the farm was carted out in horse-drawn drays to Maketu and loaded for shipment to Auckland.

All around the region there appeared to be an air of industry and enterprise with any thought of war and depredation being long since cast aside.

Mango decided that she would return to Mokoia to settle amongst the survivors of her original family whilst Maraea and Jane came to live with an uncle (***matua keke***) ***Matenga te Ruru*** and his wife ***Tikao*** who were close relatives (***whanaunga***) and lived at TeNgae where Jane would attend the Reverend Chapman's mission school.

Their stay amongst their own extended family (***whanau***) was however only to last little more than a year before they received a message from

Richard Russell asking them to return to Auckland where by then he had re-established his business and prepared a comfortable home for them both. But within that time at least, Matenga te Ruru saw to it that they should become thoroughly indoctrinated into their ancestral genealogy (*whakapapa*) and the high social standing (*mana*) that had been conferred upon them. Such prestigious principles they were each to uphold throughout the remaining years of their lives.

Maraea was left in two minds whether to remain in the tranquillity of her newly found home and family, or return to the vastly more vibrant and exciting lifestyle of Auckland. She chose the latter but for none other than her own personal and secret reason that from Auckland she would be able to look to the North to where the sea meets the sky. As for Jane, she would always be happy as long as she could be with her mother.

Jane's Story Chapter 12

Journey Through to Adulthood

Back with her mother and foster-father in Auckland, Jane continued with her education at the mission school along with her extended refugee family that had been brought together under the patronage of the Anglican Church after their retreat from Kororareka.

The bringing together of a family under such circumstances where children were to find themselves parentless and without any other family connections, was not unknown to the Maori who would take them under their care as foster-children (*whangai*) and bestow upon them the same rights and privileges as became their own extended family (*whanau*). It was in this context therefore that Jane, in her later narratives, referred to her fellow classmates at the mission school as brothers and sisters. For example her reference to a brother whom she names *Neri*, was one of the small group of refugees from Kororareka and he and a little sister were to find refuge at the Church mission at the same time as Jane. Neri's full name was *Hone te Wahahuka* whose parents had been abducted by the Ngapuhi from the *Koheriki* sub-tribe of *Ngati Paoa* who lived on the *Hauraki* coast around the mouth of the *Wairoa* River (near the present Clevedon).

Jane of course was an only child who, along with her mother Maraea (who remained unmarried for the rest of her life), was adopted by Richard Russell who remained utterly devoted to them both and cherished them as his very own family.

From the beginning, Jane was to show exceptional intelligence and adaptability and became a committed scholar who readily absorbed all of the knowledge that was imparted to her by her devoted Christian teachers and mentors at the mission school. Her academic learning was to be further enriched by the Roman Catholic brotherhood of priests who had been brought from Europe to New Zealand by Bishop Pompallier. Among them were Fathers Borgon, Justin and Euloge Reignier all of whom were later to maintain a close association with the Te Arawa people. It was from encouragement received from that fraternity that she became fluent in the French language and was introduced to classical European music, literature and culture which would continue to hold her interest throughout her long and eventful life.

In a way it was a great pity that she had not been given the opportunity to pursue a higher education in Europe. With her natural talent and insatiable thirst for knowledge, who knows what new horizons might have opened up to her? "For a rose to bloom in all its glory, it must be carefully cultivated and nurtured lest it revert to briar and bramble, – still pretty and sweet-smelling but never to reach its full potential". However it was not to be and Jane was to devote her future to the welfare of her own people by assuming a wider role in the administration of the mission school which had been extended to include the Three Kings Native Institution, a boarding school for Maori children, where she herself became a teacher at the estimably tender age of sixteen.

As she grew from childhood through adolescence to flowering womanhood, it became apparent that Jane had inherited the tall and graceful stateliness of her mother but, whereas the beautiful Maraea's limpid brown eyes were filled with wonderment and appeal, Jane's grey-green eyes could be stern and piercing, ever searching and enquiring of the truth. Her dark auburn hair soft and flowing, her fair complexion, high cheekbones, firm and stubborn chin the legacy of her Celtic father whom she had never known. She too was beautiful but in a more august and self-assuming way. One who was born to lead.

It was in the year 1854 that a group of young men from Te Arawa called at the Auckland mission station en route to the gumfields of the North where they aspired to make their fortunes extracting that rare and elusive substance from the wetlands where once stood ancient stands of **Kauri**.

At that time men (and women) from all parts of the Colony together with immigrants from other lands and in particular the Balkan States of Southern Europe could be seen journeying to the North to try their luck in the gumfields after the Government had opened up that region at the end of the Heke wars and the suppression of the antagonistic Ngapuhi.

Heading the Te Arawa expedition was a very handsome young man called *Te Kiri Karamu,* a distant relative of Maraea and a direct descendant of Ngati Rangiteaorere. He had apparently taken an instant emotional affection towards Jane and, from the sheer rapidity of the events that followed, her mutual response must have been equally as fleet.

The match easily won the approval of both Richard and Maraea who, by her own experience was to lean heavily in favour of an indigenous suitor for her daughter in preference to one who came from another land and who might one day decide to sail away and never return. And so in the following year (1855), they came together to take their vows in the Mission Chapel at Three Kings and were pronounced man and wife. Jane had now assumed the name of **Heeni Te Kiri Karamu.**

At first Jane was happy to accompany her husband to the gumfields in the North but soon after she became pregnant with her first child, she returned to Auckland where she found employment as a Governess to the family of Mr Robert Graham, a wealthy industrialist of *Ellerslie.* She was then able to persuade her husband to abandon all thoughts of making a fortune in the gumfields and come to Auckland where she had been instrumental in securing employment for him as a farm manager on Mr Graham's property on *Waiheke* Island.

Over the ensuing seven years, she shared her time between living at Waiheke with her husband and a joyously flourishing family, which began with the birth of a daughter *Sophia* in 1856 (died in infancy), followed by two sons, *Rangiteaorere* and *Atutahi* (1857 and 1858), then another daughter *Rangitauninihi* in 1860 and finally a son *Te Ngahoa* in 1861, and the resumption of her work at the Auckland Mission where she was to find herself becoming more and more involved in political affairs of state between the Government under Colonel *Gore Brown* and the *Waikato* tribes under the banner of the proclaimed Maori King *Tawhiao te Wherowhero*.

It was through her preoccupation with the education of Maori children in particular that she came to be familiar with some of the leading figures of the Maori King movement and their negotiations with the Government. *Wiremu Tamehana Tarapipipi te Waharoa* the high chief of the *Ngati Haua* tribe whose territory extended from the Firth of Thames in the North, to the Kaimai Ranges in the East, the Waikato River South of Hamilton (**Kirikiriroa**) in the West and *Putaruru* in the South, who had sent his two sons to the Three Kings School as had several other influential chiefs who were able to foresee the far-reaching value of a European education for their heirs apparent (*Aho Ariki*). These wise old counsellors were also quick to recognise the astute debating powers and the expressive articulation of the well informed young school mistress and her knowledge of formal protocol and presentation.

Jane was therefore invited to help them with their written submissions to the Governor and to appear as interpreter during the discussion and deliberations that would follow. Their confidence in her ability was not to go unrewarded as it would soon be shown that some of her documented translations of the native oratory as delivered by the Maori advocates were to be acknowledged in Government House as being quite brilliant..

As her contribution to the movement became more widely favoured, she found that the amount of time that she was able to devote to her husband and family was becoming less and less until her husband, who had not been kept fully informed of the reason for her absence and, not ever being socially inclined in any case, came to feel sadly neglected and began to look around for other more mutually sympathetic companionship.

Her children however were always well cared for and were never to be without love and affection simply because Maraea had taken them under her wing and was always there to attend their every need.

Under such circumstances therefore, it was only a matter of time before Jane should be confronted with the inevitable outcome. Her husband had become unfaithful and taken other women.

Her strict, uncompromising, almost inexorable Christian upbringing was to prohibit any thought of reconciliation. Such conduct was totally unforgivable and he would have to go.

In retrospect, it would have to be conceded that theirs was a marriage doomed to failure from the start. She of sharp intelligence, ambitious and eager for advancement, discriminating and selective of social behaviour, a champion of the rights of women and the underprivileged. He of no particular social leaning, complacent and comfortable with his place in the sun and with no desire to change the world from what it was already. The lady and the gumdigger. It had to take more than a handsome face to bridge such a formidable gap.

In the event, it has since been chronicled that Te Kiri Karamu duly returned to Rotorua with his new-found intimate *Te Kotuhi* and settled among his Ngati Rangiteaorere hapu to live out his days in far less strenuous circumstances.

Jane's Story Chapter 13

War Comes to The Waikato

Ka ngapu te whenua	The earthquake shakes the land
Ka haere nga tangata ki whea?	Where shall man find an abiding place?
E Ruaumoko	O Ruaumoko (God of the underground)
Purutia!	Hold fast our land!
Tawhia!	Bind tightly bind!
Kia ita!	Be firm. Be firm!
A - a - a ita!	Nor let it from our grasp
Kia mau, kia mau!	be torn!

This chant, which may still be heard echoing through the halls of the judiciary, tribunals and parliaments of the present day wherever Maori has been brought together to appeal their passion and sentiment for their ancestral heritage, was the rallying call of the followers of the Maori King *Tawhiao te Wherowhero* which brought war to the *Waikato* in 1863 following the breakdown of peace negotiations between the native land owners (*Tangatawhenua*) and the Crown.

In the beginning of the King movement, the more intelligent of the leadership like the wise and patriotic *Wiremu Tamihana Tarapipipi* (the "Kingmaker"), who was always a restraining force, and other Waikato chiefs such as *Patara te Tuhi*, nephew of the first King *Potatau te Wherowhero*, could see clearly that there was nothing to be gained by the severance of relations with the *Pakeha*. However, the friction caused by European encroachment into the Waikato, the treatment of the Maori by the lower class of whites, the reluctance of the authorities to grant the tribes a reasonable measure of self determination, also the *Taranaki* experience with land confiscation and the loss of so many men at *Waitara* and lately, the extension of the military road from *Drury* through the forest to the *Waikato River*, served only to reinforce the Maori disbelief in the friendly intention of the Government. Suspicion was further aggravated by the attempt to establish a Government constabulary station at *TeKohekohe*.

The natural desire of the Waikato chiefs was for a better system of government which could have been turned to beneficial account had there been a more prescient administration.

At a large inter-tribal meeting at *Paetai*, near *Rangiriri* in 1857, *Potatau*, *Te Wharepu* and other chiefs asked *Governor Gore Browne* for a magistrate and laws to be incorporated into a supreme tribal council (*runanga*) and to this the Governor responded by appointing Mr *F.D.Fenton* (later to become a judge of the Maori Land Court) to establish a civil institution but he was not given time to develop a satisfactory system before he was recalled and the whole scheme, abandoned.

Governor Browne and his Ministers consistently declined to recognise the Maori King or any separate much less authoritative Maori nationality and in 1861, after he issued a most threatening proclamation, the followers of the Maori King (now called the *"Kingites"*), forming the majority of tribes of the *Waikato* and extending as far South as the *Maniapoto,* formulated an initial plan of war.

A combined force was to come down the river to take up a position at *Paparata* (on the high ground East of the settlement now known as *Bombay*) which would be their headquarters. From thence, parties would occupy strategic positions that would menace Drury and *Papakura* in the North, military traffic along the Great South Road, and *Mauku* and other settlements in the West.

There was an alternative plan which was far more ambitious and this was to execute a grand coup to attack Auckland by night or early in the morning. The *Hunua* bush was to be the central assembly point for the main body whilst a division of the finest fighters was to cross the *Manukau* by canoe and approach Auckland from the West by way of the *Whau* Stream. The *Ngati Paoa* and other *Hauraki* coastal tribes were to concentrate on the area around the mouth of the *Wairoa* River in the South East.

This action would have been attempted had Gore Browne remained as Governor and it was only the news that *Sir George Grey* was returning that averted such a precipitate uprising. All Maori looked forward to his coming as the beginning of a different, more friendly policy towards them. But although the new Governor was to make some endeavour to meet the crisis by offering semi-independent government, he at the same time began an aggressive movement into the Waikato and by that disrespectful action it was seen by the chiefs of the King movement that compromise had become impossible and war was now inevitable. The original plan of 1861 was therefore taken up with raids on the frontier settlements with Paparata as base and camps in the Hunua forest.

With the failure of the Waikato delegation led by Wiremu Tamehana to obtain a mutually acceptable settlement after their long and protracted negotiations with the Government, the initial feeling of hope and expectation turned reluctantly to despair and resignation that war was now unavoidable.

Jane who, due to her early association with the Maori delegation, was fully appreciative of the genuine efforts of Tamehana and the other moderate Waikato chiefs to maintain peace between the races, and her disappointment that their work towards that end had apparently fallen on deaf ears after all, came to be resentful of the attitude displayed by some of the Government representatives whom she suspected were not genuinely interested in peace if it meant sharing the administration of the land with the native owners.

What incensed her more was the Government ultimatum issued on 9th July 1863 requiring all natives living North of the Waikato frontier with Auckland to either swear allegiance with the Queen and give up their arms or, for those refusing to align themselves on the side of the British, to retire to the Waikato. Those not complying with this instruction were to be ejected from their homes. That ultimatum was followed by a proclamation sent by Governor Grey on 11th July to the followers of King Tawhiao giving his reasons for the breakdown of negotiations between them and the subsequent military measures he had ordered on behalf of the Government of New Zealand.

On principle therefore and in appreciation and understanding of the genuine concerns of Wiremu Tamihana and the other Waikato chiefs for the future of their people, Jane decided to support the cause of the King movement for the retention of sovereignty over their lands. This of course meant that in accordance with the Government ultimatum she would have to retire to the South of the Waikato frontier.

There were several people living at the Mission who were also obliged to accompany her and these included her mother Maraea and the four children, her foster brother Neri and sister Hera and the sons of Waikato chiefs who had been attending the Three Kings School. Richard Russell reluctantly decided not to accompany them as he believed that he could make a more valuable contribution towards reconciliation between the warring factions by remaining strictly neutral as observed by the Church in the past. Jane was in total agreement with his decision. And so the little group of Waikato compatriots from the Auckland Mission moved South to the mouth of the Wairoa River to join with the *Koheriki* sub-tribe of Ngati Paoa under the command of the chief *Wi Koka*.

Among the meagre possessions that Jane carried away from the Auckland Mission, which had been home to her and her foster family for so long, was a special flag which she had made to express her patriotism for the Maori cause. It was a large flag of red silk and it bore the symbol of Christianity in the form of a heraldic cross on the left side and, in the centre, an open mouthed crescent moon in ascension (*Marama waha roa*) with three stars of the Pleiades cluster (*Matariki*) spaced symmetrically within its sphere of influence to represent the creation of the world in Maori mythology. Finally, the word **AOTEAROA** in large capital letters written across the bottom. This was the name that grew from the great meeting of chiefs at Pukawa, Lake Taupo in 1857 when, at the instigation of *Te Heuheu Iwikau* of *Ngati Tuwharetoa*, all gave their allegiance to *Potatau te Wherowhero* and acclaimed him as King of all of the tribes of New Zealand.

One further item among her possessions was a single barrelled, breech loading fowling piece which had been purchased for Jane by Mr Graham during her days on Waiheke Island where, in much less stressful times she would be invited to join his weekend pigeon-shooting parties and with which she was soon to display a natural proficiency.

Jane's Story Chapter 14

A Family at War

The Europeans were not without warning that the sharp and barbarous methods of Maori warfare would be revived. Wiremu Tamehana a long time advocate of peace among the races, warned Archdeacon Brown at Tauranga that his race would spare neither unarmed persons (*tangata kore ringa*) nor property and in August 1863 he wrote to the Governor cautioning him to *"bring to the towns the defenceless lest they be killed in their farms in the bush"*. "But, he concluded, you are well acquainted with the custom of Maori at war".

The war party that gathered in the *Hunua* and *Wairoa* Ranges and thence made forays against the frontier settlers was mainly from the *Ngati Paoa* tribe under the high chief *Hori Ngakapa te Whanaunga* of the upper *Hauraki Gulf.*

A strong and acutely mobile force of *Koheriki*, a subtribe of Ngati Paoa, led by the fighting chief *Wi Koka* was assembled in the Wairoa South area and joined by some *Ngati Haua* from the upper Waikato (including the two sons of Wiremu Tamehana), a number from *Ngai te Rangi* of *Tauranga* and the *Piri Rakau* from the *Kaimai* hinterland led by *Hori Ngatai* and *Titipa*. This force did not number more than 35 fighters but they were all very active and highly skilled in bush warfare most of whom were to fight right through the war and ultimately take part in the defence of *Gate Pa* at Tauranga.

Accompanying the Koheriki force with admirable courage throughout the campaign were some women and children (many of whom were to die), willing to share the hardship and deprivation of a life on the move through perilous and hostile territory just to be with their menfolk and assist with the making of camps, preparation of food, tending to the wounded, even the moulding of bullets and the recharging of cartouche cases for the firearms.

Among that intrepid group, Jane was to find herself with her four children, **Rangiteaorere** (6yrs.), **Atutahi** (5yrs.), **Rangitauninihi** (3yrs.) and the baby **TeNgahoa** not quite two years old, also her mother Maraea and foster sister **Hera**. She had brought her children with her knowing full well of the danger but with the firm resolve that as a family they would live or die together. Her children would never be left abandoned to fend for themselves as were she and her mother those many years ago. Because of her exceptional prowess with a firearm however, Jane was afforded the high veneration of a front line woman fighter (*wahine toa*) holding the same status as her foster brother Neri and the Thompson (Tamehana) brothers.

Her first encounter with her comrades of the **Piri Rakau** tribe was to hold Jane in arresting intrigue. Those who called themselves "The people who cling to the forest" (*Piri Rakau*), widely acknowledged as descendants of an ancient aboriginal stock that had settled in this land long before the third Maori migration of the fourteenth century. People who normally stayed strictly amongst themselves and preferred to live together in isolation deep in the heavily wooded country of the central North Island where they would maintain their thatched roofed slab houses (*wharepuni*) and food crop cultivations (*maara*) in shallow sunny valleys in completely concealed localities and would rarely make social contact with neighbouring tribes. Their intrinsic knowledge of the native forest with its bounty of edible plants, birds and wild-life, their uncanny ability to read sign, their unerring sense of direction and the masterly bush-craft which they were to display was to become the difference between success and failure in the turbulent months to come.

Besides their traditional hand to hand fighting weapons such as the short and long-handled tomahawk (*patiti* and *toki kakuaroa*), the Koheriki were equipped with a motley collection of firearms ranging from a few Calisher and Terry carbines 'appropriated' from retreating or fallen Government troops on the battlefield, some double-barrelled shotguns (*tupara*) and single barrelled (*hakimana*), all percussion firing, and a few elderly flintlock muskets called "duck's bill" (*ngutu parera*) named as such from the fancied resemblance of the flint holding hammer to the bill of a duck. Ammunition comprised a moulded lead bullet, measured charge of gunpowder made up into a cartridge, and a percussion cap, each to be loaded in succession to make up a primed single shot. There were occasions during this conflict, it has been recorded, when as the supply of lead bullets ran out, some of the Maori defenders resorted to using small pebbles and even peach stones, anything that could be hurled in defiance at the enemy. Each man carried an allocation of ammunition in either a captured bandolier, special hand-crafted cartouche boxes buckled around the waist, or in the pockets of a European waistcoat which came to be the prized possession of the Maori musketeer because of its close and comfortable fitting and its abundance of convenient pockets.

Their battle attire was also mixed and varied but always adaptable to the conditions under which they were living and fighting. Whereas the regular colonial soldier would be wearing a woollen shirt, blue tunic or jacket, knickerbockers, long stockings and boots, his Maori counterpart would also be wearing a shirt (if he owned one), a traditional woven fibre kilt (*maro*) or as a last resort, a kilt of any material or colour from canvas to Scottish plaid to worsted tweed, to a section of woollen blanket. Those who possessed a European waistcoat were envied by the others who had to resort to home made cartouche belts to contain their spare ammunition. Long trousers were not popular with the bush fighter as they would become saturated and heavy with mud from the continual crossing of swamps and streams and there would be rare opportunity to have them dry out. A few lucky ones would possess boots and socks but most would be either bare-footed or wearing a type of hand-crafted moccasin from canvas or sacking material and laced up with flax. The Piri Rakau also favoured their traditional rain cloak (*pake*) made of overlapping flax or *kiekie* fronds in tiers like the shingles of a roof. The women wore either European dresses or tunics with shortened (knee length) skirts, or shirts and kilts like the men.

The steep and rugged forest-clad country of the Hunua and Wairoa Ranges bordering the left flank of *General Sir D.A.Cameron's* advance into the Waikato with his combined British and Colonial armies was a natural stronghold and retreat of the so called *"Kingites"* who from that cover could raid farm settlements and ambush military convoys with little loss to themselves. Neither the regular soldiers nor the enlisted militiamen were competent in that type of guerrilla warfare and, to meet the threat, the Government resolved to form a small corps of picked men (mainly local settlers and their sons), practiced in bushcraft and willing to scout the forest and hunt out the elusive marauders.

Soon a company was formed under the command of Lieutenant (later Major) *William Jackson* who was himself a young settler of the Papakura district. Towards the end of the year a second company under the command of Captain (later Major) *Gustavus Von Tempski*, an officer of aristocratic Polish nationality, who began his military life in the Prussian Army and came to New Zealand in search of gold at *Coromandel* but only to have his old war-fever aroused when he heard of the outbreak of war with the Waikato when he decided to volunteer for a career more to his taste. Von Tempski was afterwards to serve in the concluding Taranaki wars and was killed at *Te Ngutu o te manu* in 1868.

These two select companies were named the *Forest Rangers* and it was the No.1 Company under Lieutenant Jackson that was delegated the formidable task of pursuing the raiders including Wi Koka's Koheriki party and engaging them on their own terms and in their own natural habitat.

By September 1863, the Koheriki and allied war parties who contested the Eastern front from the mouth of the Wairoa River to the high ground above Hunua, launched a series of raids on the scattered farm settlements on the lower river flats. They had been successful in driving off the outlying farmers but not without loss of life on both sides, and pillaging their houses and livestock. They had also set up patrols along the edge of the bush to cut off any attempt by the settlers to return.

By then however, the Auckland Militia had constructed and occupied the *Galloway Redoubt* which was positioned a few miles inland from *Maraetai* in a cleared area above the left bank of the river. This became the headquarters of the District Commander, *Major Lyon* and was garrisoned with a detachment of the *Auckland Rifle Volunteers.*

On 15 September the garrison was taken completely by surprise when without warning the whole of the surrounding bush suddenly erupted in a burst of rifle fire. The Koheriki had issued their challenge. This decided Major Lyon two days later to lead a detachment of 55 men up the valley towards the village of *Otau* where he directed heavy fire against the defenders who replied with volleys from numbers of men deployed in square formations with each square falling back behind the others to reload before moving forward again. In that engagement casualties were suffered on both sides before it was broken off with the militiamen retiring to the redoubt.

Before daylight next morning, Major Lyon returned with a force of 70 men and lined them along the opposite bank of the flooded river to launch a broadside of rifle fire onto the unprepared villagers who had not expected a renewal of the attack so soon. There were approximately 200 occupants of the village at the time, men, women and children who rushed about in great confusion as the bullets from over the river thudded into the walls of the huts (*whare*). Some of the men took up defensive positions and returned the fire whilst the others hastily gathered together all the possessions they could carry and rushed off to the welcoming protection of the bush. As the river was still in flood however, Lyon's force was not able to cross and follow up the attack and reluctantly was forced to again break off the engagement and return to the redoubt.

To Jane, the early morning attack came suddenly and without warning. She had just risen to begin another day by stoking up the dying fire in the crude stone hearth at the end of the large *whare*, that was being shared by her little group, and making ready to prepare food for them all. Maraea was busy getting the children up and dressed and the other youngsters were loath but slowly arousing themselves as they became aware that another day of excitement was about to begin.

As the first bullets tore into the tree-fern (*Ponga*) trunk walls, some of them passing right across the room to exit on the other side, all bedlam broke loose with children screaming, women rushing to scoop up their possessions and run and the men wildly shouting and snatching up their firearms to run out and do battle. Jane, her first thoughts for her children, called to Maraea and Hera to take the three oldest ones and run for the cover of the nearby bush. She grabbed up baby Te Ngahoa and wrapped him in a back-pack (*Pikau*) to hoist him onto her back and, taking up her firearm she rushed to follow the others and as she ran out the door she saw the chief *Titipa* fall dead in front of her. Another man called *Tipene* from Tauranga was also killed whilst others lay mortally wounded. Mercifully, the Tamehana boys whom she called upon to stay close to her side were to escape unharmed.

It was not the first time that Jane had come under fire but this incident was to bring home to her the stark reality of war and how it would not only involve soldiers battling each other to the death but also determine the fate of whole families whether they too should live or die. She had already received her baptism of fire in the raids on the settlements of the lower Wairoa where she had seen combatants on both sides shot and killed. Men who had received terrible wounds yet impatient to be patched up that they might return to the fray. But in these earlier engagements only the fighters were involved and not their old folk, women and children who were held secluded in safety and spared the horrors of the killing fields.

This latest action however, had now caught up with her own little family and had completely engulfed them in a desperate conflict the outcome of which, Jane had come to realise, was by no means assured. She observed with relief that the attack was not being followed up immediately and that there would be time for the Koheriki to re-muster its forces and decide the action that should now be taken. But here on the edge of the vast Hunua forest, she was left to ponder the future knowing that she was now the entrusted head of a family at war.

Jane's Story Chapter 15

Flight into the Hinterland

The Koheriki, now operating from deep within the Hunua Forest continued to skirmish against Major Lyon's Militia by attacking the European settlers within a short distance of his Galloway Redoubt and also further afield at *Ramarama* and *Mangemangeroa* when, very much to the dismay and consternation of Jane, several unarmed and defenceless settler families were to be caught up in the exchanges and suffer violent death. Whilst she was to witness the slaughter of people on both sides of the conflict, the innocent and culpable alike, and she had come to accept that in war it was a case of kill or be killed, her devout Christian upbringing refused to accept or justify the taking of a human life whether it be friend or deadly enemy. That conviction was to remain deeply instilled within her throughout the long and sometimes bloody encounters that lay before her.

It was inevitable that the escalating marauding actions being pursued by the Koheriki would call for urgent counter reaction and the Military Command decided to concentrate more troops against them on the Wairoa front and also to complete a line of outposts from *Pokeno* in the West, through *Maramarua* to *Pukorokoro* (Miranda) on the Firth of Thames. This would in effect cut off any retreat by the Koheriki to rejoin the main Waikato forces in the South. It would then remain for the Forest Rangers under Major Jackson to enter the Hunua Forest and flush them out.

Early in December 1863, a council of war was held by the Koheriki in the village of Urangaheuheu in the forest about four miles above Otau when it was decided that the Government troop concentrations on the Wairoa front had made further raiding across the river much too precarious and that the time had come for Koheriki to rejoin the main Waikato army at Paparata and take part in the defence of the Waikato heartland.

The plan was to travel South-west through the bush to the main headquarters of the Waikato forces at Paparata and from there down to *Mangatawhiri* on the banks of the Waikato River. But just before starting out, an old Priest (*Tohunga*) named *Timoti te Amopa* rose to warn that he had received a sign (*tohu*) from his personal god (*Atua*) *Tu-Panapana* that danger lurked on the path to Paparata and that grave ill would befall anyone that would take it. A large number of the party however dismissed it as an old man's rambling and decided to move out immediately but Jane, who was almost ready to follow them with her little family group, happened to glance up into the trees where she beheld a pair of Fantails (*Tirairaka*) fluttering excitedly towards them. They whirled and twittered above their heads and flew off in the opposite direction and then returned to repeat the performance over again. At once Maraea and Jane recognised the *tohu* that their very own *Atua* had sent them and they earnestly pleaded with the chief *Wi Koka* to heed the warning and take a path in the direction as shown them by the Tirairaka.

The chief rose to address his people and pronounce that it was right to disperse into smaller parties and meet together either at Paparata or Mangatawhiri. Those who wished to take the direct path to Paparata were free to do so but he would lead the remainder in the more Southerly direction across the high ground of the Hunua Range. The party then split into two with one half taking the direct path to Paparata and the other, including Jane and her family electing to follow Wi Koka into the unknown and trackless wilderness to the South.

The detachment led by Wi Koka would not exceed 30 men accompanied by some small families including that of Jane, Timoti the old Tohunga, fighters of the Ngati Haua and Ngai te Rangi tribes including the two Tamehana boys and lastly a section of Piri Rakau scouts who were to blaze the trail ahead and guide the party through some of the most rugged, forbidding and almost impenetrable country in the North Island. They would eventually traverse the headwaters of the *Wairoa, Mangatawhiri* and *Mangatangi* rivers through deep and broken gorges where the waters roared down from the higher reaches of the range and tumbled in rocky cascades as they snaked their way out to the more tranquil valleys and plains. All around was dense rain forest with its canopy of tall trees (including *Kauri*) blocking out the sun and its thick, dank and steaming undergrowth criss-crossed with fallen logs in various stages of decomposition as the various fungi did their work. Tangled *Rata* and supple-jack (*kareao*) vines, bush lawyer (*pohue*), bracken fern (*aruhe*), *wiwi* and *kiekie* clumps spreading across the forest floor all to block the traveller's advance and always, the seemingly incessant rain.

With women and little children in the party, progress up the range would be understandably slow. One day, after about a week on the journey, Jane, who was bringing up the rear with the children, was cautioned by one of the Piri Rakau scouts who had come back down the line to peer into the bush behind them. Jane stood stock still, listening intently and from a distance she was just able to make out the faint cry of a woman or child. Instinctively everyone sprang to the sides of the track and concealed themselves in the undergrowth and all became silent as they watched and waited.

Out from the shadows a woman came weeping. Her legs lacerated and bleeding, her arms and her fingers which she held out before her, swollen and raw. Jane at once recognised her as *Mere* the wife of *Te Paitui* who had left with the other party for Paparata. She ran forward to greet her and take her in her arms just as she was about to collapse from sheer exhaustion. Jane sat and cradled the head of the distressed woman in her lap and held a cup of water to her lips and, after a time Mere sat up by herself and related her story.

"On the day that our party had left for Paparata, we had walked until we had come to a quiet valley of the upper Wairoa River where it was decided we would camp for the night and also for the next day as it would be Sunday and we would wish to hold a Church service. Our leader was confident that by then we had put enough miles between us and the Wairoa militia to be safely out of danger of attack"

"However, on the next morning, just as some of us were bathing and getting ready for the service, there came a crashing of sound from out of the bush and suddenly a band of soldiers charged into our midst with their guns firing and shouting to us that we were to die. Some of our men were able to take up their weapons and fight back but most were caught by surprise and were shot down without mercy. My husband *Te Paitui* was shot through both hips and lay terribly wounded. His older brother *Te Tapuke* ran back to help him but he was shot through the head and fell dead at his brother's feet."

"When the firing stopped, and the soldiers had left after burying our dead and carrying away their own, I ran back to my husband and washed and tended his wounds but he was only to last the rest of the day before he raised himself up to bid me farewell and then fell back dead. I wept over him all that night and in the morning I tried to shift him to where the soldiers had buried the others but he was too heavy for me so I dug a grave next to him by myself and buried him there by the side of the river."

"After that I left him and decided to walk back the way we had come as I had heard from the soldiers talking that Paparata was no longer in Waikato hands. Some of our party had managed to escape into the bush before me but I could not catch up with them and just had to keep walking for as long as I was able".

Jane and the others listened in awe as the realisation struck home that the signs read by the tohunga *Timoti* and again by Jane and Maraea with the timely appearance of the *tirairaka* were very true and that they were indeed fortunate that they had taken heed. They had also come to realise that the Government had unleashed a new force against them in the form of the Forest Rangers who were even now deployed as a strike force that would operate between the regular Militia encamped North of the Wairoa River and the newly established line of outposts South of the Hunua Ranges. In effect, the Koheriki had not only been hemmed in by the permanent forces surrounding them but would now have to contend with the roving Forest Rangers in their midst.

This called for extreme caution from now on not to betray the whereabouts of this now fugitive party to an enemy whose special unit of bush-trained hunters could now be hot on their trail. They must always keep under cover of the bush during the day, there would be no talking out loud or babies crying during the march nor in the evening camps, no longer would they be able to shoot wild pigs and pigeons for food lest the sound of their shots be heard and there could be no more lighting of cooking fires. All evidence of their passage through the bush must be obliterated and disguised in order to cover their tracks and deceive and delay their pursuers.

Jane was first to reflect on the enormous reliance that would now be placed on their Piri Rakau friends to guide them through this threatened impending peril.

The official account of the clash between the Forest Rangers and the detached group of Koheriki on the track to Paparata was much as Mere described it. The Ranger patrol of eight men was led by Ensign Westrupp. They left four Maori dead and sustained only some (stretchered) wounded of their own. Te Painui was laid out on a blanket before they left as there was little else they could do for him.

The date was Sunday 14 December 1863.

Mere was not to know however that a tin box containing three flags was captured by the Rangers that day and that one of them was the red silk AOTEAROA flag made by Jane and presented to Wi Koka. It would be many years later before Jane was to become reunited with it at the Auckland Old Colonists' Museum (now the Auckland Institute and Museum) where it remains to this day.

Jane's Story Chapter 16

The Great Escape

After the warning they had been given of the new threat of Major Jackson's Forest Rangers being in the area, the depleted fighting force of Koheriki, led by Wi Koka, decided to press on as fast as they could to the Southern side of the Hunua Range where they would seek an escape route through the line of heavily manned military outposts which were barring their way to freedom and the relative safety of the upper Waikato.

Progress was painfully slow however and made so much more difficult because of the restrictions placed upon them in avoiding detection by the enemy forces. Not being able to replenish the food supply with fresh meat as they were accustomed and no longer having access to cultivations of potato and kumara, they were now having to survive entirely on wild berries, shoots of special plants, wild honey and cold water. Again, it had occurred to Jane that it was to the eternal credit of the Piri Rakau and their infinite knowledge of the bush with its precious and carefully guarded bounty that they were able to prevail at all. The terrain was also becoming more and more formidable as they traversed the headwaters of the Wairoa and the Mangatawhiri rivers and prepared to negotiate the Mangatangi.

To Jane and the other women, the plight of the children was most pressing. The little ones were already suffering the effects of prolonged exposure to the cold and rain and of not being able to warm and dry themselves by a fire also the need for hot and more nourishing food. The very young like Jane's baby Te Ngahoa were subjected to the additional discomfort of having to have their mouths bound shut whilst being carried on their mother's backs only because they were not old enough to understand why they should not cry out at any time. For those like Maraea and Jane who were shouldering the extra burden of tending and escorting their little families through the harsh and unfamiliar countryside as well as being called upon to set up the evening camps and help prepare what little food there was to go around, morale was sinking lower as they were gradually being overtaken by fatigue and beginning to despair that it would never end.

Now amongst the men of Ngai te Rangi who accompanied the party was a man called **Penetito** and he was one of those rarities who can only be described as a compulsive conversationist - quite irrepressible and remembered as one who was constantly being scolded for not keeping his voice down. He wandered down and sat amongst the women during a rest period one day to tell them a story. It was about the olden day warriors of his own sub-tribe (*hapu*) whom he claimed had learned how to overcome the pangs of hunger, just as they were suffering from that day. They would hang a strip of dried shark from one ear and a similar strip of dried kumara from the other. When their hunger grew unbearable therefore, they would pass the strip of dried shark across under the nose from one side and then follow up with the dried kumara from the other. They would even nibble them sometimes if they wished to taste the flavour. Thus were they able to stave off their ravenous hunger for extensive periods of time.

Ever the pragmatist, Jane of course didn't believe a word of it but she could not suppress a giggle at the thought as she came to realise that idiots would always exhibit themselves even in times of war.

For several days after they had crossed the headwaters of the Mangatawhiri, the party camped in a deep valley whilst the forward scouts sought an escape route which would safely navigate a crossing of the more difficult Mangatangi River and thence infiltrate the military lines which were barring the way to the South.

Jane was called forward to join the scouting patrol not only because she had become an expert bush fighter with her astute perception and proven skill with her gun but also for her acute sense of hearing and knowledge of the English language. She was able to overhear the soldier's conversations and impart their meaning to her comrades.

They at length successfully reconnoitred the opposing military encampments and the sentry cordons that were stationed across the way and finally, after a brief conference the decision was made to attempt a breakthrough. That night with the Piri Rakau in the van and the other fighters following, the women and children bringing up the rear, their babie's mouths bound shut and the other young ones sworn to absolute silence under fear of death, the entire column crept up like shadowy spectres to the right bank of the Mangatangi where the scouts had earlier located a log bridge that had been thrown across a place where the very deep ravine had narrowed.

Because the bridge consisted only of a pair of crudely trimmed logs, it was to take an anxious and fearfully long time for them all to get across but at last, with everyone accounted for, two of the Piri Rakau men were left to begin the perilous task of cutting down the bridge with their bush axes without arousing the soldiers who were stationed nearby. Once the bridge had been successfully cut away, any threat from the rear had been effectively removed but there still lay ahead the military picket lines to be negotiated.

To further frustrate any attempt to slip through their lines, the soldiers had lit a line of fires in the fern but rather than deter the fugitives it only helped them by providing a smoke screen. There were times also when they passed so close to some of the soldier's tents that they could hear them laughing and talking and on one occasion, they were astounded to hear the bizarrely outlandish strains of an accordion.

This would have been near the *Esk Redoubt* between Paparata (Surrey) and Pukorokoro (Miranda). Some of the troops were mounted men of the Waikato Militia and C.D.F. Cavalry but their pursuit was forestalled with the cutting down of the log bridge over the Mangatangi.

And so the remnants of Koheriki who had defended the Eastern front at the Wairoa until they were forced to retreat under sheer weight of numbers, had emerged after their long and arduous traverse of the Hunua Ranges quite unscathed after their ordeal, weary and weakened with hunger but mercifully left without any further molestation.

After they had cleared the military lines, the party was forced to wade through deep swampland in the general direction of *Rangiriri* where it was hoped they might join up with the main Waikato forces. The going was very exhausting but they knew that they would have to press on until they had put a safe distance between them and any possible chasing columns.

At last they came to dry ground which appeared as an island surrounded by swamp on the Northern side but more open water to the South. This turned out to be the Northern arm of *Lake Waikare* (near the present *TeKauwhata*). A camp was quickly set up and the men lost no time in fishing and hunting for food until an abundant supply of wild pork, pigeons and eels, even fresh vegetables from a recently abandoned garden, was brought to the awaiting cooking fires and everyone was soon to eat their fill for the first time in several weeks.

Jane called her extended family together and led them in prayers of thanks for their deliverance from the terrible misery and privation they had suffered, and to pray that the time would soon come when all of the people of Waikato would again be able to live in peace.

Since the arrival at this place, Jane had become more and more puzzled and apprehensive. They had found only deserted dwellings and recently abandoned cultivations, even canoes pulled up on the shore but, where were the people?

She remembered that during their enforced sojourn in the Hunua Ranges, there were days when she could hear the distant boom of cannon fire rising up from the direction of the Waikato River and she surmised that it was coming from General Cameron's gunboats as they attacked the fortified strongholds (*pa*) of the main Waikato forces at **Meremere** and **Rangiriri**. It had occurred to her that this place could not be more than a few miles from either of those *pa* yet there was neither sight nor sound of any activity. Her astute mind had already come to the conclusion that both Meremere and Rangiriri had fallen to the British forces and that the Waikato had since retreated further up the river possibly as far as Tawhiao's own headquarters at **Ngaruawahia**. She must therefore consult with Wi Koka. New plans would have to be made and a new evacuation route decided.

Jane's Story Chapter 17

A Parting of the Ways

After two days of rest and recovery, the party prepared to leave that friendly little island and resume their quest for reunion with the main Waikato resistance force. They crossed the lake in the canoes that had been left abandoned on the island and continued on their journey now in a South-easterly direction away from the Waikato River and over a line of low hills towards the valley of the Piako which lay within the territory of the Ngati Haua tribe under the high chieftainship (*Rangatiratanga*) of Wiremu Tamehana Tarapipipi.

When they reached the river, they followed it up until they came to the village of Piako (near the present Morrinsville) and from there they swung further to the East until eventually after several days altogether of marching, they reached their destination of Matamata. There they were greeted by *Te Raihi* a Ngati Haua chief whose sub-tribe (*hapu*) had remained remote from the present conflict preferring to leave their allegiance with Queen Victoria. Although befriending the Koheriki party, Te Raihi advised that they should go on to *Peria*, a large village just to the West of Matamata and close to the river where Wiremu Tamehana had prepared a great gathering place for all tribes dedicated to the cause of the Maori King.

Jane was delighted to be reunited with her old friend and mentor Wiremu Tamehana and more than relieved to be able to deliver his two sons safe and sound after such a long and eventful absence. She was also pleased to renew acquaintances with *Pokai* and *Hori Ngakapa* of the Ngati Paoa tribe who had fought alongside them in the Wairoa campaign until they had become separated when the Koheriki was forced to withdraw into the Hunua forest. Apparently the Ngati Paoa had also been compelled to retreat and had already been dispossessed of their lands bordering the Western shore of the Firth of Thames and the lower Piako. There were also prominent people from other tribes aligned with the King Movement including *Ngati Rangiwewehi* of Te Arawa and *Ngati Porou* from the East Coast.

Wiremu Tamehana took great pride in showing his honoured guests including Jane over his model village of *Peria* (the Maori form of the Biblical Beria) which was laid out in traditional European style with streets and a civic centre, containing clusters of houses for family groups, a large meeting house, post office, flour mill and a schoolhouse with boarding accommodation for a hundred pupils. There was also a church and a burial ground on a hill and all around there were orchards and fields of wheat, maize, kumara and potatoes. For some years prior to the outbreak of war, a flourishing trade had already been established for the supply of milled flour, grain and agricultural products from Peria and other centres in the upper Waikato not only to Auckland and around the developing Colony but also for export to New South Wales and Victoria in Australia. Unfortunately however, due to the present ill-conceived conflict between a prescience lacking government and a fiercely patriotic Waikato for the retention of authority over their lands, this grand enterprise had come to a halt.

All this was seen by Jane as another example of the devoted statesmanship, patriotism and foresight of Wiremu Tamehana who could see even then the advantages to be gained for both races by living and working together in harmony and sharing in the abundance of wealth that this country had to offer. Tamehana never did advocate war and tried everything in his power to prevent it. Prophetically therefore it would be many years later that Jane would indeed live to see the two races working in harmony together but it had to be in another time of war when they lived and died for a common cause against a common enemy.

It was early in January 1864 when the Koheriki arrived at Peria and it was decided that they should stay for the remainder of the summer. War was now raging in the upper Waipa region and the main Waikato forces were preparing to make a stand along the Pikopiko Stream at Paterangi (just West of TeAwamutu).

Jane however was called upon to work alongside Tamehana and the other chiefs to decipher captured British despatches and also to maintain written correspondence with the Governor in Auckland with whom Tamehana was still trying to negotiate a ceasefire and honourable settlement with the cessation of hostilities. It was Jane's special brief to translate into the written language, Tamehana's gift of logical argument expressed in plain words and his deep knowledge of the Scripture to convey his true intentions to Governor Grey and his Ministers. The land always the land was foremost in his submissions. "Surely" he proposed, "because the land is unoccupied now, is no reason why it should always remain so. I hope the day will come when our descendants will not have more than they really require. As to a King, do you begrudge us a king as if it were a name greater than that of God? If it were so that God forbade us, then we would bow to His command – but he forbids us not."

During this spell of relative peace and inaction at Peria, Jane was however forced to come to terms with a gnawing problem that had bothered her ever since the escape from Hunua. Maraea and the children should never again be exposed to the ravages of war. In all innocence they had been caught up in a conflict no part of which was of their making yet for too long already they had been placed at frightful risk. They were fortunate to have escaped without harm befalling any of them so far but that could change at any time. They were all still existing on an immediate war footing and in any case it would be only a matter of weeks, even days before the Koheriki party was called to the front line again.

There were people here who came from the *Ngati Rangiwewehi* hapu of TeArawa and it was evident that they were keeping in contact with their home base with messengers alternating between centres quite regularly. This was an opportunity to have Maraea and the children escorted to *Hamurana* on the shores of Lake Rotorua where they could arrange for a canoe to take them across to Mokoia Island where they would be safe in the care of the ever faithful Mango. However reluctant she was to part with them, Jane felt compelled to let them go.

It was not difficult to arrange with Ngati Rangiwewehi for the safe deliverance of her family to Hamurana. After all that hapu was closely related to Ngati Rangiteaorere and Ngati Uenukukopako to which Maraea and her family belonged and who had together with Ngati Whakaue of Ohinemutu from ancient times been made custodians of Mokoia Island. The only difference being that Rangiwewehi, probably through its close geographical proximity to the Ngai te Rangi (Tauranga) and Piri Rakau (Kaimai) lands, had thrown in its lot with the King Movement whereas all the other tribes of Te Arawa remained strictly neutral and loyal to Queen Victoria. (It was the Arawa high chief *Temuera te Amohau* who, at a grand meeting of Waikato tribes, rose to say "We will not join the King tribes." *"Taku kingi ko kuini Wikitoria"* - ("My King is Queen Victoria").

All too soon the time came for the little family to separate. The tall and stately Maraea, still beautiful with her proud head held high, little TeNgahoa held snugly in a pikau on her back, the two little boys (Rangiteaorere and Atutahi) and the girls Hera (Jane's foster sister) and Rangitauninihi (her only daughter) gathered in a group waiting for their escort to lead them away and, standing together to wave them goodbye, Jane and her (foster) brother Neri their hearts heavy with love (*aroha*) but knowing that they still had a job to do before they too could make the journey to lasting peace and reconciliation.

And as they stood and watched the little group move away, there came darting and frisking out from the fringe of the tall enshrouding forest, a little female *tirairaka* to circle excitedly above Maraea then to swoop and cavort towards Jane to twitter a happy song before returning to encircle Maraea and the children again before departing for the sanctuary of its forest home. Jane at once grasped Neri in delight. Their loved ones would be delivered safely. Their own Atua had given that assurance.

The news from the front grew steadily worse for the supporters of the King Movement as the summer of 1864 drew onward and slowly gave way to autumn. The vast farmlands and granaries of **Rangiaowhia** (just South of TeAwamutu) which had been the main source of food and provender for the Waikato forces had since fallen to the advancing armies of General Cameron, the numbers of able bodied fighting men were fast becoming grievously depleted whilst those of the opposing side had increased into their thousands and, dwindling supplies of powder and ammunition had fallen to dangerously low levels with no immediate prospect of improvement. The time had come therefore to decide how next to advance the Waikato cause.

At a council of war amongst the surviving chiefs whose own numbers also had not escaped grievous depletion, it was the dauntless **Rewi Maniapoto** who stood in defiance of any capitulation and rallied the sorry remnants of the once majestic tribes of Waikato to fight on to the death. He would make a stand at *Orakau* (near Kihikihi) at the gateway to his beloved Maniapoto homeland and there in glory would they live or die in defence of their noble cause. In sheer admiration of Rewi's courageous stand, Wiremu Tamehana resolved to demonstrate his allegiance and unflagging support by making his own stand at *Te Tiki o te Ihingarangi* (on a cliff top above the Waikato River opposite the present township of Cambridge), on the Western border of his Ngati Haua country.

At length therefore, the Koheriki party under their chief Wi Koka were to take up their weapons and march Westward with Ngati Haua to reinforce the Waikato defenders in their fortified pa on the upper terraces of Te Tiki o Ihingarangi. Jane and Neri, carrying their arms and provisions marching along with them but pausing for a moment to look back in the direction that their beloved family had taken only a few days before. Two paths going in opposite directions, the one in peace, the other in war. Would they ever come together again and which would prevail?

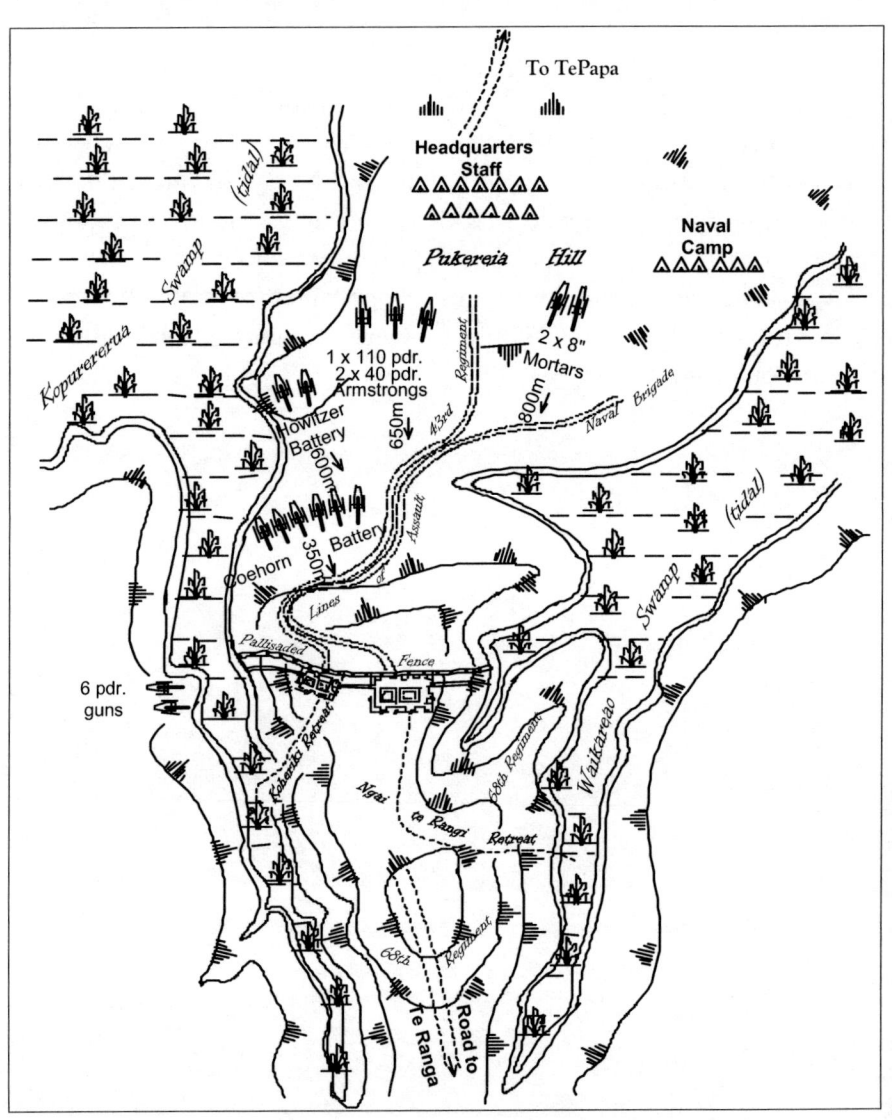

Plan of Attack on the Gate Pa (29th April 1864)

The smaller Pa on the left was defended by 50 mostly Koheriki warriors under Wi Koka and including Jane. It was there that Colonel Booth was mortally wounded as he led the assault by a detachment of the 43rd Regiment. The larger Pa on the right was commanded by Rawiri Puhirake with Henare Taratoa and garrisoned by 200 Ngai te Rangi. In the night of the 29th April, both Pa were abandoned.

Jane's Story Chapter 18

A Woman of Passion

The support column that marched out of Peria that day numbered more than 200 fighting men (and women) made up mostly from Ngati Haua (the home tribe) and Ngai te Rangi (Tauranga) but also volunteers from Piri Rakau (Kaimai), Rangiwewehi (Te Arawa), Ngati Porou (East Coast), Ngati Paoa (Hauraki) and of course the Koheriki under Wi Koka.

When she arrived at the Waikato River, Jane gazed in awe at the scene before her. The river differed markedly from the broad and placid waterway that she knew in the lower reaches and was here a raging torrent that had cut its way down into a narrow gorge. On the other side, towering above them from the cliff top was the ancient fighting *pa* of *Te Tiki o te Ihingarangi* (directly opposite the present township of Cambridge) heavily palisaded and seemingly bristling with rifle loopholes or embrasures and parapets on all sides.

The shell trumpet (*putatara*) was sounded from the visitors' side and duly responded to in kind after a period of close scrutiny by the sentry in the lookout tower high above them. Canoes were then sent across to ferry the new arrivals over the swiftly flowing current. There was a second much smaller pa further up the slope which served as a dormitory for the overflow of reinforcements that had been summoned to the 'barricades'. There they all awaited word of the outcome of the battle of Orakau just a few miles to the West.

On 2nd April 1864, word came through that Rewi Maniapoto had been defeated at Orakau after suffering crippling casualties and had been forced to retreat with the remnants of his army into the Maniapoto hinterland (later called the King Country).

Meanwhile Wiremu Tamehana had received word that the Government had ordered a total blockade of the Port of Tauranga in an attempt to cut off the supply of food and munitions to the native forces and had also begun to amass troops at Tauranga to engage Ngai te Rangi and other tribes who were hostile towards "Her Majesty's Colonial Authority". As many of the Ngai te Rangi fighting men were at Te Tiki o te Ihingarangi, a hasty council of war was held immediately and it was unanimously agreed that they should return to defend their homeland without delay and also, because Orakau had now fallen and Rewi and the surviving Waikato loyalists were in retreat, it was doubtful that a depleted garrison at Te Tiki o te Ihingarangi would hold out against a concentrated attack by the British and therefore, the pa would now be abandoned and everyone would retire to Peria and prepare to support Ngai te Rangi in the defence of Tauranga.

Already a detachment of mounted militia had been seen scouting from the Maungatautari area in the West and, to avoid a confrontation it was decided that the evacuation would be carried out that night. A decision which caused Jane much consternation as she imagined the crossing of the river would be even more hazardous in the dark. However it was something that she would have to contend with when the time came.

In the event, the dangerous feat was accomplished without mishap despite the swift current and the threatening rapids below the crossing place, men women and children all safely reached the Eastern side and marched across the plain to Peria and, on the following day when an advance guard of the British arrived at Te Tiki o te Ihingarangi, they were confounded to find the place totally deserted.

Jane and her compatriots of the earlier expedition therefore had marched to war and back again without firing a shot.

The entire returning party paused only long enough at Peria to re-provision with food, gunpowder and ammunition before thrusting East over the Kaimai Range to set up a ring of fortifications on the edge of the great forest overlooking a broad expanse of the Bay of Plenty. The majority of Ngai te Rangi chose to concentrate at *Waoku* on the Eastern side whilst others including the Piri Rakau and the small band of Koheriki under Wi Koka took up positions at *Kaimai, Poripori, Wairoa* and *Tawhitinui* strung out along the fringe of the forest towards the North-west.

Tawhitinui was a palisaded pa on a hilltop above an established track up from *Te Puna* on the Western outskirts of the Tauranga township. This was the stronghold of the venerable chief *Te Moananui* whose ancestral home was on *Matakana* Island in the Tauranga Harbour and who had lately brought his people to Tawhitinui to construct a fort against which he hoped the British would launch their attack. His Ngai-te Rangi followers numbering about seventy fighters were reinforced by thirty or so Koheriki (including Jane and Neri) and about the same number of Piri Rakau.

At Waoku where the Ngai te Rangi was concentrated in greatest numbers, their chief *Rawiri Tuaia Puhirake,* after completing the fortification of the pa, issued an invitation to the British commander at Tauranga to *"use at his own convenience and in his own time, the new road that had been built for them so as not to tire his troops unduly, so that they might engage in honourable combat at Waoku."* To Rawiri's extreme chagrin and disappointment however, his rather impertinent challenge received neither acknowledgement nor reply.

Growing impatient with the inactivity and perhaps being a little too cocksure, Rawiri sought to hasten a confrontation with his adversaries by moving his forces down to *Poteriwhi* on the *Wairoa River* and from there he issued a similar invitation to the British commander to come out and fight, but again there was no British response or sign of agitation from their redoubt at *Te Papa* on the Tauranga waterfront. Finally, a council of war was held amongst the Ngai te Rangi and its allies when it was decided that all outlying forces would come together at *Pukehinahina*, a ridge of elevated ground lying about two miles from the Tauranga Landing, to build new fortifications from which they could launch their own attack on Te Papa.

This place (Pukehinahina) was known to the European settlers as "*The Gate*" because it was there that a gate had been erected on the boundary between land which had been sold to the Europeans and that which remained in Native hands. The gate had been erected in the boundary fence at the request of the Church missioners who had convinced the Maori owners that access should be provided for the passage of carts engaged in normal community fare. Hence the fortifications built by Rawiri on this spot became known as *"The Gate Pa"*.

Physically the Pukehinahina ridge was a natural barrier against any advance into the Ngai te Rangi hinterland as it was narrow and, on both flanks it dropped away sharply into deep tidal swamps that ran up from the Tauranga Harbour. Looking North towards the Tauranga township, these swamps were named *Waikareao* on the right or Eastern side and *Kopurererua* on the left (West). Its elevation gave it a commanding view over all of the land running down to the harbour so that any movement by the British forces could be kept under close observation.

The old fortifications had however fallen into sorrowful disrepair and required extensive renovation. Trenches had to be re-excavated and deepened along the full length of the fence line and all old and collapsed post and rail sections renewed completely. On the highest point of the ridge, the main redoubt was reconstructed in the form of a rectangle with inner and outer trenches inter-connected and fortified against infilading fire. Underground pits (*rua*) were positioned for shelter against shellfire and all were solidly roofed over and covered with earth to allow safe passage during action.

To further strengthen the defences on the left (Western) side, a smaller second pa of similar design was being constructed but, unfortunately it was not to be fully completed before the first attack came. Throughout the whole re-fortification however, there was a desperate shortage of heavy timber for the palisades. Some posts and rails were "appropriated" from settlers' stockyards and fences and also from around the British camp but in many places the protection was reduced to only manuka stakes (*tupakihi*) and even flax sticks (*korari*).

The main stockade (*pa*) on the top of the ridge was garrisoned by about 200 fighters mostly of Ngai te Rangi with some Ngati Porou (from the East Coast) and Ngati Rangiwewehi (from Te Arawa). The lower (smaller) pa which was separated from the main one by a ditch and parapet was manned by Wi Koka and his Koheriki party together with some Ngai te Rangi from Tawhitinui and a small group of Piri Rakau (altogether about 50 fighters). This was to present a combined total of not more than 250 fighters to stand in defence of Pukehinahina under the supreme command of Rawiri Puhirake and his close adviser and strategist **Henare Taratoa** a chief from *Otaki* who had in his youth converted to Christianity and eventually became a minister of the Church of England.

Women as well as men were to be seen toiling diligently during the building of the barricades as well as preparing and storing food and provisions of war against any prolonged siege but, when the British attack became imminent, all the women were ordered by Rawiri to withdraw to the safety of the villages in the hinterland to the South. There was one exception however and that was Jane who flatly refused to go. She strode indignantly up to Rawiri and declared, *"I shall not leave this pa without my brother Neri. If it is right that he should stay, then it is my own right also. I have fought and suffered beside him all through this war and my gun has been no less silent nor less willing than his."*

Wi Koka stepped up behind her and held his long handled tomahawk (*toki kakuaroa*) high in acclamation, "*Tenei i aku wahine toa*" ("behold my woman warrior") he pronounced and at once Rawiri gestured in approval and spoke *"Aue kei te pakanga, ko wai he taane? ko wai he wahine?"* ("Alas in war, who are the men? who are the women?").

Rawiri and his councillors were soon to learn the reason for the apparent reluctance of the British commander to engage with them. He was awaiting the arrival of reinforcements from Auckland and also his supreme commander General Cameron who had delayed his arrival until 21 April when he landed from HMS *"Esk"* and set up his headquarters at Te Papa and it was only towards the end of April that it was confirmed that sufficient forces had been amassed to launch an offensive.

By 27 and 28 April the main body of troops and heavy guns had been moved up to within 1200 metres of the pa and dug in on a hill called *Pukereia* and on the night of 28th, Colonel Greer and his 68th Regiment numbering 700 men crossed the Waikareao swamp below the pa on the Eastern side and took up positions well in the rear of the Maori fortifications. A detachment of the Naval Brigade from the "*Miranda*", "*Esk*", "*Harrier*" and "*Falcon*" joined the 68th to close off any retreat to the South. The troops engaged in the attack which took place on the following day (29th) totalled about 1650 officers and men made up of a Naval Brigade of about 420, 50 Royal Artillery, 300 of the 43rd Regiment and 700 of the 68th besides 180 of a movable column consisting of detachments of the 12th, 14th, 40th and 65th Regiments.

The battery of guns and mortars assembled at Pukereia Hill was the heaviest used in the entire Waikato War and was grossly excessive considering the weak and flimsy character of the defences they were arrayed against. The artillery consisted of a 110-pounder Armstrong (used for the first time in New Zealand), two 40-pounders and two 6-pounder Armstrongs, two 24-pounder howitzers, two 8-inch mortars and six Coehorn mortars.

And so the stage was set for what would go down in history as the second of the three final deciding battles of the Waikato Wars of 1863-64. A brave and defiant band of warriors numbering not more than two traditional *hokowhitu,* the measure of their fighting ancestors, armed only with a few captured military carbines (*pu*), some single and double barrelled shotguns (*hakimana* and *tupara*) and a further few ancient flintlock muskets (*ngutu parera*). Their short (in-fighting) weapons consisting only of long and short handled tomahawks (*toki kakuaroa* and *patiti*) to be pitched against the fixed bayonet of their battle hardened opponents. A hopelessly out-gunned partisan group aligned against the vastly overwhelming numbers and firepower of the cream of the British Colonial Army.

A demand was conveyed by Colonel Greer from General Cameron that the Ngai te Rangi cease hostilities and give up their guns. But to this Rawiri replied, "*E kore au e whakaae kia ho atu aku pu; engari ka aea atu koe a ka parakuki au ki Te Papa*" ("I cannot consent to giving up my guns, but if you wish, I shall take breakfast with you in Te Papa"). This was Rawiri's way of saying that he would meet the General but only on equal terms and, even though in his heart he knew he could never hope to surmount such overwhelming odds, he remained duty (*mana*) bound to stand in defence of the land of his ancestors (*tupuna*) and fight on to the very end. He could never concede defeat.

Perhaps the good General could be excused for not appreciating the depth of sacrosanct reverence the Maori held for his land such that his mana should demand that he stand against such impossible odds, but not so Governor Grey who had often professed a profound empathy with the inherent custom and beliefs of the Maori. He could have called a halt to the conflict at any time but elected to let it proceed.

Was it because he could see no more convenient way of acquiring land for his new settlement than through confiscation by way of reparation against *"those who wage war against Her Majesty, or remain in arms, threatening the lives of Her peaceable subjects"* (his words)?

Jane's Story Chapter 19

A Woman of Compassion

Soon after daybreak on the morning of 29th April 1864, the great guns and mortars assembled on Pukereia Hill, opened up against the hastily constructed fortifications at Gate Pa. The fire was chiefly directed at the left angle of the main redoubt on top of the ridge with the intention of breaching an opening through which an assault party could enter. At noon a second 6-pounder Armstrong was hauled across an arm of the Kopurererua swamp and mounted on a hill overlooking the Maori left flank to enable enfilading fire.

The flimsily built palisading soon began to disintegrate under the relentless fusillade and earth from the freshly mounded parapets was sent showering into the air. Rawiri strode fearlessly up and down the barricades exhorting his warriors to stand firm and hurling his defiance at the enemy. *"Kia u! Kia u!"* he cried *"Kaore e tai mai te Pakeha!"* ("Stand fast! Stand fast! The Pakeha will not enter"). And as the big guns roared their lethal intention, he shouted to them *"Tena! Tena! E mahi I to mahi!"* ("Go on! Go on! Do your worst work!") and turning to his followers he urged *"Ko te Manawa rere, Ko te Manawa rere, Kia u! Kia u! aue a te riri"* (Trembling hearts be firm! be firm! Aha it is war!").

Before the first shot was fired that morning, Jane was among an assembled Koheriki party in the shelter of the smaller stockade, further down the (West) slope below the main pa, where they were holding their matinal service as was their devotion at the beginning (and ending) of each day in accordance with their Anglican Faith and, just as their lay reader *Hori* was about to pronounce the final blessing, the first shell came down upon them. She was standing on the inner edge of the trench with Hori on one side of her and another Church priest named *Iraihia te Patu Witi* (Elijah the wheat thresher) on the other. Just below her in the trench crouched *Timoti te Amapo* their old tohunga (he of the timely warning of danger that day in the Hunua forest) who, not being a Christian adherent, chose not to participate in the service but to focus his attention on the big guns below.

Hori was uttering the closing verse of the prayer *"Kia tau Ihu Karaiti ki runga ki a tatou katoa"* ("may the blessing of Christ rest upon us all") when suddenly old Timoti caught hold of Jane's skirt and pulled her down into the trench on top of him. Next moment the two clergymen between whom Jane had been standing, the chaplain Hori and the priest Iraihia te Patu Witi, were killed instantly by the first shell of the battle with Hori being so badly mutilated that he was quite unrecognisable. To Jane's everlasting gratitude and admiration Timoti had acted immediately he caught the flash of the gun as it fired and was quick enough to grab her and pull her down into the trench. He had snatched her from death by an instant.

As she climbed up out of the trench, Jane realised that the shell had not burst immediately it struck the two men but had carried on to explode in the cooking area ten metres away amongst a heap of potatoes that had been scraped for the hangi on the previous evening, sending them flying into the air and all over the place. She heard the soldiers laughing and cheering as they watched to see the effects of their first shot and when they saw the potatoes flying they imagined them as white feathers.

All that morning the great guns roared their relentless raging fury. Their shells brushing aside the flimsy palisading in absolute disdain, bursting above the motionless defenders huddled in their trenches and hurling earth and shattered debris high into the air. And all the time a booming thunder rolling up through the hills and valleys of the hinterland, striking terror into the hearts of all who dwelt therein from the shy Piri Rakau in their secluded bush-clad havens, to all the wild creatures of the forest now being exposed to a frightening sound that had never before been heard in the aeons of existence of this land. Jane, as she crouched in the meagre shelter of her rifle pit, allowed her thoughts to ponder this sacrilegious intrusion as she envisaged her own beloved tirairaka huddled together in awe on a bough of their favourite tree, heads tucked tightly under their wings and waiting for the first heavy drops of rain to come shafting down through the canopy above but this time waiting in vain for with this storm, no rain would be forthcoming.

It was some hours later that a column of infantry moved up within range of the defenders guns and, on Rawiri's command, *"Puhia"* ("fire!") Jane and the others fired several shots but they found that it was taking some time to reload their guns as their trench was not very deep and they had to crouch down to avoid becoming exposed as they primed the fresh charges.

At 4 O'clock in the afternoon the breach in the West corner of the main battlements was considered large enough to allow a storming party to enter and General Cameron ordered an assault. The 43rd Regiment under **Lieutenant Colonel H.G.Booth** and 150 seamen and marines under **Commander Hay** of *HMS "Harrier"* advanced in column of four, with two soldiers and two sailors abreast, towards the entrenched defenders. **Major Ryan's** movable column was brought up closer to the front to draw fire from the rifle pits and later to fall in behind the assault column. The rest of the Naval column and the 43rd Regiment were to follow in reserve. At the same time the 68th Regiment under Colonel Greer, alerted by rocket signal of the impending assault, moved up closer to the rear of the main pa to cover any likely break out.

Jane, who was observing all this movement from her forward post in the lower pa, called back a warning that a detachment of soldiers had peeled off to attack their wing whilst the main column, chiefly of blue jackets, continued on towards the main redoubt. As their palisades had already been smashed down early in the shell bombardment, they were fully exposed to a frontal attack and Jane could only watch as the British officer leading the charge leapt, sword in hand, over the trench and into the midst of the defenders who rose up altogether to meet the assault and a furious hand to hand battle ensued. Some were firing and withdrawing to reload, others were swinging their tomahawks and clubbing with the butts of their guns. Jane fought side by side with Neri to prevent all but a few soldiers from entering their trench. She did not club her gun but determined to jump into the trench time and again to reload and climb back out to re-enter the fray.

The British officer, who led the charge had thrust his way several metres into the rear of the forward trench before he was felled by a young man called *Piha,* one of the Koheriki who stepped over him and took his sword which the officer had held up to him, and also his watch. Piha afterwards said that he was about to kill the officer when the call came to man the trenches again.

At length victory came to the defenders and the soldiers were driven out leaving their officer and several men dead and wounded within the compound. The victorious Koheriki, Jane among them and the redoubtable Wi Koka leading with his *toki kakuaroa* rushed down the slope in pursuit of the retreating troopers firing upon them as they fell back in disarray. In the excitement of battle the whole party had by then taken themselves right outside the fence to harass the retreating soldiers until finally the call came for them to return to the trenches. They fired several more shots after re-entering the pa as the soldiers tried to regroup and all the while a pall of gunsmoke hung over the scene. A light drizzly rain began to fall and it became almost dark.

In the meantime, the larger military assault party which had carried on to storm the main redoubt in which Rawiri and his Ngai te Rangi were waiting, was met with determined opposition and there developed the most ferocious hand to hand fighting with neither side prepared to yield a backward step.

Navy cutlass meeting toki kakuaroa, fixed bayonet thrusting against clubbing gun butt, resolute lumbering soldier fronting agile leaping warrior, the vanquished falling smitten to the ground, the victor thrusting onward to the fray.

At first it appeared that the initial onslaught would carry the day as the defenders were forced to the rear of the pa to become dispossessed of their front line trenches but, upon falling back they were to be met by a withering hail of fire from Colonel Greer's 68th Regiment which had been waiting for just such an opportunity. That fire however was fatally misdirected as it served to prevent the main assault party from pressing home their attack and it was distressing to observe several of their own troops being shot down as they also became caught in Greer's crossfire.

Thus there arrived the critical deciding moment of the battle as the Ngai te Rangi, being driven back by the fire from the 68th Regiment, intensified their attack on the now confused frontal party and finally succeeded in forcing them out of the compound and down the sloping glacis which they had earlier scaled with considerable loss of life. Many of their officers had been shot down in the first charge and soldiers and sailors were left milling about desperately striking out at their foes but all the while being hampered by lack of organised leadership whilst falling back in confusion before the now rampant Ngai te Rangi. Captain Hamilton of the "Esk" leading the Naval reserves made a heroic attempt to stay the panic but he was shot on the top of the outer parapet while calling on his men to advance.

And so the British attack was aborted with the entire complement of forces thrown into disorderly retreat. Some men striving desperately to carry their wounded comrades with them with others limping and clutching their terrible wounds, frantically struggling to keep up with the rest and not be left behind. The triumphant Ngai te Rangi and their indomitable allies shrieking their terrifying war cries as they hounded their enemy on its way, picking off the stragglers and firing after those in stricken flight. Until at last the call comes down from Rawiri standing on the tattered ramparts: *"Heoi ano! Kati te whawhai! Waiho ma te whakama e patu"* ("Enough! Stop the fight! Leave them to be punished by their shame").

Such was the unremitting price of war that Commander Hay was mortally wounded and nearly every other officer fell. Four captains of the 43rd lay close to each other just within the pa and Lieutenant Hill of HMS "Curacao" (the senior officer saved from the wreck of the "Orpheus" at the Manukau in 1863) was shot when he had reached the centre of the fort. More than a hundred of the assault column were casualties leaving the glacis and interior of the pa strewn with dead or dying. The Maori defenders had suffered as well but not so severely.

When the Koheriki returned to their lower pa after receiving the call from Rawiri, they took up their positions in the rifle pits to await any possible counter attack from a regrouped enemy. Jane, who found herself alone to regather her thoughts whilst they waited in silence, heard a plaintive cry for water uttered in English and coming from the interior of the compound behind her. She at once remembered the British officer who had led the first charge against them that morning and that there were other soldiers left lying there after the battle also, some of whom were severely wounded.

When she heard their cries, something stirred deep within her. It was compassion - that which crosses all frontiers and knows neither hatred nor malevolence towards any in the image of the Lord whether friend or foe. She was reminded of a passage from Romans 12:20 of the Bible, "*Ki tematekai tou hoariri, whangainga: Ki te matewai, whakainumia*" ("If thine enemy hunger, feed him: If he thirst, give him drink"). She remembered also the pledge that the morning assembly had made before the fighting had begun that if any person asked for mercy, it was not to be refused for to ignore such plea would invoke the wrath of God (an *Aitua*).

The sight of the foe, their life blood flowing from them seemed to elate some of her comrades but not so Jane who could only feel pity. She intuitively slung her gun and rose up from the trench to turn and run back to the cooking area where she knew there was water but, her brother Neri called to her in alarm " Where do you think you're going? Don't you know you are exposing yourself to the enemy fire?" "I am going to fetch water for the dying soldiers who are crying out for it and I cannot disobey the call" she snapped back at him. Neri shook his head in resignation and stood resting his hands on the muzzle of his *tupara,* his anxious eyes following her every move, and uttered not a word.

Because the outer palisades had by then been almost completely demolished, she became perilously exposed to the enemy riflemen for several seconds before she reached the shelter of the cooking area but only to find that the pot in which she expected to find the water had been capsized and broken. There was still a large iron nail can remaining full but it was so heavy that she had to spill half its contents before she could lift and carry it in her arms to the suffering soldiers.

She came first to the British colonel to kneel by his side and take his head on her knees and whisper in English "Here is water" and she cupped some of the water in her hand and held it to his lips that he should drink. He looked up at her and in a faint voice uttered "God bless you" and drank again from her hand. Three other soldiers she attended in the same way until finally, her work done, she placed the nail can securely amidst them so that it would not spill and ran back to the trenches.

When at last darkness fell over that scene of devastation, Rawiri, his gallant band of fighters now in sorrowfully depleted numbers, his ammunition almost exhausted, decided to abandon the pa. The Koheriki in their own dilapidated fortifications down on the left flank concluded that their wisest course would be to retire also. Their defences had been considerably weakened after the thorough battering they had taken from the artillery and it was certain that the British would be launching another storming attack next day. So that night, under cover of the darkness and a drizzling rain, they stole away into the Kopurererua Swamp and melted into the vastness of the Kaimai hinterland. Before leaving, Jane returned amongst the wounded soldiers to give them more water and there she left them after setting the container by their side.

It was not until the year 1867 that Jane learned the identity of the English officer to whom she had given water. A Colonel St.John came to her one day at Maketu and, taking her hand he said "I did not know until lately that it was you who gave the water to my dear friend Colonel Booth at the Gate Pa". He then went on to tell her that Colonel Booth, when dying in hospital at Te Papa, informed the surgeon, Dr Manley, that it was a Maori woman who spoke English that gave him the water.

Long after the war a friend sent her a picture by a New Zealand artist showing a man with a calabash carrying water to the dying Colonel Booth. It amused Jane to be depicted as a man (though she might have fought like one) and there was also no calabash but only an old iron nail can.

Jane's Story Chapter 20

A Last Call to Arms

Again it was due to the uncanny tracking skills and masterly bushcraft of the few Piri Rakau amongst them, their ability to merge with the landscape and silently pass through the enemy lines without being seen or heard that enabled the whole Koheriki party to escape without detection through the Kopurererua Swamp and up into the heavily wooded country of the Kaimai Range to the South. It was determined by Wi Koka that they should rejoin Te Moananui in his hilltop fortress of Tawhitinui there to await further developments. There was, at that stage, no knowledge of Rawiri and the main Ngai te Rangi force who had earlier made their exit via the Eastern route through the Waikareao Swamp which required them to infiltrate the lines of Colonel Greer's 68th Regiment which had been placed there to prevent any such attempt. The Koheriki would therefore be called upon either to join forces again with Rawiri at Waoku or remain to support Te Moananui should the British decide to accept his challenge to come up and fight at Tawhitinui.

As for Rawiri and the Ngai te Rangi, they had departed Gate Pa in good spirits after collecting arms and accoutrements from the British dead and wounded and, after splitting up into small groups, made their way skilfully through the enemy lines, some being spotted and fired upon but generally making good their escape into the hills without serious harm save for only a few wounded. They travelled on until they reached the Waoku Pa where they rested and took time out to recount the events of the day and take stock of their own losses.

The British casualties numbered more than a third of the total storming force that scaled the glacis and assaulted the two defensive fortifications. Ten officers were either killed or died of wounds and four more were wounded. Of the non-commissioned officers and men, twentyone were killed and seventysix wounded making a total of 111 officers and men killed or wounded. The 43rd Regiment lost their colonel, four captains and one lieutenant killed and one other with two ensigns severely wounded. Among the killed were two brothers, Captain and Lieutenant Glover. Nearly all the Naval Brigade officers were killed or wounded. The official return of officers killed and wounded was as follows:-

Naval Brigade: Killed: - Captain Hamilton HMS "Esk", Lieutenant Hill (late of "Orpheus") - "HMS "Curacao", Mr Watts, Gunner HMS "Miranda". Wounded: - Commander Hay (abdomen - mortally)- HMS "Harrier", Lieutenant Duff (back in two places - severe) - HMS "Esk", Lieutenant Hammick (shoulder - severe) - HMS "Miranda".

43rd Regiment: Killed: - Captain R.C.Glover (head), Captain C.R. Muir (tomahawk, right axilla), Captain R.T.Hamilton (head), Captain A.E.Utterton (neck), Lieutenant C.J.Langlands (chest). Wounded: - Lieutenant-Colonel Booth (spine and right arm - mortally), Lieutenant T.G.E.Glover (abdomen - mortally), Ensign W.Clark (right arm - severe), Ensign S.P.T.Nichol (scalp - slight).

A bluejacket named Samuel Mitchel, captain of the foretop of HMS "Harrier" was recommended for the Victoria Cross for carrying Commander Hay, who was mortally wounded, out of the Pa.

The Maori losses in killed totalled about 25 including the Ngai te Rangi chiefs Te Rewiti, Eru Puhirake, Tikitu, Te Kani, Te Rangihau and Te Wharepouri. Te Moananui received three gunshot wounds whilst Te Ipu, was another warrior badly wounded. Te Rewiti had received six or seven bullet wounds and had his legs broken.

Upon finding the Pa completely abandoned the next day, Captain Pye with his Colonial Defence Force Cavalry scouted the lower fringe of the Kaimai Forest but did not attempt to carry the pursuit into the bush proper and contented himself by occupying the abandoned settlements in the area including the remains of Gate Pa itself. A portion of the British force with all of the warships excepting the "Harrier", returned to Auckland.

Meanwhile the Ngai te Rangi, under Rawiri had been strengthened with new reinforcements from Rotorua including volunteers from the sub-tribes of Ngati Rangiwewehi and Ngasti Pikiao who had declined to espouse the general Te Arawa edict of remaining loyal to Queen Victoria, to side with the Kingites. In addition, there was a small party from Ngati Porou, chiefly of the Whanau ia Hinerupe from Pukemaire in the Waipu Valley on the East Coast. These determined warriors were led by Hoera te Mataatai.

This revitalisation of his forces prompted Rawiri to issue one more challenge to his supercilious adversary General Cameron. He chose a site for a new fortified Pa at Te Ranga which was on a prolongation of the Pukehinahina Ridge about three miles to the South and East of the Gate Pa. This was also on a narrow neck of land flanked on either side by steep to undulating wooded valleys with swamps and water courses and with the Eastern (right) flank falling abruptly away into a deep gully. The ridge top was quite level and the approach from the coast, along which the British were expected to advance, fell back in a long gentle slope.

The decision to make a stand at Te Ranga being affirmed by the assembled fighting chiefs, everybody was put to work digging the trenches and collecting materials for the construction of the breastworks and palisades. This work however was never to be completed and the glorious and defiant stand that was intended to flaunt the might of the British Colonial Army was to end in the most devastating defeat to be inflicted upon the Maori in all of the Waikato war.

On the morning of the 21st June 1864, a strong reconnaissance column under the command of Colonel Greer, whilst following along the ridge from the Gate Pa, came suddenly upon a large working party of Ngai te Rangi busily engaged in digging trenches across a high point of land in front of them. There were no palisades yet erected and the trenches were still quite shallow. Here at last, it occurred to the Colonel, was an opportunity to catch the enemy out in the open. He already had at his command a fully armed force of 600 men composed of the 43rd Regiment under Major Synge, the 68th under Major Shuttleworth and the 1st Waikato Militia under Captain Moore with which he could launch an immediate assault whilst a rider would be despatched to Te Papa with a request for reinforcements and an Armstrong gun.

At once skirmishers were sent forward to engage the unsuspecting warriors in the trenches whilst the 43rd and a portion of the 68th were sent under cover to the flanks on either side to maintain steady enfilading rifle fire. After about two hours of this long range fighting from cover, the Armstrong gun and the infantry reinforcements arrived and the time had come for Colonel Greer to order the bugler to sound the "Charge". Forward thrust the 43rd, 68th and 1st Waikato's shouting as they ran and, in a few minutes they had reached the trenches where the Ngai te Rangi and their staunch allies rose up as one to meet the charge unflinchingly matching tomahawk and clubbing rifle butt with fixed bayonet in the most desperate and ferocious of hand to hand battles. Even after being bayoneted some warriors fought on to fell their foe before finally falling to the ground locked together in death. But sheer valour was to no avail against such overwhelming numbers.

Warrior upon warrior fell to the relentless British onslaught until at last all the fires of resistance were extinguished and only a few survivors were able to break for the sheltering cover of the bush.

Thus for a comparatively minor casualty list of thirteen privates killed, six officers and thirty-three other ranks wounded, the British exacted a terrible vengeance for their defeat at Gate Pa. Fully 120 of the defenders were killed by rifle fire in the initial surprise attack and the hand to hand fighting that was to follow.

The intrepid Rawiri Puhirake was among the last to fall as he strode amongst his comrades shouting his defiance and exhorting them to *"Kia u! Kia u!"* ("Stand fast! Stand fast!"). His close friend and adviser Henare Taratoa (the Otaki mission teacher) died there also and, of the allies of Ngai te Rangi who stood with them, the small Ngati Porou party resisted to the death with thirty killed, the Ngati Pikiao unit from Rotoiti was almost completely wiped out and the Ngati Rangiwewehi suffered so severely that the survivors of that hapu were never to accept the hand of friendship with the Pakeha for as long as they were to live.

So ended the final battle of the Waikato Campaign with the British emerging victorious after little more than a year of conflict. An inevitable ending when a small however earnestly patriotic band of warriors, unfamiliar and under-equipped with the discharge and weapons of modern warfare, is pitched against a professionally trained and disciplined army with an unlimited supply of manpower, weapons and supporting ordnance stemming from the might of the most powerful nation in the world. As with the Colonisation of new and uncontained lands throughout history, it was never the quality of the fighting spirit that failed the indigenous defenders, only the overwhelming superiority of the war machine used against them.

Some of the Maori wounded were taken to the military hospital at Te

Papa whilst others elected to crawl off into the bush to await their fate whether left to die alone or be found and rescued by their fellow survivors. Most of the dead were laid out in three long rows – thirty in one row, 33 in another and 34 in the last. They were then dumped into the trenches, that they themselves had freshly dug that day, and buried over. Others were buried where they fell as they sought to find the safety of the bush. The improvised mass grave however had been dug scarcely deep enough to accommodate the number of bodies thrown into them and, to the distress of some of the survivors crouching in concealment in the bush, soldiers of the burial fatigue were observed to be tramping down protruding limbs in order to cover them over completely.

Several years later, the remains of Rawiri were re-interred in the military cemetery at Tauranga, by the side of his adversary Lieutenant-Colonel Booth who was mortally wounded at Gate Pa. It was also intended that a Maori monument be erected at Te Ranga to mark the sacred spot where so many gallant warriors fell.

It was on the body of Henare Taratoa that Rawiri's "Order of the Day" was found in which a strict code of combat was drawn up forbidding any mutilation or violation of the fallen enemy. The wounded were to be given comfort and protection and were not to be abandoned nor left to suffer unattended. Possibly it was the discovery of this code of conduct on the body of Henare that connected him with the revered act of compassion at Gate Pa when water was carried to the dying Colonel Booth.

There exists to this day a stained glass window in the private chapel of the Bishops' Palace in Lichfield, England which was placed there by the first Bishop Selwyn to commemorate the Gate Pa incident which was mistakenly attributed to Henare Taratoa but however, whilst there can be no doubt of Henare's chivalry and devoted adherence to the Christian faith, it was Jane who rightly deserved the credit for that memorable act of humanity.

As Jane herself recounted some years later, neither she nor any of her Koheriki comrades, who defended the lower Pa against Colonel Booth and his assault column, knew anything of the code framed by Rawiri and Henare in the main Ngai te Rangi fortress at the time and that she had simply obeyed her own Christian conscience when she attended the call from the dying officer and his soldiers.

Jane's Story Chapter 21

Champions for the Return Home

With the loss of Rawiri and so many high ranking chiefs of Ngai te Rangi in the fighting at Gate Pa and Te Ranga, there remained only *Te Moananui* and *Hori Ngatai* of sufficiently high authority (*mana*) to assume the leadership (*Aho Ariki*) of the extended tribe (*Iwi*). Te Moananui however had been carried to Tawhitinui on a stretcher as he had received three near-mortal gunshot wounds in the fighting at Gate Pa and was unable to continue the fight. It would take many months of tender care and attention from his wife and her aides to administer the traditional curing treatments (*tahutahu*) to his wounds if he was ever to recover. It therefore fell upon Hori Ngatai to call together the remnants of the tribe in a council of war (*runanga pakanga*) to decide their future action. The meeting was held at Tawhitinui and was joined by Ngai te Rangi from surrounding settlements including *Waoku, Kaimai, Poripori and Whakamarama* for it was from those places that came the majority of fighting men followers of Rawiri.

Hori began his address by affirming his allegiance to the Maori King Movement and the principle of *Tino Rangatiratanga* which gave Maori sovereignty over their own lands as was guaranteed under the Treaty of Waitangi. "My warriors (*toa taua*) have followed me into battle at *Meremere* on the Waikato, *Otau* in the Wairoa and thence to the Gate Pa (*Pukehinahina*) and our numbers are now few as are they of other hapu of the proud Ngai te Rangi. We did not go to Te Ranga for had we done so, we too would be lying with Rawiri in that long and shallow grave."

"To those of you who are left I say:- These are the lands we would not give up for if we did so, we would be left like sea birds (*manu o te moana*) perched on a rock and when the tide flows the rock is covered and the birds have to fly off and there is no place for them to rest. But alas we must now abide the endless flooding tide of the Pakeha and his soldiers that will crash against the rock that stands in the ocean (*toka tu moana*) so it will soon be buried under its surging spume".

"We no longer have the numbers nor the strength to stand against such overwhelming force and therefore I say to you we have fought a good fight, our dignity (*mana*) has been upheld but now it is time for us to lay down our arms and seek an honourable peace (*Rongo taketake*)".

There then rose a long and plaintive chorus of lament (*apakura*) from the seated assembly as they slowly came to accept the sound judgement as delivered by their *Aho Ariki*. Many were the tears shed amongst the survivors as they remembered their loved ones who had died or suffered terrible wounds fighting for their cause (*take*) yet all in vain as now they must bear the ignominy of defeat.

Wi Koka sprang to his feet and, holding his *toki kakuaroa* erect before him acclaimed, "I shall not accompany you to Te Papa to make terms with the Pakeha though I agree with Hori Ngatai that Ngai te Rangi has had enough of war and the time has come to put aside your weapons and seek peace. But I and my Koheriki hapu shall leave you and return to Peria there to rejoin Wiremu Tamihana and his Ngati Haua. We shall abide by his wise counsel whether to continue the fight or make peace also for we cannot rest until we are permitted to return to our own standing place (*turangawaewae*) in Ngati Paoa.

There remained a few Ngai te Rangi with survivors of Ngati Rangiwewehi and also some of the Piri Rakau fighters who were not convinced that they should give up the fight and they elected to retire deeper into the bush where they would live in seclusion with the Piri Rakau and await the outcome.

Then there were left Jane and Neri sitting quietly together amongst their grieving comrades, listening respectfully to the speeches of their elders (*kaumatua*) and contemplating whither should their own path into the future take them.

Jane had long since come to recognise the futility of further resistance against such boundless and overwhelming odds and that with the continued sacrifice of their finest leaders and fighting men would come the tragic degeneration of a once proud and noble people. She agreed with Hori Ngatai that for the sake of their own survival, Ngai te Rangi must cease hostilities now.

She turned to her brother and spoke, "Neri I know that you really belong to the Koheriki hapu even though you came to Auckland from Tai Tokarau as I did. But I am of Te Arawa and I wish now to return there to my children and my mother Maraea. You are free to go to Ngati Paoa with the Koheriki if that is your desire but I shall always look upon you as my dear brother and will cherish your memory always. Neri looked at her and smiled, "Dear lady you have dominated my life ever since I came to school with you in the Auckland Mission. We have lived together, fought together and were willing to die together. I could not let you go your own way now. I have no special ties with Ngati Paoa so I shall come with you to live in Te Arawa.

In the days that followed, Hori Ngatai sent his message around the wider region calling on the chiefs of all hapu of Ngai te Rangi to bring their fighting men (*toa taua*) with their guns and ammunition to the military redoubt at Te Papa there to lay down their arms before the British commanding officer in token of complete cessation of hostility and a desire to live on in peace. And so on the chosen day, they marched down from the hills and valleys of the Kaimai hinterland to join their coastal brethren arriving in canoes from the outer islands and points North and South to form up on the great barracks square in front of the commandants quarters at Te Papa to ceremoniously move forward one by one to lay their arms in neat and orderly rows before the table of the seated British Commander and his aides-de-camp who, in a gracious gesture of recognisance, had invited Hori Ngatai to sit beside them on that solemn and momentous occasion.

It is most gratifying however to record that in the years that followed, the peace pact ratified on that day was loyally observed on both sides and that Hori Ngatai was eventually to lead and encourage his people into the farming industry and, within a short time they were to become the largest growers of wheat and maize in that region.

Meanwhile back at Tawhitinui, the Koheriki were preparing for their departure after rendering every assistance towards the recovery of their esteemed host Te Moananui. They would need to cross the Kaimai Range in the South and then descend into the farmlands of Ngati Haua where they would seek out Wiremu Tamihana in his headquarters at Peria.

The time had now arrived for Jane to bid farewell to her grand patron warrior chief Wi Koka and his redoubtable band of followers whom she accompanied throughout the long and bloodied campaign. For she and Neri at last it was over and they would soon be retiring to the sanctuary of their island home in Te Arawa. For the Koheriki however, they would have to fight on until peace came to all of the Waikato and they would be free to return to their home on the Wairoa.

Jane walked among her adopted hapu to take the hands of Wi Koka, his wife and the other women who shared with her the hardship and self abasement of their long and demanding ordeal together, the special warriors who would never show fear and the few Piri Rakau who had chosen to fight on with the Koheriki and not return to their bush homeland. Men whose exploits had never ceased to fascinate Jane throughout the long and hazardous campaign. There were tears of melancholy and deep sorrow as they bade each other farewell and in their thoughts knowing that their paths might never come together again.

Jane looked toward Wi Koka and praised him in thankful acclamation and acknowledgement of his wise guidance and determined leadership which had delivered them all safely through that cruel and ultimately un-winnable war.

Wi Koka drew her to him and placed his great arms gently upon her shoulders and spoke, "Farewell my brave little woman warrior (*wahine toa*) but do not despair. "*E pai ano te whawhai he mahue hinga; Ka kore te whawhai whakamahi*" ("Far better to have fought and lost than not to have fought at all").

As Jane and Neri gathered together their meagre possessions ready to depart the now almost deserted pa, they were surprised to see a group of others happily preparing to leave with them also. There were two of the Piri Rakau scouts who had accompanied them through the Hunua forests and were now prepared to guide them through the *Kaimai* and *Mamaku* forests to *Hamurana*, there was old Timoti Te Amapo the *tohunga* who had decided to go and live with the Rangiwewehi and there was also that effervescent personality *Penetito* who announced that he was going along to find fresh and more appreciative audiences in Te Arawa. There were other mostly younger people who held hereditary links with Te Arawa and wished to return and claim their tribal affiliation. Among them were two young sisters *Raiha* and *Mereana Ratete* who had become orphaned during the Ngaiterangi campaign and whom Jane had taken upon herself to see safely home to Mokoia. Jane found it incredible that she would have attracted such a large personal following.

The long and laborious walk up through the Kaimai and Mamaku ranges to the summit was slow but uneventful as on this occasion at least there was no ominous threat of contact with hostile forces. When they reached the settlement of *Tarukenga* they emerged from the bush to catch the first glimpse of Lake Rotorua with its sentinel island of Mokoia basking contentedly in the sunshine. They pressed on down to the waters edge and around the Western shore until at last they came to Hamurana the headquarters of the Ngati Rangiwewehi and journeys end for all but Jane, Neri and the two Ratete sisters. There they were fortunate to meet a man named *Moihi* who had come across from Mokoia by canoe and who cheerfully offered to take them along with him on his return.

When at last the canoe pulled in to the landing place at Mokoia and the tired and weary occupants stepped out onto the hallowed soil of their ancestors, a great wailing cry (*karanga*) of anguish rose up from the people assembled on the shore. Their children (*tamariki*) had at last come home and their families (*whanau*) would be united again. Jane rushed up to gather in her own little family and weep over them with tears of joy and relief. And standing there amidst their own tears of profusion, their hearts aching with the outpouring of their love for their daughter delivered safely home to them at last were the graceful Maraea and the ever faithful Mango extending their arms in greeting and drawing them ever closer.

Jane looked up to the sky and offered up her prayer of thanksgiving and dedication   Secure amongst her loved ones again, the long and brutal conflict now ended. The year is 1864 and she is yet only 27 years old.

Jane's Story Chapter 22

Wars End and Losers Weep

There can be little doubt that General Cameron's convincing victory at the battle of *Orakau* in which the battered remnants of the Waikato tribes under Rewi Maniapoto, in a last desperate stand, were soundly defeated, was the decisive blow which brought an end to all organised resistance by the Maori King movement in that area.

With the subjugation of their Ngai te Rangi and other East Coast allies after the battles of Gate Pa and Te Ranga which followed, there remained only a token resistance at best which could be offered amongst the scattered sub-tribes (*hapu*) of Ngati Maniapoto in their wild and largely uncharted country South of the *Puniu River* (the point at which the pursuit of Rewi and the survivors of Orakau was broken off). Such token resistance was in fact organised with fortifications being thrown up in the area of the *Upper Waipa* at *Otorohanga, Otewa* and *Mangaorongo* extending to the *Rangitoto Range* in the East, and between the *Mangaokewa* and *Mangapu* Streams at *Hangatiki, Haurua* and *Waitomo* to *Te Anga* in the West. The full strength of *Ngati Maniapoto* was represented in these defensive works by such powerful chiefs as *Wahanui, Rewi, Raureti, Wetini, Paku Kohatu, Te Rangi ka haruru* ("The thundering heavens"), *Hauauru* and his brother *Patena* of *Ngati Matakore* and also *Topine te Mamaku* from the upper *Whanganui*.

However as it transpired, none of these preparations were to be put to the test because General Cameron's advance had ended at the Puniu River and *Kihikihi* became the most Southern outpost of his troops. It was obvious therefore that to extend the campaign into the rugged and inaccessible Maniapoto would require a total change of strategic planning and could well result in long drawn out guerrilla type warfare the cost of which would need to be weighed against the value of the land in that region that might be expropriated.

It was at the *Ngati Raukawa* village of *Ara Titaha* (near the present *Pukeatua* on the Southern slopes of *Maungatautari*) that the last shots of the Waikato War were exchanged. Acting on a report that an armed Maori party was seen in the area, *Lieutenant Rait*, a mounted artillery commander who was on patrol around the forward posts, joined a detachment of the 65th Regiment under *Captain Blewitt* to investigate the incursion and became engaged in a long range skirmish near the village, but without much effect due to the rapidly increasing distance between them. *Ensign Gilbert Mair*, (the younger brother of *Major William Mair* of battle of Orakau prominence), was armed with the only long range carbine and it fell to him in returning the Maori fire to trigger the last shot of the campaign to mark the belated end of a long and mindless conflict The entire territory between the Waipa and Waikato Rivers had therefore been effectively cleared of all resistance and, with the defeat of the Ngai te Rangi on the Eastern front, there was left only Wiremu Tamihana and his Ngati Haua in the middle.

Soon after the fortified pa of Te Tiki o te Ihingarangi was evacuated by Wiremu Tamihana when he agreed to release his Ngai te Rangi allies to return to Tauranga to defend their own lands, General Cameron made preparations to shell the place and had gathered a strong battery at *Pukerimu* but, on finding it already abandoned, he at once set up a redoubt on the site of the upper pa which remained garrisoned for some time after the cessation of hostilities.

At his headquarters at Peria, Wiremu Tamihana anxiously awaited the outcome of the Ngai te Rangi effort against the British at Tauranga for it was from that source that future supplies of arms and provisions to sustain the war effort must come as also would warrior reinforcements drawn from *Ngati Awa, Whanau a Apanui* and

Whakatohea of the Eastern Bay of Plenty, *Tuhoe* of the *Urewera* and *Ngati Porou* of the East Coast. But when Wi Koka and his Koheriki party arrived with news of the devastating defeat of Rawiri at Te Ranga and the subsequent decision of Hori Ngatai to press for peace with the British at Te Papa, Tamihana was forced, however reluctantly, to concede that the long and hopeless struggle was over. He was now bereft of support from his allies of the Waikato in the West and now the coastal tribes in the East. There was no alternative therefore but to make his own peace and so, on 27th May 1865, at *Tamahere* (on the Southern outskirts of the present city of Hamilton), in the ancient noble gesture of concession, he lay down his taiaha before *Brigadier-General Carey* and signed a document acknowledging complete obeisance to the law of Her Majesty Queen Victoria. His tribe of Ngati Haua was eventually to lose part of their lands by confiscation but by far the heaviest losers were the Waikato who were dispossessed of all of their territory East of the Waikato River and the lower Waipa basin bounded by *Mount Pirongia* in the West, the Puniu River in the South and the Maungatautari Range in the East. Those people would be forced to remain on the lands of their friends of Ngati Maniapoto for nearly a generation after the war.

Te Awamutu remained the headquarters of the Waikato Army of occupation and, after the government fixed the confiscation lines, the Puniu River was made the frontier and no attempt was made to drive the defeated Kingites any further South. Four thousand regular troops remained at Te Awamutu and the outposts until the end of 1864 and, as they were withdrawn, the military settlers already embodied in the regiments of the militia took over from them and established frontier villages with each defended by a redoubt and, in time they developed into townships as the occupation of the surrounding land increased. The 1st Regiment of Waikato Militia were allocated sections of land at Tauranga and the other three regiments garrisoned and later settled the Southern Waikato as follows: The 2nd at *Alexandra* (now *Pirongia*) and Kihikihi, the 3rd

at Cambridge and the 4th at Hamilton (formerly *Kirikiriroa*). The river steamer *"Rangiriri"* landed the first of the military settlers at the present site of Hamilton on 24th August 1864 and numbered 120 men under *Captain W. Steele*. Each military settler received a grant of one town acre and a section from 50 acres upward according to rank. The Forest Rangers of Majors Jackson and Von Tempsky were given land at *Rangiaowhia, Te Rahu, Kihikihi* and *Harapepe*.

South of the frontier, the remaining renegade Waikato preferred to live in isolation to contemplate the re-conquest of their lands but deterred from continuing the war until such time as sufficient good arms were again procurable. It was not until 1881, when *Tawhiao te Wherowhero* laid his gun at the feet of Major William Mair at Alexandra, that Waikato and Ngati Maniapoto definitely and finally made their peace with the Colonial Government. So came to an end the conflict between the followers of the Maori King anxious to retain sovereignty over their lands and a Colonial government eager to obtain land for the settlement of their new colonists.

The leaders of the King Movement wanted to see Maori and Pakeha living together in peace. Chiefs like Wiremu Tamihana had already established thriving centres of agriculture and trade and they could see no reason why the Maori King and the British Queen could not work together in partnership as, in accordance with their interpretation of the Treaty of Waitangi, the mana of chieftainship and the mana of the Crown would both be held in the highest reverence. Government officials thought differently as did most Europeans. The King stood for Maori independence and this irritated most officials and settlers who wanted the central North Island opened up for settlement. Some thought that colonisation and the treaty were incompatible whilst others held to the belief that the Crown was morally bound to uphold the treaty compact. Many and finally most Europeans concluded that a war to assert British sovereignty was inevitable.

War did come despite efforts by many Maori and European leaders to avoid it but with the government and the King movement holding different views of sovereign rights, a meeting of minds was near impossible. As the fighting dragged on into the mid 1860's, the British officers and their troops came to realise that they were only being used to fight a war for land on behalf of settlers against an enemy that had earned their profound respect. Many settlers too, were deeply disturbed that the two races who had aimed to build a new nation together, should end up fighting each other.

By 1870, after the war had drawn to an untidy end, the last British troops had left for home and the British government had made it known that it would pour no more money into New Zealand. The Colonial government now fully responsible for the Maori people, came out more openly and bluntly to assert that the Maori people had signed away their mana in 1840. It was true that the Maori people had been made humbly aware that their mana had become gravely diminished after the fighting in the 1860's but they would still not accept that by recognising British sovereignty they would be forfeiting altogether the mana of chieftainship (*Tino Rangatiratanga*). For them this was a quite new interpretation of the treaty. It was some time before the Maori leaders fully realised that the responsibility for their affairs had been passed from the British into the hands of the New Zealand Colonial Government. They could not believe that the Queen and her British Parliament would wash their hands of the Waitangi covenant. But sadly, they had done so.

The New Zealand Settlement Act of 1863, under which the confiscation of native lands was carried out, set forth in the preamble that it was necessary "that some adequate provisions should be made for the permanent protection and security of the well disposed inhabitants of both races for the prevention of future insurrection or rebellion, and for the establishment and maintenance of Her

Majesty's authority and of law and order throughout the colony". It was enacted that the Governor in Council might take native land where desirable in order to set apart sites of settlements. The money derived from the sale of the land was to be devoted to recouping the expenses of the war, the construction of public works, the establishment of schools and other public institutions and in promoting immigration for the colonisation of confiscated territories.

An enormous area of the Waikato and neighbouring country was confiscated under this Act. It embraced the whole of the Waikato-Waipa basin from Mangatawhiri, South to the summit of Mount Pirongia (near Te Awamutu), thence along the Puniu River to the Waikeria (near Wharepapa) and from there across the foothills of the Maungatautari Range to the Waikato River, thence North through Ngati Haua country to the Firth of Thames. Portions of this area were afterwards returned to sub-tribes (*hapu*) who had not shared in the war but by far the greater portion was divided up for white settlement.

It was however significant that although peace pacts were entered into at the end of the war with each party generally in agreement, there were always among the warring hapu a few dissentients who refused to concede defeat and, instead of laying down their arms with their compatriots, elected not ever to recognise Pakeha authority but to retire to their tribal hinterlands there to await any new opportunity to continue the conflict.

History records that such opportunity did in fact arise when many of those malcontents were brought together under the rebel religious prophet *Te Ua Horopapera Haumene* to engage in the most malicious, vindictive and rapacious atrocities against Pakeha and non-aligned Maori alike and thereby arousing such outrage that the country again found itself at war. But this time more people of the two races found themselves united in the cause of Christianity against the adherents of a strange, fanatical faith which first surfaced amongst the dispossessed tribes of Taranaki and was originally founded on the Christian bible but, as it spread through the rest of the country, it became manipulated by zealots to become a vehicle of evil. So much so that Jane, now living in comparative tranquillity in her island home on Mokoia, was impelled to again take up her gun.

Jane's Story Chapter 23

Seeds of an Ill-conceived Insurgence

The settlement of their confiscated lands with large bodies of ex-militiamen as an assurance that peace would prevail after the defeat of the Waikato and allied tribes by General Cameron's Imperial Army, by no means secured the total pacification of the dispossessed Maori owners. The confiscation of land of the so-called rebels which ignored the just protests of such men as Bishop Selwyn and Sir William Martin, the appropriation of Maori land which for centuries had been the property of larger tribes, and the denial of adequate consideration of the rights of those hapu who remained loyal to the Queen during the conflict and also the innocent children of the native belligerents was inevitably to lead to a bitter and unrelenting animosity, even hatred towards the Pakeha "conquistadors".

The crude and unjust manner in which the Colonial government rewarded its forces with land grants and also the unconcealed wish of many colonists and even some politicians for a war of extermination of the Maori altogether, only served to strengthen the belief that the white man's desire for their land was the all empowering factor. The Waitara seizure remained always in the Maori mind and the injustice done to Te Ati Awa by that act of spoliation would never be atoned for. It was inevitable therefore that as the result of these perceived injustices, the Maori reaction, fuelled by renegade dissidents who never did concede defeat despite the eventual capitulation of their home tribes, would harden to bitter resentment and develop into a kind of holy war and racial struggle. The Maori blood would always be prone to flair into belligerence at any threatened intrusion when wartime chivalry would become debased and raw barbarity emerge unrestrained.

The early governments failed to completely appreciate the depth and strength of the Maori regard for his ancestral land and they could not understand why any race should fight to the death for a country which for the most part lay in waste. The land always the land from the days of the first settlements by Wakefield onward remained the root of all the trouble (*putake o te riri*) and when the fire of fanatical religion fused the people into a federation of hatred against the Pakeha, all was merged into a struggle of race mastery. Thus was the doctrine of *Pai-marire* spawned among the impressionable and essentially religious Maori nature to spread like fire through dry fern to reach and incite tribes, even some who had no grievance whatsoever against the white man, to cast themselves into battle for the retention of Maori independence and sovereignty.

The *Pai-marire* or *Hauhau* religious cult which bonded so many tribes in passionate hatred against the Pakeha was partly a reaction from the teachings of the early Christian missionaries (which the people had once embraced with devotion but now looked upon in disillusionment), and partly a recrudescence of the long discredited but not altogether extinguished influence of the Maori *tohunga*. It was therefore a blend of ancient spells and incantations (*karakia*) with smatterings of English knowledge and phrases with perverted fragments of church services. Ridiculous as they were when analysed, the sum of the teachings held the impressionable Maori in total obeisance and, more importantly, it appeared just at the hour when the hostile tribes, embittered by heavy losses of people and property, were in a mood for insurrection and a renewed effort against the Pakeha intruder.

The *Pai-marire* faith had its origin in the hallucinatory mind of a Taranaki Maori named *Te Ua Haumene* who had taken the Scriptural name Zerubbabel (*Horopapera*). He had absorbed the teachings of the missionaries and was a keen student of the Bible particularly of the Book of Revelations. He developed his own interpretations of visions which appeared to him only and related curious visitations that came to him through angels (*anahera*), particularly the angel Gabriel (*Kaperiere*) from whom he received inspiration and the revelation of a new religion which would give the Maori race domination over all the Pakeha hosts. Te Ua promulgated this new faith and, although little regarded at first, gradually drew a devoted band of believers around him. His supreme deity was the "Good and Peaceful God" (*Atua Pai-marire*) a phrase that came to be applied to the religion which he founded.

The term *"Hauhau"* by which the disciples of the new faith came to be known, had its origin in the exclamation *"Hau"* used at the end of the charms (*karakia*) which they chanted. *"Hau!" "Hauhau"* or *"Whakahau"* is also a battle cry meaning "Strike!" "Attack!"

Literally *"hau"* means "wind" but it also has another more esoteric significance as it was the term applied to the life-principle of man. *"Anahera hau"* or "wind angels" was one of the curious phrases Te Ua coined as reference to the fancy that the angels came down to the Maori on the winds of heaven and that they ascended and descended by ropes left dangling from the yardarms of a sacred mast called the *"Niu"* which was the central symbol of worship under Te Ua's dispensation. The term *"niu"* was the olden day Maori word for the short sticks used by tohunga in their mystic arts of divination particularly before battle. Te Ua's *"niu"* was a tall pole or flagstaff around which the faithful would march in procession chanting their peculiar karakia. The first niu erected in Taranaki is said to have been part of one of the masts salvaged from the steamer "Lord Worsley" wrecked near Cape Egmont in 1862. Crossed with a yard rigged with stays and halliards and adorned with flags of curious indigenous designs, it was the first visible representation of the Pai-marire religion. Often a wood carving of a bird was placed on the truck of the pole representing a dove (*rupe*) and carved knobs sometimes decorated the ends of the yard or the crosstrees. One of these knobs was called *Rura* and the other *Riki* the names of two of Te Ua's gods. Each hapu as it fell convert to the new religion, set up its own niu under the direction of Te Ua or his sub-priests. By the end of 1865, a niu stood in nearly every large village from Taranaki to the Bay of Plenty (excepting Te Arawa) and from North of Wellington to the Waikato frontier.

Te Ua and his disciples impressed their adherent converts with the belief that implicit faith in Pai-marire and the observance of the rules laid down by the founder would ensure success in war. A cardinal principle in the religion as first practised was the belief that Pakeha bullets could be averted by certain magic spells. Thus the faithful marched into battle chanting their karakia and, at first sight of the armed enemy, they would hold up the right hand, palm towards the enemy and level with the face, and shout (almost bark like a dog) *"Hapa, hapa! Pai-marire, Hau!"*

"Hapa" means to pass over or ward off and the incantation was meant to avert the bullets from the true believer. In precisely the same way, the Arabs of the Sudan charged upon the British squares, and the wild tribes of the North-west frontier of India came rushing down against rifle and machine-gun.

Even repeated defeats and the deaths of their first war-prophets, did not impair the faith in the incantations and the magic sign of the upraised hand (*Ringa Tu*). Not only were the fanatical followers of the faith completely entranced by the chanting in battle but people on the opposite side also seemed to become captivated with a curious blending of fear and fascination which came over them as they watched and listened from their entrenchments. The political value of such faith was enormous and Pai-marire even succeeded in attracting many who had no particular affinity with Te Ua but were nevertheless sympathetic with their fellow Maori in lamenting the deaths of their people in the Waikato wars and the loss of their lands and also supportive of a renewed effort to sweep the land clear of the Pakeha.

Like wildfire the movement flared from its first kindling among the tinder dry umbrage of the *Ngati Ruanui* tribe at *Taiporohenui* beneath the Taranaki Mountain, into full conflagration throughout the Island to reach as far as the Eastern seaboard, uniting all tribes having grievances against the Government into a common body of bitter anarchy. It was indeed fortunate for the Government at the time that no military genius or intellectual redeemer like Wiremu Tamihana should be included among the Pai-marire numbers, capable of exploiting such a widespread alliance to the full. *Te Kooti* was one who could have taken full advantage of the opportunity but fortunately for the frontier settlers, who were the most vulnerable, he arrived three years too late. There can be no doubt however that Te Ua charged his disciples when visiting the distant tribes to carry out their missions peacefully and to refrain from acts which would lead to all out war. But unfortunately some of his missioners chosen to carry the message were not of high mental or principled capacity and such uncultured apostles such as *Kereopa* when left to his own devices resorted to savagery and murder which inevitably resulted in arousing the country into a war of retribution.

It was perhaps inevitable that if the cult of Pai-marire was to gain a foothold in Te Arawa territory, it would do so through the Ngati Rangiwewehi hapu who were the only sub-tribe of Te Arawa to have broken rank and joined the Kingites in the Waikato wars in defiance of the general Arawa edict that the tribe should remain loyal to Queen Victoria. It was Ngati Rangiwewehi that suffered such devastating losses in the rifle pits of Te Ranga and, it was the few survivors of that battle that returned with their stories of the unscrupulous advantage taken of them by the British and the merciless slaughter that followed. Moreover, the prophet *Kereopa* was a member of that tribe and it was natural that he would wish to establish his newly adopted faith among his own hapu first. It transpired therefore that only two *niu* were ever to be erected in Te Arawa and both were in Ngati Rangiwewehi territory, the first being at *Puhirua Pa* on a hill overlooking the North-west shore of Lake Rotorua and the other at *Te Kiri o Tautini* about three miles inland on the edge of the great forest which extended into the Tauranga district.

It was at Puhirua that Jane became first acquainted with Pai-marire. She had become curious upon hearing of this strange new religion which was fast spreading throughout the land and decided to cross from her home on Mokoia Island to observe for herself this apparent change in direction of conventional worship. Seated on the marae with other invited dignitaries of the Anglican and Catholic Churches of Rotorua, she witnessed her first manifestation of a full Pai-marire ritual service as its devotees gathered at the foot of the niu pole and marched in procession round and round the mast chanting in chorus the Pai-marire incantations taught them by the prophet. Such chanting, although sounding quite musical, was to Jane spoken in some meaningless language neither common Maori nor English and it was not until some time afterwards that, upon some urging from converts of that faith who came to her and said "Our Gods taught us this; it is English and therefore you ought to know it", she discovered what it all meant. Her alert mind finally recognised that much of the language used was merely strings of English words rounded into the softer Maori intonation whilst others were mis-pronunciations of parts of the litany used by the Church of England with a sprinkling of Latin borrowed from Roman Catholic ritual. Some phrases were actual military commands picked up from the parade ground.

"Porina Hoia!" ("Fall-in soldiers!") was the order when the prophet marched up to the niu and took his stand at its foot, whereupon the people fell-in in military order and marched round and round the mast, reciting in a high pitched chant the following curious medley in

the belief that it was a most potent incantation brought down to them by the angels:

Kira, wana, tu, tiri, wha – Teihana!
Rewa, piki rewa, rongo rewa, tone, piki tone, - Teihana!
Rori, piki rori, rongo rori puihi, piki puihi – Teihana!
Rongo puuihi, rongo tone, hira, piki hira, rongo hira – Teihana!
Mauteni, piki mauteni, rongo mauteni, piki niu, noriti, koroni – Teihana!
Nota, no te pihi, no te hihi, noriti mino, noriti, koroni – Teihana!
Hai, kamu, te ti, oro te mene, rouna te niu, - Teihana!
Hema, ruira wini, tu mate wini, kamu te ti – Teihana!

(Translation)
Kill, one, two, three, four – Attention!
River, big river, long river, stone, big stone - Attention!
Road, big road, long road, bush, big bush – Attention!
Long bush, long stone, hill, big hill, long hill – Attention!
Mountain, big mountain, long mountain, big staff, long staff – Attention!
North, north-by-east, nor'-nor'- east, nor'-east-by-north, north-east, colony – Attention!
Come to tea, all the men, round the niu – Attention!
Shem, rule the wind, too much wind, come to tea – Attention!

Then the measure of the incantation changed and took a less staccato and more musical tone. "*E te Matua, pai-marire*" ("O Father good and gracious") the leader began, and all the people responded *"Rire, rire hau!"* Then they chanted in a wild cadence, sometimes falling away softly, then rising and swelling in volume that throbbed with intense fervour, the ritual of *"Waiata mo te ata"* or "Morning song" beginning with this karakia:

> *To mai Niu koroia, mai merire!*
> (My glorious Niu, have mercy on me!)
> *To mai Niu kororia, mai merire!*
> (My glorious Niu, have mercy on me!)
> *To mai Niu kororia, mai merire!*
> (My glorious Niu, have mercy on me!)
> *To rire, rire!*
> (Have mercy, mercy!)

(The words *"mai merire"* were a transliteration of the Latin *"Miserere mei"* in the Roman Catholic prayers). Another burst of "Morning Song" followed:

> *Atua pai merire,*
> (God the Father, have mercy on me)
> *Atua paimerire,*
> (God the Father, have mercy on me)
> *Atua paimerire,*
> (God the Father, have mercy on me)
> *Rire, rire!*
> (Have mercy, mercy!)

> *Atua Tamaiti, pai merire*
> (God the Son, have mercy on me)
> *Atua Tamaiti, pai merire*
> (God the Son, have mercy on me)
> *Atua Tamaiti, pai merire*
> (God the Son, have mercy on me)
> *Rire, rire!.*
> (Have mercy, mercy!)

> *Atua Wairua-Tapu, pai merire*
> (God the Holy Ghost, have mercy on me)

> *Atua Wairua-Tapu, pai merire*
>   (God the Holy Ghost, have mercy on me)
> *Atua Wairua-Tapu, pai merire*
>   (God the Holy Ghost, have mercy on me)
> *Rire, rire!.*
>   (Have mercy, mercy!)

This chant, rhythmic and haunting in its frequent repetitions was taken from the Church of England prayer book and it called upon God the Father, God the Son and God the Holy Ghost to "have mercy upon us – mercy, mercy." In the evening assemblies, in the meeting house, there was much chanting of hymns and prayers. This was one of the hymns:

> *To tangikere Pata, mai merire,*
>   (Oh Father, have mercy on me!)
> *To tangikere Pata, mai merire,*
> *To tangikere Pata, mai merire,*
>
> *To tangikere titekoti, mai merire,*
>   (Jesus, have mercy on me!)
> *To tangikere titekoti, mai merire,*
> *To tangikere titekoti, mai merire,*
>
> *To tangikere Orikoti, mai merire,*
>   (Holy Ghost, have mercy on me!)
> *To tangikere Orikoti, mai merire,*
> *To tangikere Orikoti, mai merire,*
> *To rire, rire!*   (Mercy, mercy!)

A maorified version of the Benediction was chanted in chorus with all the people holding up the right hand (***Ringa tu***) on a level with the head as the canticle was intoned:

Kororia me te Pata,	Glory to the Father, and to the Son
Ranei tu,	and to the Holy Ghost, as it was in
Ranei to,	the beginning and ever shall be,
Riiko – e	world without end – (and instead
Te wai te pikine,	of "Amen", "Rire, Rire, hau!")
Huoro Pata	
Hema ta pi	
Wai wi rau te,	
Rire,rire, hau!	

It did not take Jane long to dismiss all these chants as simply "pidgin" English which merely copied the sounds with no attempt to convert the words into proper Maori. She also gleaned from the converts their stolid belief that when they had learned all of the incantations well, their Gods *Rura* and *Riki* would give them power to walk upon the water and perform many other miracles.

To judge from the hymns and prayers that were rendered with such reverent devotion, goodness and mercy were the distinguishing attributes of the Pai-marire or Hauhau faith but perhaps it was because she was a little more worldly wise or just downright pragmatic, Jane remained sceptical that it might not all form part of a scheme designed to exalt the impressionable Maori to spiritual and material advantage over the hated Pakeha and that the "good and peaceful" refrains would soon become war cries and incite them again into a desperate racial struggle. Her intuition being nevertheless right or wrong, she would have none of it.

Jane's Story Chapter 24

A Battle of Minds and Divine Intervention

It was at *Te Ahuahu* in Taranaki in April 1864 (just prior to the battle of Gate Pa and the end of the Waikato wars) that adherents of the Pai-marire faith first actively clashed with the Government forces. A company of soldiers of the 57th Regiment and some newly enlisted Taranaki Militia Settlers under Captain Lloyd, who had only recently arrived from England and was new to Maori warfare, was ambushed by a *Hauhau* war party and caught totally by surprise whilst they rested with their arms stacked as they awaited to re-establish contact with a forward scouting party on the hill. The Maori warriors leaped from their well concealed cover of dense fern and charged amongst the startled soldiers, some firing their guns (*pu*) and others wielding their long handled tomahawks (*toki kakuaroa*) and shouting their war cry *"Pai-marire hau! hau! hau!"* which sounded like the baying of hounds to their panic-stricken victims. Captain Lloyd ordered his men to take cover and return fire but only for those who attempted to essay the order to be ruthlessly cut down whilst the others scattered in all directions to hide amongst the fern and await nightfall before making their way towards the ocean beach about two miles away.

Seven soldiers were killed and twelve wounded in the action and the forward party on the hill, under Lieutenant Clarke, were fortunate to make their escape northward by track along the ranges. It was Captain Frank Mace of the Taranaki Mounted Rifles who, after hearing the firing of shots from the redoubt at Oakura, was first to come onto the scene to find the naked and decapitated bodies of Lloyd and his men lying gruesomely among the fern. The heads of the slain soldiers including that of Captain Lloyd, were delivered by their assailants to the Pai-marire prophets who had several of them preserved by the ancient smoke-drying process (*mokomokai*) for the purpose of brandishing them from tribe to tribe to enlist new Hauhau recruits. One of the heads was recovered in 1865 and returned to Taranaki and mistakenly buried as Captain Lloyd's but, some Maori came forward later to state that Lloyd's head was taken by *Kereopa te Rau* across the Island as far as Opotiki whilst another, believed to be that of Private Gallagher was carried by *Patara Raukatauri* to the tribes of *Ngati Porou* between Gisborne (*Turanganui*) and the East Cape (*Waipu*).

The Pai-marire faith had now entered a far more ferocious phase than that which Te Ua as its founder had at first visualised. To adjust to the new circumstance therefore, he claimed to have received a further adjuration from the angel Gabriel to exhibit the Pakeha soldiers' heads throughout the tribes of the Island and, after all the tribes had been visited and converted to Pai-marire, the Maori people would become endowed with such power and wisdom that they would emerge victorious in their struggle with the Pakeha and restore the land to its original owners. This would only be achieved through absolute faith in the ceremonies and prayers (*karakia*) of Pai-marire.

In pursuance of this dictum, Te Ua appointed special apostles to promulgate the doctrine throughout the land. Principally among these were *Hepanaia Kapewhiti, Matene te Rangitauira, Patara Raukatauri, Kereopa te Rau and Horomona*. Little could Te Ua have imagined at the time that the fire of resentment that he had kindled amongst his own Taranaki people in the form of Pai-marire, would flair and fluctuate throughout the Island for the next twenty years until finally being extinguished with the pardoning of *Te Kooti* in 1883 and also, that of the principal apostles he had chosen to carry his word, all but one would come to violent ends in battle or at the hands of the public executioner. The only exception being Patara Raukatauri who lived to see the return of peace to the land.

The three prophets despatched by Te Ua early in 1865 to the East Coast to carry his word and convert the tribes to the Pai-marire faith were Kereopa te Rau, Patara Raukatauri and Horomona. Of them, Kereopa was by far the most authoritative and it was he who carried the barbarity, which was far in excess of anything that might have been condoned by Te Ua, to his own outrageously brutal ends.

Although, originally, Kereopa had accompanied his kinsmen of Ngati Rangiwewehi in disregard of the main Te Arawa resolve that they should remain loyal to Queen Victoria, and fought on the side of the Maori King in the latter stages of the Waikato wars, he was always an inveterate savage of the very worst excesses, even cannibalism. It was therefore not inconceivable that he should choose to disregard Te Ua's instructions which were to conduct a peaceful crusade across the Island until he reached TeKani-a-Takirau of the East Coast who was recognised as the highest chief in all of Aotearoa, to whom he was to present Captain Lloyd's head.

That Te Ua did not authorise further murder or indeed hostile acts of any kind on their introductory mission to the East Coast can be confirmed by the following translation of a written instruction given on the eve of their departure to the three prophets at *Matakaha,* Taranaki on December 8th 1864:

"(*From Te Ua Haumene to all settlements in the Island, extending to every boundary)*".

"*These are directions regarding the head which is being sent forth to the districts of the Island.* This is the route to be taken: Go direct from here to *Waitotara,* then pursue a course inland until *Pipiriki* is reached; thence go direct to *Taupo* and from there to the *Urewera,* thence on to *Ngati Porou* until you reach *TeKani-a-Takirau.* There ends the journey. Let your proceedings be correct, not like those of *Te Rangitauira* whose actions were not in accordance with my teachings in the land. Let your conduct be good in carrying these my instructions to the various parts of the Island, even until you come to *TeKani* who will convey the teachings peacefully to his European acquaintances there. "This letter you must make known to all the villages. Should it become soiled in the swamps, you must copy it onto new paper so that it may be conveyed properly to the settlements visited, and so on until you reach *TeKani*. That is all, From *Te Ua Haumene*".

History records that Kereopa, Patara and Horomona did in fact obey the instructions by travelling inland from Waitotara, skirting the lower Whanganui territory of the *Ngati Hau* and *Ngati Pamoana* (who, as with the people of Te Arawa, remained hostile to Paimarire), until they reached Pipiriki and thence through the North Taupo territory of Ngati Raukawa to the Southern fringe of the Urewera Country before deviating East to avoid contact with Te Arawa, thence to emerge in the Eastern Bay of Plenty at Whakatane.

Meanwhile Jane, on her visits to the surrounding settlements from her island home on Mokoia, had begun to feel concern and alarm as she observed the growing influence of the Pai-marire religion particularly amongst the people of Ngati Rangiwewehi on the North-western shores of the lake and northward into the Ngai te Rangi and Piri Rakau bush regions of the Kaimai, Te Irihanga and Whakamarama. It troubled her to find that so many of her erstwhile friends and comrades of the Waikato wars were now being persuaded to enter into new conflict in the cause of some magical, messianic resurgence which she had already exposed as a totally false and irresponsible profanation, completely alien to the principles upon which an enlightened Christian civilisation should be founded.

This then would become a test of determination whether as a nation, Maori would move forward and share in a policy of mutual advancement and coexistence for the future now being offered them, or revert to the ancient ritual of *Tohunga Maori* with its paganism and fanatical worship of gods and demigods in whose name the blood of thousands in the past was shed as the flames of tribal warfare were left to flare uninhibited and without restraint.

Jane thought of her beloved father, Richard Russell, and how he devoted his all to the welfare of his adopted family in their time of desperate need. Of her tutors and mentors of the Anglican and Roman Catholic Missions who guided and educated her through her tender years and introduced her to the classical world of music, literature and culture. She remembered Wiremu Tamihana who, with other forward thinking chiefs of their time, tried their utmost to avoid war but rather to share in the prosperity of the land together. For her therefore there could be no turning back. She would advance the cause of Te Arawa and the other truly circumspect and responsible tribes and reject all approaches from Pai-marire in favour of true Christianity as the only way forward for her people.

There shortly came a time however when Jane herself would become confronted with a test of determination after she had discovered that during her absence, some of her own family had succumbed to the lure of the new religion. Her mother Maraea, brother Neri, his sister Hera and her own daughter Rangitauninihi, whilst staying with relatives at Puhirua in Ngati Rangiwewehi territory, had become infatuated with the rising popularity of Pai-marire amongst their peers and had themselves become prospective converts.

Neri, who had by then taken a wife of Ngati Rangiwewehi and was living permanently at Puhirua, came out to greet her as she arrived at the village and forcibly uttered the strange, scarcely intelligible words of a Hauhau incantation and after he had finished, his expression became relaxed and he was then able to explain that he had been endeavouring to persuade her towards accepting the new faith. But when she scolded him for even imagining that she would entertain such profane and blasphemous heresy, he smiled and shook his head in submission and confessed: "I should have known that no power on earth could move one so firm in her conviction as my beloved and unshakeable big sister."

She witnessed the curious hypnotic power that the chants of Te Ua, combined with the influence of *Tohunga Maori,* held over the people of Puhirua. The prophet of the *niu* at Puhirua was a Tohunga named *Tiu Tamihana.* The title *Tiu,* the Maori version of "Jew", was used often among the devotees of Pai-marire because it was considered under Te Ua's dispensation that Maori was the chosen people of God, just as the Jews were in the Old Testament. "We are the *Iharaia* (Israelites) and are one with the chosen people whose ancestors came from the land of Canaan" it was taught.

As *Tiu Tamihana* led his disciples in the rites of Pai-marire, they were seen to be wholly oblivious to all terrestrial things and seemed to be possessed of spirits as they circled round and round the *niu,* appearing to be half dazed with their hands held aloft, reciting their prayers in a sing-song chant, their bare legs and arms perhaps covered with sandflies (*namu*) and being apparently immune to their bites.

As Jane sat on the marae and watched, she particularly noticed and admired a lithe young chieftainess named *Hikairo* who was dressed only in a beautiful white cloak (*korowai*) of fine dressed flax fibre fastened over her right shoulder, leaving that arm free, and reaching below her knees. Her bare and graceful arm was upraised in the gesture of the *Hapa Pai-marire* as she marched with dignified step around the *niu* pole and she, like the others, seemed to be totally entranced and oblivious of all else around her. It saddened Jane that such promising, young influential talent as personified in that young woman, should be sacrificed to this morally corruptive abomination that was now being inflicted upon these people.

Later on that day, Jane was astonished to see a white man, shaggy-haired and wearing tattered clothes, emerge from the bush and walk up to the *niu* pole and begin to chant the Pai-marire incantations and, as he walked around the pole with his hand upraised, the people looked on cautiously before moving to join him in the service. It appeared to Jane that this man, whom it was obvious by his tattered uniform was a deserter from the Tauranga Militia had, for his own self preservation, deliberately gone straight to the *niu* immediately he arrived at the village thereby assuring himself of a friendly reception.

She was subsequently told of several renegade white men, decried by their fellow countrymen as "Pakeha-Maoris" who had "taken to the blanket", who had become as fanatical about Pai-marire (or "*Hauhauism*" as it became more commonly known) as any of its native perpetrators and participated fully in many of the acts of barbarism that had later been brought to the attention of the authorities.

Jane's presence in the village and her perceived abstention from the Pai-marire conventionality did not go unnoticed by Tiu Tamihana and the higher ranked priests at Puhirua and they secretly resolved to invoke the superior powers of the gods **Rura** and **Riki** to bring her to submission and obedience to the faith. Therefore, at a singular evening séance especially arranged in the communal meeting house (*wharepuni*), the people were called together under the prophet and his disciples to call down the spirits of the wind (*nga wini*), who normally would dwell in the *niu* but could be brought to the wharepuni at night, to concentrate their powers on Jane and gain her as a convert.

On this occasion however, there was another unbelieving visitor named **Nohoroa Koki** who had been summoned to join Jane in the ceremony. They were each called upon to stand in the centre of the room whilst the people, led by the prophet , circled continuously around them reciting prayer (*karakia*) after prayer in chorus to try and draw the winds (*wini*) down upon them to lodge in their hearts and minds and charm them into submission. But perhaps it was due to her devout Christian upbringing and her English education that Jane should prove to be a most difficult subject, so much so that she could not suppress her laughter which earned her a severe reprimand from the people who told her that it was very wrong to treat the gods so disrespectfully. Nohoroa laughed at first also but, as the chanting became more earnest and intense, he began to tremble and shake and shortly lapsed into a kind of trance or fit. He opened his mouth to speak and out poured the weird pidgin English incantations of Pai-marire, "*piki mauteni, rongo mauteni*" and so on until finally the last vestige of scepticism had been exorcised and he became a complete convert.

But they never succeeded with Jane. Oh the force was there alright and she would be first to acknowledge it though she never let it show. She recalled that as the incessant, remorseless chanting droned on, she sensed a shroud of suffocating blackness descending upon her and she imagined she was standing in a darkened cavern and all around there were weird fiendish, bat-like creatures of some kind shrieking and scuttling for cover deeper into the darkness. She felt abandoned and afraid that soon she would yield to the overwhelming pressure that was bearing down upon her. Desperately she wrenched her gaze away from the depths of darkness and looked up to the heavens and then fleetingly there came to her these words of the 23rd Psalm - "*The Lord is my shepherd; I shall not want. Yea though I walk through the valley of the shadow of death, I will fear no evil, for thou art with me; Thy rod and thy staff shall comfort me.*" She turned and stepped out into the light and she knew that she had triumphed.

Early next morning she left Puhirua for her home on Mokoia and, with her in the canoe, were her mother and the two girls none of whom felt the slightest urge to look back over their shoulder.

And as Moihi brought the canoe up to the mooring place at the sacred *totara* tree named *Atuahu* on Mokoia, and the ladies stepped once more onto the hallowed ground of their ancestors (*papakainga*), there came to greet them from a certain *hinau* tree at the edge of the bush, two excited little *tirairaka* darting and cavorting in the air above them, twittering their cheerful little song of welcome as they led their returning family along the path to the village. Maraea and Jane looked at each other in mutual understanding. Their own special guardian spirit (*Atua*) whose symbol (*Aria*) appears in the form of the tirairaka, had once again brought them reassurance that evil would not befall the female line of the descendants of Rangitauninihi who, on that special day, on this island of Mokoia, had been given under the protection of the goddess *Kura Ngaituku.*

Jane's Story Chapter 25

A New War, A New Cause

Reference has already been made of the events following the battles of Gate Pa and Te Ranga in 1864 after which the majority of the Ngai te Rangi survivors under Hori Ngatai made their peace with the Colonial Government when they surrendered their arms to the British Commander at Te Papa (Tauranga) and resigned themselves to sharing in the development of their lands with the new settlers for the mutual benefit of both races. However there remained those among some Ngai te Rangi and Piri Rakau sub-tribes (*hapu*), chiefly the bush dwellers of the Kaimai hinterland, who refused to accept defeat and preferred to remain in isolation in the rather forlorn hope that there might some day be a resurgence of hostilities. These were the people who had now aligned themselves with the *Hauhau* movement to become devotees of Te Ua's Pai-marire religion and join with the Ngati Rangiwewehi to control the heavily bushed region from the North-western shores of Lake Rotorua, throughout the Mamaku and Kaimai forests as far North as Whakamarama on the Eastern slopes of the Kaimai Range.

It had disturbed Jane to find that many of these people had been old friends and comrades, who had fought alongside her so valiantly in the Waikato wars, but had now become inveigled into supporting this far less honourable, in fact totally repugnant and discreditable cause.

The leader of this insurgent group was *Hori Tupaea* who had refused to accompany Hori Ngatai in his peaceful submissions to the Government authorities at Te Papa and elected to remain in seclusion in the bush. He had become a declared devotee of the Pai-marire faith and determined to throw his whole weight behind Te Ua and his disciples in their crusade to "sweep the Pakeha from the land and back into the sea from whence he came". The prospect of gaining such a formidable ally, already firmly established in the Western Bay of Plenty, prompted Te Ua to send a messenger to Hori Tupaea with an invitation to meet with his senior emissary and prophet *Kereopa te Rau* at *Te Huruhuru* on the upper *Rangitaiki* River on the fringe of the *Urewera* Country where he was assembling a war party of Urewera warriors in preparation for an expedition to the *Whakatane-Opotiki* headquarters of the *Ngati Awa* and *Whakatohea* tribes. It would greatly heighten the prestige (*mana*) of the expedition should Hori Tupaea agree to accompany it.

Although the invitation was favourably received, Tupaea was nevertheless aware that to bring about such meeting, he and his attendant party would need to pass through the forbidden territory of Te Arawa where the Pai-marire cult had been strictly outlawed and no exponent of that faith would be permitted to pass. If he was to attend the meeting therefore, he would have to move by night to avoid detection and capture by Te Arawa and in particular the Ngati Pikiao hapu through whose heartland they would have to pass.

It was early in the summer of 1865 that Jane was called by her uncle *Wiremu Matenga te Ruru* of *Ngati Uenukukopako* to accompany him to a meeting of Arawa chiefs in a council of war (*runanga pakanga*) at *Kahuwera* a heavily fortified pa on a promontory on the Northern shore of *Lake Rotoiti*, not far from the present *Otaramarae*. There it was made known that the Ngai te Rangi rebel chief Hori Tupaea was preparing to cross Arawa territory to join Kereopa te Rau and other Hauhau protagonists in the Urewera Country to the South. The council therefore determined that every track should be closely guarded and that canoe patrols would scout the lake and maintain watches day and night and, as this was Ngati Pikiao territory, it would be fitting that the overall command be entrusted to the redoubtable *Matene te Auheke* of an earlier successful repulse of a *Tai Rawhiti* intrusion.

Matenga te Ruru pledged the full support of both Ngati Rangiteaorere and Uenukukopako although he was himself suffering ill health. That was his reason for inviting Jane to accompany him as he was well aware of her reputation as a fearless fighter and expert in the use of firearms. She would join him in one of the canoe patrols where she would not only lend armed support but also a sharp pair of eyes.

Daily they patrolled in their small canoe, scanning the shoreline for any sign of recent disturbance until one morning they discovered an empty canoe drifting about in the middle of the lake. Jane at once fired a shot to raise the alarm and soon there came a scurry of other canoes racing up towards them when a quick examination showed that the abandoned canoe had been cast adrift only minutes beforehand and that the occupants would have gained only a short head start and should still be fairly close by.

They made for the shore at its nearest point and it was not long before Jane's keen eyes spotted the disturbed sand where the fugitive canoe had beached at the foot of the cliffs between *Hauparu* and *Ruato* Bays on the Southern shoreline. A tuft of grass with fresh earth still clinging to its roots had landed on the beach from the heights above and this infused the party to quickly scale the cliff where they came upon the footprints of a group of people leading into the bush. Then began a wild chase South from Ruato in the direction of *Lake Okataina* and suddenly they came upon the fleeing party with Hori Tupaea among them. Jane recognised their leader as the elderly prophet (*kai karakia*) from Puhirua *Tiu Tamihana* ("Jew Thompson") and also among them was her old friend *Timoti te Amopo* the tohunga who had saved her life at Gate Pa.

Matenga at once called on the party to stop, threatening to fire on them if they did not and, as seemed very odd to Jane, Hori Tupaea and his companions, whilst showing no sign of fear nor apprehension, halted without any show of defiance yet made no move to surrender as if their pursuers were of no consequence. Instead, they gathered around the prophet and began to chant their Pai-marire incantations calling on their gods to strike their persecutors blind and, for the following few minutes, there was nothing the Arawa party could do but sit and listen patiently to the karakia.

Others among the Hauhau party besides Hori Tupaea, Tiu Tamihana and old Timoti, were Hori's old wife *Akuhata,* his young wife and child, a half caste called *Hoani Makaraoti* (John McLeod) all of Ngai te Rangi, Te Hati and several from other hapu including Piri Rakau and Rangiwewehi numbering about twenty in all. Old Timoti had turned Hauhau and had undertaken to guide the party across the Ngati Pikiao territory. Having camped for a time in the bush on the North side of the lake, they had succeeded in crossing unseen very early that morning and were making their way to the Urewera Country when they were discovered. They were all unarmed without even a stone club (*patu*) among them but, unknown to all of the others, old Timoti was secretly carrying a short-handled tomahawk (*patiti*) under his shirt. The party had done their utmost to escape detection by crossing the lake under cover of darkness and by dragging brushwood back and forth on the beach where they landed but all to no avail.

The elders Hori Tupaea and the prophet when approached, called on their gods (*atua*) Rura and Riki to blind the eyes of their pursuers and prevent them from seeing and then Tiu Tamihana led off with this Pai-marire chant:

Koterani, teihana!
Karaiti titi Kai.
Kopere, teihana!
Rire, rire, hau!

And, as they chanted, all of the Hauhau devotees raised their right hands above their heads in the regular Pai-marire gesture and recited more karakia seemingly convinced that they would be made immune from danger. The prophet then led them into the Maori version of *The Benediction* in which they all chorused:

> *Kororia me te Pata,*   *Te wai te pikine,*
> *Ranei tu,*   *Huoro Pata, hema ta pi,*
> *Ranei to,*   *Wai wi rau te,*
> *Riiko – e!*   *Rire rire hau!*

("Glory to the Father, and to the Son, and to the Holy Ghost; as it was in the beginning and ever shall be; world without end" and, instead of "Amen", "Rire rire hau!" Jane well remembered that karakia as she heard it chanted on that day but it was not until long afterwards that she was able to identify and relate it to the appropriate passage of the Bible.

Those people lived always in the belief that when they had learned all of the karakia well enough, their gods Rura and Riki would bestow upon them the power to walk upon the waters and perform other supernatural deeds which would elevate them to the levels of the demigods themselves. "Then why did Tupaea not walk across the lake instead of taking a canoe" asked some of the Arawa party? "Oh because he had not yet learned the karakia well enough" was the irrepressible reply.

When at length the prayers were ended, and the circumstances remained unchanged, Matenga te Ruru asked Jane to run out to the edge of the bush and fire a shot to alert the other Arawa searchers of their find and, soon afterwards they came up eagerly to escort the captives back to the beach and into the large war canoe of Matene te Auheke to be carried in triumph back to Kahuwera. Jane's small party under Matenga te Ruru joined the triumphant flotilla in their own canoe, the youthful company chanting their war-songs in time with the paddles until they were met with a tumultuous greeting from the Kahuwera people who came dashing out into the water brandishing their weapons and threatening to despatch Tupaea and his followers there and then. Matene te Auheke however called for calm and waited for the excitement to die down before landing his quarry. Hori Tupaea remained impassive throughout and even offered to go ashore and brave the anger of the people alone, then resumed his Pai-marire karakia in the firm belief that his faith would preserve his life and strike his enemy helpless. His Arawa antagonists however jeeringly reminded him of his position, pointing out that he was their prisoner now and could never again call himself a high chief (*Rangatira*).

Then followed as by traditional custom (*tikanga Maori*), a call (*mihi*) for all of the prisoners to be brought ashore and escorted into a large tent where a plentiful supply of food had been prepared for them, pork, kumara, potato and freshwater mussels and crayfish (*kakahi* and *koura*) and so on, but as Jane observed, they were still all feeling very sorrowful and it was perhaps understandable that they were not able to eat very much.

From Kahuwera, the captives were taken out to the coast at Maketu and from there shipped under guard to Tauranga where they were given over to the Military Commander at Te Papa. Hori Tupaea was to be held prisoner at Tauranga for some time before eventually being released to his hapu at the end of the Hauhau wars. When old Timoti was searched in the Tauranga Gaol, his short-handled tomahawk (*patiti*) was found tucked under a flax girdle beneath his shirt. Tiu Tamehana, on hearing of this, complained that he had expressly ordered that no weapons were to be carried on their secret mission and it was because Timoti had disobeyed his instructions that a bad omen (*aitua*) had descended upon them and brought misfortune.

Jane's Story Chapter 26

Hauhau Venom Broaches the Surface

When word came through of the capture of Hori Tupaea by the Ngati Pikiao at Rotoiti, and his ensuing incarceration in the Tauranga gaol, Kereopa, who had been waiting to receive him at the Tuhoe pa of Te Huruhuru on the edge of the Urewera forest, decided to proceed without him on his errand to the Ngati Awa and Whakatohea tribes of the Eastern Bay of Plenty at Whakatane and Opotiki. By then he and his fellow Pai-marire prophets Patara Raukatauri and Horomona had assembled a war party of Tuhoe warriors to strengthen the original company (*Wakataua*) which had accompanied them from Te Ua's stronghold at Matakaha in Taranaki. Among the (original) escort were two deserters from the British forces, one of whom was Louis Baker, a half-breed French-Canadian-Indian who came to New Zealand as a stoker on a British steam-powered man-o-war. He was assigned the duty by Kereopa of carrying the head of Captain Lloyd which would be paraded at each place they visited as a symbol of the all-consuming might of the Pai-marire religion which, it was pretended by the prophets, had the power to make the dead mouth speak.

In February 1865, Kereopa and his band of Hauhau fanatics arrived at Opotiki where, as it would evolve just one month later, he was to commit by far the most heinous atrocity not only of the Hauhau war but of any of the previous New Zealand wars ever to have involved Maori and Pakeha in conflict.

In those earlier campaigns, Christian missionaries had always been respected for their impartial charity and compassion towards all mankind particularly in times of war when often, at grave risk of their own safety, they would go resolutely among the combatants to administer their benefaction to either friend or foe. Such an honourable man was the Reverend *Carl Sylvius Volkner* of the German Lutheran Church who had come to New Zealand to work among the natives. He became a member of the Church of England body and worked among the Whakatohea people in the Eastern Bay of Plenty. He built a fine church which he named Zion (*Hiona*) at Opotiki which, after the disastrous incident which occurred on 2 March 1865, became known as the *Church of Saint Stephen the Martyr* and was preserved as the Anglican place of worship in the present township of Opotiki. The Whakatohea people had always held their missionary in very high regard and had become deeply appreciative of the kindness and Christian teachings that he had brought them. But that was before the advent of Pai-marire whose prophets everywhere set out deliberately to undermine the influence of the Christian ministers by preaching revulsion against them by portraying them as infiltrators that were sent among the Maori by the Pakeha to slyly prepare the way for white settlement. They succeeded in turning many of the native deacons against their own ministers and some had even been induced to take up arms against them.

When the apostles of Pai-marire arrived at Opotiki, Mr Volkner was absent in Auckland and Patara Raukatauri decided to despatch a message to him advising that he should not return as, from now on Pakeha missionaries would no longer be permitted to remain among the Maori people. Evidently Mr Volkner's conceived offence was that during the Waikato war, he had tried to dissuade the Whakatohea from joining in that conflict. He was therefore accused by some as being a spy for the Government. In the following days, a flagstaff of Pai-marire worship (*niu*) was erected at *Pa Kowhai* at the entrance of the Opotiki Harbour and, Kereopa proceeded to conduct his fanatical rituals to bring the people to the niu to indulge in and rehearse the Pai-marire prayers and incantations. He flourished the head of the slain Captain Lloyd to excite the people to the new religion and its professed invincibility.

On the 1st March, the schooner *"Eclipse"* which was owned and operated by *Captain Levy*, a Jewish trader, arrived at Opotiki from Auckland and among the passengers were Mr Volkner and a brother missionary the Reverend *Thomas Grace* whom, it was made known, had recently been forced to abandon his station at *Pukawa* in *Taupo South* under threat from marauding Hauhau. Both men had been warned in Auckland that it would be dangerous to return to Opotiki at that time but they could not be dissuaded from what they regarded as their bounden duty.

Mr Volkner was distressed to find that in his absence his house which was situated some distance from the church at a place called *Peria*, (after the biblical "Beria" in Macedonia), had been sacked by the Hauhau and the contents carried off in all directions. The *"Eclipse"* was boarded and looted of all its cargo but the lives of Captain Levy and his brother were spared and given their liberty fortuitously because they were Jews and therefore to be treated as brothers by the Pai-marire who, from the teachings of Te Ua, were themselves descended from the *Iharaira* (Israelites) from the land of Canaan. The two missionaries were however arrested and held in confinement. Kereopa who had by this time established his supremacy over the greater part of the tribe, summoned a meeting of the people that evening to announce that Mr Volkner (*Te Wakana*) would be tried before him next day and that Mr Grace would remain a prisoner.

On the afternoon of 2nd March, Mr Volkner was taken out of his prison hut by an armed guard of Hauhau and marched into his church which was filled with a highly volatile and excited people. Kereopa, standing by the altar, summoned the missionary before him and announced that he must prepare to die. He was stripped of his long frock coat and waistcoat, which Kereopa immediately put on, and led outside and up to a large willow tree standing on a hill about 100 metres away where he was prepared for execution by hanging.

A line and block, looted from the "Eclipse" was rigged to a stout branch of the tree and the noose placed around the condemned missionary's neck. He knelt down to pray for his deliverance unto his maker and for the souls of the people who had now forsaken him and shook hands with some of those around him until swiftly the executioners hauled on the rope and the missionary's body was lifted and held until at length it hung lifeless from the gallows tree. It is said also that Kereopa fired several shots into the body as it hung there kicking.

After about an hour, in which it was hauled up and down several times, the body was lowered to the ground and taken back to the steps of the church where the head was cut off with an axe used by a man named *Heremita*, whereupon the people crowded around to chant their newly rehearsed Hauhau ritual. Kereopa had by then taken the silver communion chalice from the church vestry and filled it with the spouting blood and he carried it along with the severed head into the church and all the people followed in procession. That gruesome scene outside the church that was known as Zion (*Hiona*), and that which was to follow, was of a character of such revolting measure as was never exceeded by either Maori or Pakeha at any time in their most darkest days. It was as if the devil himself had entered into the lives of the frenzied people of Whakatohea and indeed it had in the human form of Kereopa to terrify and fascinate them by his sheer savagery.

Standing in the pulpit before them, dressed in his victim's frock coat, Kereopa placed the dripping head onto the lectern before him and by its side he placed the communion cup of blood. "Hear Ye of Israel!" he cried, "This is the word of the God of Abraham, Isaac and Jacob! We are the Jews who were lost and persecuted". "Behold!" and gripping the head he gouged out both eyes and took one in each hand between thumb and forefinger. "Listen Oh Tribe" he called "This eye is the Parliament of England, and this one is the law of New

Zealand!" He then swallowed them one after the other, but the second eye was seen to stick in his throat and he called for a drink of water to wash it down. He picked up the head from the floor where he had dropped it and set it upon the lectern in front of him again. Then the cannibal priest held up the communion chalice and drank of its contents. He then passed it to his attendant priests who sipped from it in turn before passing it around the congregation some of whom put it to their lips whilst others dipped leaves into the cup and sprinkled themselves with the blood of their one time revered missionary. The empty cup was carried back to the desecrated pulpit where the head lay and, where the stains of the martyred missionary's blood remains indelibly in the wood of the lectern to this day.

That monstrous act of barbarity earned its enforcer the epithet "Kereopa the eye eater" (*"Kereopa te Kai Karu"*) but, six years afterwards, when he was finally captured in the Urewera Country, he said that he had always known that he would meet with a violent end sooner or later because of that one eye of Mr Volkner (*Te Wakana*) which stuck in his throat. It was a bad omen (*aitua*) and a portent of death.

From the church, Volkner's head was taken to the house of the Roman Catholic priest where it was set upon the mantelpiece for a time and then carried to its own house at Peria and every other place that was sacred to the Christian mission; the object being to render them common (*whakanoa*) by pollution with the blood of the downfallen. The after history of Volkner's head as narrated by native witnesses has it preserved by the smoke-drying process (*mokomokai*) and carried by Kereopa on his travels inland to the Urewera Country and later to Southern Taupo where it is said to be hidden in a cave at *Rotoaira* under *Tongariro* Mountain.

Not all the Whakatohea participated in or approved the slaying of the Reverend Volkner and there were two sub-tribes (*hapu*) in particular, the *Ngati Ira* of *Waioeka* and *Ngati Ngaere* who expressed their disapproval but were powerless before Kereopa and his armed followers and were also held in fear of his gods and magic incantations. Kereopa impressed upon his followers that by tasting the blood of the missionary, they would acquire a knowledge of the English language and would be able to work miracles. This was obviously a revival of the ancient Maori belief that by eating the flesh of the enemy, his *mana* would be acquired by his victor

The fate of the other missionary Mr Grace, remained precarious for some time as he was accused of having preached false doctrine amongst the people of South Taupo. It was highly probable that he too would have been sacrificed like his friend Mr Volkner had it not been for Patara who offered to exchange him for Hori Tupaea who had been captured by the Ngati Pikiao at Rotoiti while attempting to join Kereopa and his party in the Urewera. Mr Grace was kept in suspense for a fortnight whilst Patara awaited a reply from Tauranga but he at last contrived to slip away in a boat from the schooner "Eclipse" which was about to sail for Tauranga and Auckland. They were met on their way out by two armed cutters from *HMS "Brisk"* (Captain E. Freemantle) which had just arrived to investigate reports of Volkner's murder and this fortuitous midstream encounter ensured their escape to safety.

Some weeks after the events at Opotiki which led to the ritual killing of the Reverend Volkner, the Pai-marire scourge descended upon nearby Whakatane where *Horomona*, one of the original prophets chosen by Te Ua, had persuaded the *Ngati Awa* and *Whanau o Apanui* tribes to embrace the new religion. The small coastal trading cutter *"Kate"* , chartered by *Mr James Fulloon*, a half-caste man of great ability who was in the employ of the Government as an interpreter and native agent, arrived at the mouth of the Whakatane River. Fulloon, who was a surveyor by profession, was well known among the Whakatane people to whom he was related through his mother who was an East Coast chieftainess. He was given the Maori name of *Te Mautaranui* after a locally famous forefather.

When HMS "Brisk" was sent down the coast to investigate the reported murder of the Reverend Volkner, Mr Fulloon accompanied Captain Freemantle as a guide and interpreter and, after armed parties were landed up and down the coast in an attempt to apprehend Kereopa and Patara, he decided to transfer from the "Brisk" to the smaller "Kate" and sail for Whakatane where he had arranged to meet local leaders on official business. Horomona, upon hearing of the arrival of the cutter at the mouth of the river and that it was waiting at anchor for high water before crossing the bar, at once urged his followers to capture the vessel and kill all those on board. A party of Ngati Awa, led by the renegade chief *Mikaere Kirimangu* waited until nightfall before boarding two longboats to come up quietly alongside the cutter and steal aboard. Entering the cabin they found Fulloon sleeping soundly in his bunk and, without waking him a young boy gently removed his revolver from under his pillow and handed it to Kirimangu who did not hesitate to place it against the sleeping man's temple and shoot him dead. The rest of the crew consisted of two white men who were killed immediately and two half-caste youths who were taken ashore and allowed to go free. A *Mr Bennett White* who was also on board, was spared from execution as he was married to a local Maori woman and was the father of one of the half-caste youths.

The cutter was later brought up the Whakatane River to a landing opposite the settlement and thoroughly looted. Her mast was chopped off at deck level and taken ashore to be erected a short distance away at *Kopeopeo* where it was set up as a niu under Horomona's directions. The local hapu of *Patutatahi* and *Ngati Pukeko* who had recently been brought under the fanatical influence of Pai-marire were led through the ritual processes around the foot of the niu, chanting the new incantations as taught them by Horomona.

The old chief *Te Apanui* who was adamantly averse to the new faith and the excesses of Hauhauism, was nevertheless compelled to participate in the ceremony by taking his place at the foot of the niu and, with his people revolving around it with right hand raised in absolute subjection.

The sequel to these deeds was the despatch, after considerable and frustrating delay, of a Government punitive expedition and the ultimate capture of many of those actively involved in the murders of both Volkner and Fulloon. Of these, *Horomona, Kirimangu, Mokomoko, Heremita, Kahupaea* and *Hakaraia te Ruwhi* were tried in Auckland and hanged at Mount Eden Prison on 17 May 1866. *Te Uhi* a Whakatane chief was imprisoned for his part in the killing of Fulloon and the crew of the "Kate". Note however that Kereopa and his henchman Patara were able to escape capture by retreating deep into the Urewera Country where they rallied the Tuhoe people to their cause and join forces with *Te Kooti* eventually to prolong the Hauhau wars for a further seven years.

Providentially perhaps, Jane was spared the horrors of witnessing the deaths of the two men each of whom she had known from her time at the Anglican Mission in Auckland. Mr Volkner was an old friend who was revered not only by the people at the Mission but also among the Arawa people of Maketu on the coast where he was a regular and very welcome visitor. Mr Fulloon was known to Jane through her earlier work with Wiremu Tamihana and the other chiefs who had endeavoured but failed to reach a peaceful conclusion with the Government to the dispute which ended in the Waikato War.

However, word of the murders quickly spread throughout the other tribes of New Zealand from Ngapuhi in the North to Ngai Tahu in the South and such was their shock and revulsion that none would condone the action and all but a few remaining dissidents chiefly among the Taranaki and Tuhoe tribes called for the immediate apprehension of the perpetrators. Te Arawa in particular were so incensed that they called together a force of 400 men consisting of the finest warriors from, *Ngati Tuwharetoa* (Taupo), *Tuhourangi, Whakaue, Rangiwewehi, Pikiao, Uenukukopako, Rangiteaorere, Tuara and Rangitihi* all of whom would be placed under the command of the Government appointed Major **William G. Mair (RM),** remembered for his service in the Colonial Defence Force Cavalry at the Battle of Orakau.

The utter savagery displayed by Kereopa with the mutilation of Mr Volkner's body was enough to convince Jane that the diabolical evils of Pai-marire, which she had already recognised in her earlier experiences with that abominable cult, had inevitably surfaced as she knew it would and it had now become vital for the future of Maori and Pakeha alike that it should be stamped out urgently and completely.

She thought of the chivalry shown by the fighting chiefs of old to their opponents in battle. From Heke and Kawiti in the Northern wars, to Wi Koka and Ngakapa of Ngati Paoa, Tamihana of Ngati Haua, Te Huirama, Mohi, Rewi and Tawhiao of the Waikato wars and the magnificent Rawiri and his written code of conduct at the battle of Gate Pa. These were honourable people fighting honourable causes. Not so the Hauhau who represented no-one but themselves and discriminated not between Maori or Pakeha, woman or child but killed without hesitation any who refused to accede to the faith.

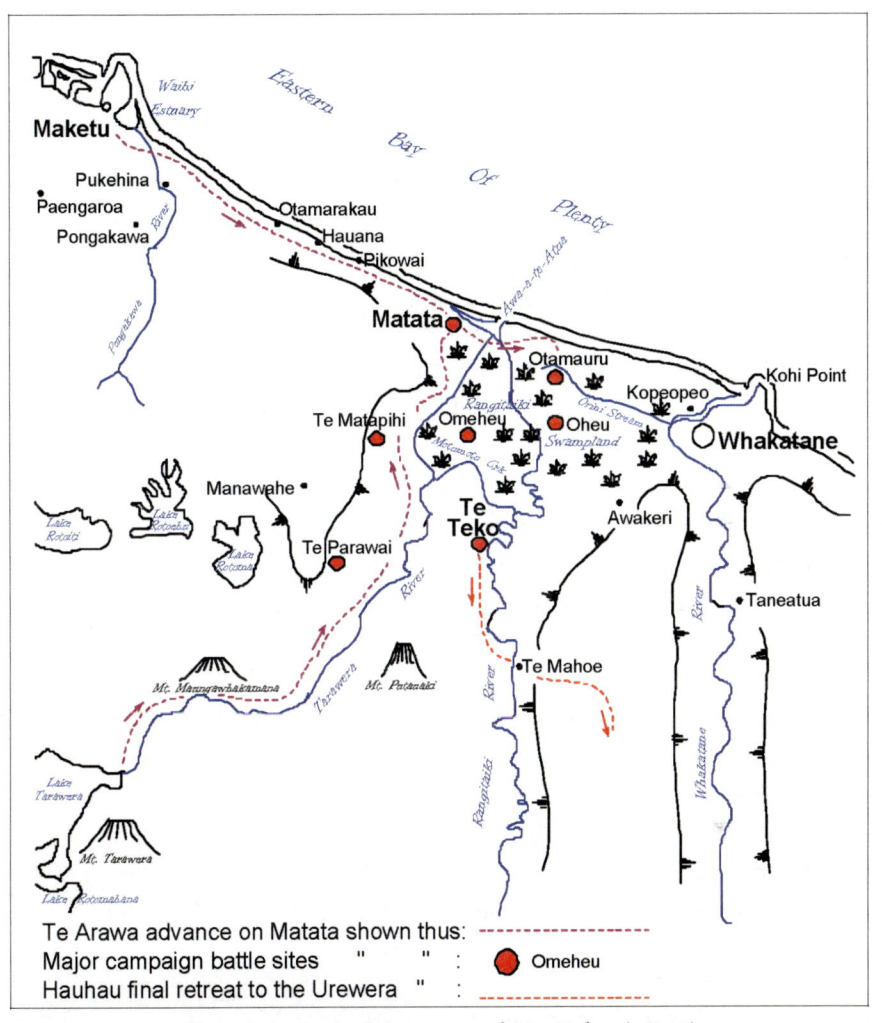

Operations At Matata and Te Teko (1865)

Notes:

The Rangitaiki Swamplands as shown on the map, no longer exist and the Tarawera and Rangitaiki Rivers have since been given new outlets to the sea.

Twentyone years after these operations, Tarawera Mountain erupted and the Pink and White Terraces were destroyed

The townships of Kawerau and Edgecumbe were as yet non-existent.

This was Jane's last campaign.

Jane's Story Chapter 27

End of an Era for Jane

When Major William G. Mair R.M. came to Rotorua at the behest of the New Zealand Government to organise a force of Te Arawa to suppress the rise of Hauhauism amongst the tribes of the Eastern Bay of Plenty after the murders of the Reverend Carl Volkner and Mr James Fulloon, he made it a first priority to pay a visit to Jane at her home on Mokoia. It was his wish to pay homage to the renowned woman warrior (*wahine toa*) who fought so valiantly against the might of the British Imperial Forces with whom he was himself a serving officer, yet found within her the compassion to answer the plea from the dying Colonel Booth in the heat of battle and, under intense fire, to carry him water in complete disregard for her own safety. Besides, he could think of no better ally than she to assist him in rallying support for the raising of a strong fighting force of Te Arawa to put down this new threat to peace and the civilised development of the new Colony. With the powerful influence (*mana*) commanded by her uncle *Matenga te Ruru* throughout the region, together with her own standing amongst her peers as a *wahine toa* of the highest acclaim, there would be no more inspirational delegation to arouse the fighting spirit of all of the hapu of Te Arawa.

It took only a short time therefore before Major Mair had assembled a force of more than four hundred volunteers from the nine major hapu of Te Arawa to form an expeditionary force consisting of a flying column chiefly of *Ngati Pikiao* led by their principal fighting chief, Major Fox (*Te Pokiha Taranui*), based at *Maketu* on the coast, and a main Rotorua force made up of fighters from *Ngati Tuwharetoa* (from Taupo), *Tuhourangi, Whakaue, Rangiwewehi, Uenukukopako, Rangiteaorere, Tarawhai* and *Rangitihi* all under his personal command. Attached to his headquarters staff, at his special invitation, was Jane who would prove invaluable to him not only as an experienced and knowledgeable interpreter and advisor but also a practised markswoman to be entrusted with one of the two only *Minie* rifles available to the company. The other one would be retained by the Major himself. The rest of the Arawa force was armed only with single and double barrelled shotguns (*hakimana* and *tupara*) and some old flintlocks (*ngutu parera*). That the Minie rifle was a superior weapon was demonstrated on several occasions one of which involved Jane during a skirmish in the swamps when she brought down a Hauhau who was poling a canoe across a lagoon at a range of at least 500 metres. Another was when the Major himself, during the siege of the pa on the scarped hillock of *Oheu* in the *raupo* swamp, shot a Hauhau through the forehead from *Te Rangatai* on the opposite bank of the *Tarawera River.*

The Hauhau influence had by this time spread as far West of Whakatane as *Matata* at the mouth of the *Te Awa o te Atua* River where the waters of the *Tarawera* and *Rangitaiki* Rivers ran into the sea after flowing through a labyrinth of reed fringed waterways navigable only by small canoes and winding among islets that rose slightly above the water level to provide camping grounds for eel-fishers and hunters of wild fowl. This whole area, which has long since been drained and converted into fertile farmland, provided a link between the *Tarawera* River in the West and the *Whakatane* River in the East by way of the *Orini* and *Awaitipaku* Streams which at that time were navigable waterways but have since been incorporated into a flood control canal system by the Bay of Plenty Catchment Commission. The Hauhau, consisting of the *Whakatohea, Ngati Awa, Whanau Apanui* and *Ngai te Rangi Houhiri* tribes and some *Tuhoe* from the Urewera, had established two fortified positions at *Parawai* and *TeMatapihi* on the high ground on the Western side of the Tarawera River and also three swampland strongholds at *Oheu, Otamauru* and *Omeheu* inland of the coastal belt of high sand-dunes at the extreme Western end of which was the main pa of *Matata*.

Major Mair, after arranging to rendezvous with Major Fox (*Te Pokiha*) and his Maketu column at Matata, assembled his Rotorua force and crossed the *Tarawera* Lake to *Tapahore Pa* and then, after enlarging his force with a considerable number of *Ngati Rangitihi* fighters, marched down the Tarawera River skirmishing with scouting Hauhau parties as they advanced but avoiding the heavily fortified pa of Parawai which was considered too impregnable for a frontal attack, until at length they joined forces with Te Pokiha and his men to lay siege to the main pa at Matata which was taken with surprisingly little resistance. Then followed further skirmishing on the Western side of the Tarawera until both strongholds Parawai and TeMatapihi finally fell to the superior Te Arawa forces. The Hauhau, thus deprived of their high ground strongholds, were forced to retreat into the swamps where they believed they would be safe from conquest because of the difficulty of approach by their pursuers into an unknown and inhospitable terrain. Major Mair however, took a strong detachment of Ngati Pikiao and Whakaue up the Orini Stream by canoe to land in the rear of *Otamauru*, a large palisaded and entrenched pa about five miles to the East of the Tarawera River towards Whakatane and there they waited until a second detachment from Matata, led by Te Pokiha, marched along the beach under cover of the sand-dunes, taking care not to alert the Hauhau of their presence until they reached a point opposite the pa where they swung inland to silently work their way through the fern and reed infested swampland to come up on their enemy from the opposite side. Thus between them the two columns now had the stronghold completely surrounded.

The successful storming of Otamauru and the capture of so many disillusioned Hauhau who believed that they would be safe there, seemed to have the disparaging effect of breaking all resistance in the

Rangitaiki swamps and, after the subsequent fall of *Omeheu Pa* on another island a short distance South of Otamauru, the Hauhau retreated up the Tarawera River in their canoes and crossed to the Rangitaiki River by way of the *Motumotu Creek* which ran roughly parallel with the Orini Stream. There they occupied a strongly fortified pa, complete with firing trenches and double palisading, at TeTeko on the left bank of the Rangitaiki and about 25 miles inland from the coast.

The coastal areas now cleared of the enemy, the Te Arawa embarked on a foraging expedition right into the township of Whakatane and there they loaded their canoes with quantities of provisions which they carried in triumph back to their headquarters at Matata where they made ready to continue their pursuit of the Hauhau and their ultimate expulsion from the entire Eastern Bay of Plenty region.

When his scouts reported that the Hauhau had entrenched themselves at Te Teko on the Rangitaiki River and were preparing to make a stand there, Major Mair despatched his forces by war canoe up against the swiftly flowing current to within a short distance of the pa where they encamped whilst forward scouts were sent out to reconnoitre the strength of the enemy. He decided that it would not be practicable to launch a head-on assault as the pa was too well protected not only by the six metre high frontal palisading but also the natural lay of the land with the river on one side and a broad exposed area on the other. At the rear, there was a cleverly concealed walkway cut obliquely down the bank to the river which, at that place was about six meters below. On the opposite bank there was a small supporting pa called *Pa Harakeke*, fully manned and well within range of its companion fortress. The garrison at Te Teko numbered about 170 men and there was also a large accompaniment of women and children. The Te Arawa force totalled at least 400 including some women and, of course, Jane.

At a hastily called conference among the military heads and strategic advisors, it was agreed that, to avoid the heavy casualties that would likely result from a full frontal attack, the pa would be approached under cover of sap. Major Mair, it will be remembered, had taken part in the siege of Orakau in the previous year and had closely observed the methods employed in the successful sap used in those operations when a series of zigzag trenches were carried right up to the defensive ramparts to provide cover to the advancing troops. Here was an opportunity to make a similar approach and indeed improve upon it. There was an old riverbed which wound around the Western side of the pa to meet the river again some hundreds of metres down stream and that natural depression would present an ideal base from which the saps could be started. Five lines of sap would be opened from the old river bed with each being allotted to a different hapu, the deliberate intention being to engender fierce competition among them to be first to reach the enemy ramparts. The most Southerly line which would be the longest and most exposed, would be given to Ngati Pikiao because they were the strongest party. The lines were therefore allotted as follows:

(1) Ngati Pikiao, Uenukukopako and Tarawhai (Maketu and Rotorua North).
(2) Ngati Whakaue (Ohinemutu, Rotorua South),
(3) Ngati Rangiteaorere and some Uenukukopako (Te Ngae, Rotorua East)
(4) Ngati Rangiwewehi (Awahou, Rotorua West)
(5) Ngati Tuwharetoa (Taupo), Tuhourangi and Ngati Rangitihi (Te Wairoa and Tarawera)

As the saps advanced towards the stockade, demi-parallels of about six metres in length were opened up on either side to enable marksmen to be stationed to protect the diggers, and the main trenches were also filled with musketeers as they were pushed forward. The head of each sap was just wide enough for one digger with three or four others working behind widening and deepening to about a metre or more.

Women as well as men shared the hard work and among the most energetic of them was Jane who, when not digging, was exchanging fire with the enemy from one of the side trenches. Another dauntless lady was *Ana Pene* from TeNgae, Rotorua, conspicuous for her fearlessness by exposing herself to enemy fire while she urged the warriors onward. Jane recalled that while the saps were being dug, with each hapu striving furiously to be first to reach the palisades, high above the noises of battle Ana's voice could be heard inciting the tribe to fight on ("*Riria e te Iwi, Riria!*"). Besides Ana, her husband and two brothers were also among the fighters.

Jane described another exciting episode when an old tattooed warrior named *Hakawa* from Ohinemutu, stripped naked and covered himself all over with red ochre mixed with shark oil (*kokowhai*) and, taking a long length of white calico (used by all of the Arawa to make headbands to distinguish them from the Hauhau), he tied it around his head, leaving the greater part streaming out behind him and to complete his adornment he stuck turkey feathers in his headband. Then, like a Red Indian chief on the warpath, he burst out into the open and dashed up and down in front of the stockade, shouting insults and thrusting out his tongue in defiance and all the time inviting the astonished Hauhau to shoot him if they could. He ran the length of the ramparts several times while hundreds of shots were being fired at him yet miraculously he managed to emerge unharmed until at last Major Mair intervened and demanded that he return to the trenches. When finally he appeared before the Major, the old warrior explained that his object was to induce the Hauhau to expend all of their ammunition on him so that presently the Arawa would be able to storm the place without losing any men. Hakawa would declare ever after that the Hauhau had wasted more than three hundred cartridges on him.

Shortly it became necessary to silence the small *Pa Harakeke* on the opposite bank of the river as its garrison was maintaining an effective crossfire against the sappers as they neared the main stronghold. About twenty Ngati Pikiao crossed the river by small canoe to establish a landing place from which their leader *Te Pokiha,* with *Mita te Rangituakoha* and one other strode boldly up to the pa and called on the occupants to surrender as they desired to take peaceable possession and avoid the unnecessary shooting of several of their own kinsmen who were among them. The chief in command of the garrison was a man named *Maraki,* of Ngati Pikiao connection, who immediately led out his companions and surrendered.

The Ngati Pikiao were the first to carry their sap close up to the main Te Teko stockade and when they came within a couple of metres of the South-western flank, they prepared for the assault. Strong ropes were brought up and heavy stones were attached to the ends for the purpose of throwing them up and over the palisades and hauling back down on them to breach an entrance. In the other saps, the men were working furiously to complete their tasks whilst maintaining heavy fire into the stockade to divert the enemy attention away from the storming column. The defenders were now running short of ammunition and they were troubled also that their access to the water had been cut off. All was ready for the assault when *Te Pokiha,* from the head of the sap, called out to the garrison, "*Where are the Tawera?*" He wished to give that hapu a last chance to escape slaughter; "*Come out Tawera that you may be saved!*" As Jane recounted the events that followed, the response from the garrison was quite astonishing and far exceeded all expectations. A white flag appeared above the ramparts and the entire garrison surrendered.

The Hauhau were ordered to file out and lay down their arms and, as they came one by one to stand before their captors, their heads bowed in humiliation, the Arawa sprang up from their trenches and launched into a furious *haka* of triumph. Ngati Pikiao danced and chanted their ancient battle-song "*Koia ana te peruperu*", then "*Kia kutia au au!*" The Ngati Tuwharetoa men from Taupo with Tuhourangi burst in with their own "*Uhi mai e waero*" as they leapt in perfect time high off the ground, their legs tucked under them like birds in flight, their guns gripped by the barrel uplifted at full arms length. Then the tribes united in one grand haka delivered with terrific ferocity in front of their silent and bewildered captives.

Several Hauhau had been killed in the three days of siege but there were no losses amongst the Arawa. All of the prisoners were escorted down river to the Arawa headquarters at Matata where another haka of victory was celebrated on their arrival. Some days later, Major Mair marched about a score of the principal offenders to Opotiki for trial by Court Martial. Among the men captured was *Horomona* the Pai-marire prophet sent by Te Ua from Taranaki, the chief instigator of the murder of Mr Fulloon. He was a venerable figure with long snow-white hair and beard, a mystic sage (*tohunga*) of the ancient type. Others were the Ngati Awa chiefs *Te Hura* and *Kirimangu* who were concerned in the death of Fulloon.

Jane again recalls that when they arrived back at Matata with their prisoners and marched onto the marae, Te Hura was confronted by an Arawa chieftainess named *Puhou* from Maketu . Her nephew *Tamarangi* had been killed in the swamp skirmishing at *Mana Whakatane* opposite the fortified pa of *Te Matapihi* . Puhou, in a frenzied state of rage and grief, declared that she would avenge the youngster's death and, clothed only in a waist mat and clutching a whalebone club (*patu*), she rushed up to Te Hura where he was seated on the marae and caught him by the hair. She violently shook him and would have killed him had she not been forcibly restrained. And all the time Te Hura uttered not a word nor made any movement but just sat there like a statue.

The capture of Matata and the fortified Hauhau strongholds of

Parawai and Te Matapihi on the West side of the Tarawera River, the swampland strongholds of Oheu, Otamaura and Omeheu inland of the coastal sand belt, and the final siege of TeTeko Pa, was to occupy Major Mair's Te Arawa expedition for nearly two months during which time they had successfully driven the Hauhau from all of the Whakatane region right to the fringe of the Urewera Country where they would be kept confined never to return to those parts again.

The final outcome of the action in the area bounded by the Tarawera River in the West, the sea front from the main pa of Matata and extending Eastward towards Whakatane, then South up the Rangitaiki River to Te Teko, was concluded with the permanent allocation of some, but not all of those lands to the Te Arawa hapu of Ngati Rangitihi and sections of Tuhourangi and Ngati Tarawhai in recognition of their military services. Ngati Pikiao, Uenukukopako and the others marched back along the coast to Maketu, some returning to their homes and others to rest for a few days before continuing inland to Rotorua.

Jane accompanied her uncle Matenga te Ruru and the Uenukukopako party to Maketu also but it was her intention to travel on from there by coastal trading vessel to Tauranga and thence to Auckland to visit her beloved foster-father, Richard Russell who she had been told was now ailing, and also old friends at the Anglican Mission before returning to Rotorua and her home on Mokoia. When she left Matata that morning however, she was not to know that it was at the siege of TeTeko that she had fired her last shot in anger, that her arrival at Maketu after her march up the coast with her compatriots of TeArawa would mark the final curtain fall on a boldly resolute and exemplary interval in her life and, that a brief interlude during an overnight stay at Maketu was about to change her life forever.

Jane's Story Chapter 28

A Momentous Change of Direction

It was early in the spring of 1865 that Jane and the Ngati Uenukukopako party arrived at Maketu after their march up the coast from Matata. The campaign had been long and exhausting and, being kept constantly on the move over difficult and hard to negotiate terrain, had taken its toll on the moral as well as the physical fortitude of the ultimate victors but they were all relieved that it was now over and they could return to their homes and families. Jane was certainly no exception.

The weather had become much warmer and already the plantations of kumara, potato (*riwai*) and corn (*kaanga*) had taken on their lush new mantles of green. All through the bush the bird life was active and full of joyful chorus and, the demure and delicate flowers of the bush clematis (*puawananga*) could be glimpsed cascading down in veils from the dense canopy above. High in the sky out over the sparkling sea, flocks of diving seabirds could be seen wheeling and circling over shifting shoals of migrating fish and, down on the rocks along the foreshore, pairs of cormorants (*kawau*) preening their creamy white breasts and hanging out their wings to dry in the sun while digesting their earlier catches and preparing for the next foray into the gently lapping waves.

Foremost on Jane's mind after arriving at the village however, was to find some place where she could take a long and luxuriating hot bath, and after that a hearty home-cooked meal and finally, a full and undisturbed night's sleep. Such a place, surprisingly enough was available even in that small and isolated settlement. The fact that Maketu was a port of call for the now quite numerous coastal trading vessels plying the Bay of Plenty from Tauranga as far as Opotiki and around the East Cape, had attracted the attention of one *Denis Stephen Foley* late of County Galway, Ireland who, with his brother Thomas, had come to the new colony to pursue their fortunes together in the hostelry trade with which they both served their apprenticeships in the mother country. Thomas was first to establish himself in Auckland as 'mine host' of a flourishing hotel on the waterfront and Denis, the younger and the more adventuresome of the two, had sought the excitement of frontier life by setting up the *"Travellers' Rest Hotel"* at the crossroads of the East at Maketu. This was no "grog-shop" as abounded all along the sea coast North and South during that early period to serve the heavy drinking fraternity of seafarers of the time, but rather as its name suggested, a well appointed, comfortable and convenient stop-over for the numerous civil, clerical and military assignees, merchants, traders and travelling public who were obliged to pass through Maketu en-route to Tauranga, Auckland, Rotorua, Whakatane, Opotiki and points beyond.

Denis had quickly gained a reputation as a popular and friendly host, totally dedicated to the comfort and welfare of his guests and, he had also won the absolute confidence and trust of the local Maori population and the several Pakeha settlers who had come to Maketu to live amongst them. All of this was no doubt made so much easier to achieve by his inherent beguiling Irish charm which, when aligned with his rather striking physical appearance, tall and masculine, smiling blue eyes and shock of tousled brown hair, would serve to be his most compelling attribute.

So it was that when Jane called to enquire of his hospitality, she in her battle-worn and dishevelled tunic, looking weary and bedraggled after her long march, her rifle slung over her shoulder, she at first appeared to him as a young lad until he beheld that proud and haughty gaze, that determined and stubborn chin and, of all things, her dainty slippered feet. This then was the venerable and highly exalted Heeni Te Kirikaramu, the famous woman warrior, veteran of some of the bloodiest and most highly contestable battles of the Maori wars yet, as she stood there before him, he saw only a wistful, slightly distressed slip of a girl.

In due deference, he tipped his forelock to her and welcomed her inside and that night, Jane was to be afforded all that she had wished for and when at last she pulled the freshly starched sheets about her and buried her head in the softness of her pillow, all the events of the past few months seemed to be floating further and further away and she was being left to look around her and observe a softer, more gentle world where the sun rose high above the clouds of war.

The new day dawned clear and bright and Jane rose early to prepare for her trip North on the sailing cutter which was due to leave on the outgoing tide. She was surprised to find Denis already up and about and directing the business of the day. He had ordered breakfast for his honoured guest and greeted her with a cheery "Top of the morning to you my lady". He found it difficult however to hide his bland astonishment at the transformation that had taken place in her appearance from the bedraggled waif that had wandered up to the reception desk last evening, to the now well composed, self assured young lady, dressed in more effeminate wear, standing there before him. He announced over breakfast that he had undertaken to personally escort her to the boat landing and see her safely on board ship, apologising for such liberty that he might have taken of her.

And so it was that a horse and trap was drawn up in front of the Travellers' Rest later that morning and Jane was driven down to the jetty where she was introduced to the Captain who was placed under strict instructions from Denis that he should take good care of her. He appeared to be in no hurry to return to the hotel and was content to sit in the trap, allowing the horse to stand quietly while he watched the cutter move slowly out into the stream and set its sails for the voyage. He smiled and waved to a now bemused Jane who quite subconsciously waved back. "I'll be waiting here for you when you return" he called and she smiled and waved in response before turning away to join the other passengers in the cabin. It had been such a long time since she was treated like a lady that she had quite forgotten how much it could flatter and exalt her and, however reluctant she might have been to admit it, she would be secretly looking forward to her return to the Travellers' Rest in Maketu.

During the scheduled stop-over at Tauranga on her way to Auckland, Jane took the opportunity to inquire after the health of her old friend *Te Moananui* who had received three gunshot wounds during the battle of Gate Pa and had been carried on a stretcher to his fortress pa at *Tawhitinui* there to attempt a recovery. There was also **Hori Ngatai** the chief who had negotiated the peace pact with the British Military at Te Papa and had encouraged his people into farming the land in concord with the new colonists. Happily she found them both in good spirits, fully recovered and rapidly extending their interests in the welfare and prosperity of their people.

Jane also paid a courtesy visit to Colonel Greer, the commander of the military establishment at Te Papa who had in the previous year, officiated at the signing of the peace pact when *Ngai te Rangi* laid down their arms. He recognised her instantly and strode forward to seize her by the hand. "It is indeed an honour to receive a visit from the heroine of Gate Pa" he exclaimed. He also took the opportunity to thank her on behalf of the Government for the support she had so willingly given Major Mair during the recruitment of the Te Arawa expeditionary force and the successful campaign against the Hauhau insurgents in the swamps of the Rangitaiki and again at the siege of TeTeko. But in the exchange of pleasantries that followed, Jane found herself inclining more towards a future that would move on from the tensions of the past that had divided the fledging nation into conflict, to put it all behind them so that all peoples whatever their ethnic origin might look towards the dawn of a peaceful and promising new era. Assuredly, the time had come to move on.

It was night when the cutter pulled alongside and tied up to the wharf at Britomart on the Auckland waterfront and a group of weary travellers prepared to disembark. Jane looked about her in wonder at the changes that had taken place to the lower township since last she was there. Taller and larger buildings seemed to have sprung up everywhere, the streets were bustling with activity, horse-drawn wagons and carts of every style and livery jostling for position, busy people rushing to and fro and all around an air of progress and prosperity. Because it was evening and it would have been a long way for her to walk, she decided to take her very first ride in a hansom cab all the way up to Three Kings and the Anglican Mission where she knew she would find her foster-father.

When she walked into the familiar surroundings of the Mission house however, she sensed a strange quietness about the place and, when one of the Sisters came to greet her, they hugged each other but neither raised their voices. "He is sleeping now but he will be so pleased to see you when he wakes" softly spoke her companion as they sat down together. "He has not been very well for some weeks now and the doctors don't seem to know what it is that ails him. Rest and more rest is all that they have prescribed." Jane stole quietly into the room and her emotion welled within her as she found others sitting there in silent vigil. Old friends whom she recognised and concerned young people all had come to pray. Such was the measure of love and reverence held by all for this kind and gentle man.

All night she sat at his bedside, dozing off occasionally but always ready to respond to his slightest need and, when at last he opened his eyes and smiled up in recognition, she became overwhelmed with compassion and, clasping his hands in hers, she knelt before him and gently rested her head upon his shoulder, "Papa my dear Papa" she cried. Here was the man who came to the aid of her distraught little family those many years ago, rescued them from the burning and ransacked Kororareka, brought them all to Auckland, adopted them and gave them his name, saw to their welfare and education and remained devoted to them along with the many other young people left abandoned and homeless and sought no greater reward than the pleasure of serving his Church and his God. Had the time now come for him to rest from his labours and (according to Maori proverb), prepare to follow along the path from which no messenger returns? ("*E haere I te ara karere kore ki muri?*").

In the days that followed, he would rally occasionally sufficient to learn from Jane all about her adventures in the war and also news of the others of the family, Mango, Maraea, her own children, Neri and Hera, how they had fared, where they were now living and what they were doing. He was able to speak of his own work and expectations at the Mission and there were also times when he spoke of returning to his hereditary home in Sunderland, England.

It seemed that Jane's arrival at the Mission and the love she had brought with her had contained the magic 'elixir vitae' needed to breathe new life into the flagging spirits of her sadly ageing father and his steady improvement became such that her thoughts at length were drawn towards home and her own little family on far away Mokoia Island. As long as her father continued to improve, she decided, it should be safe to leave him there at the Mission in the best of loving care and medical attendance whilst she returned to her other responsibilities. It was therefore only a short time before she found herself aboard the cutter and bound for Maketu on her homeward journey.

True to his word, Denis was waiting at the landing to greet her on arrival, all ready to escort her up to the Travellers' Rest where the finest room in the house had been reserved for her. Their conversation that evening could only be described as exploratory as each was getting to know the immediate as well as the future ambitions of the other. Denis looked towards quitting the hospitality trade as soon as he had saved sufficient finance to buy a block of land that he could develop into a productive farm. His ancestors back in Ireland had always been of the land and although he and his brothers had chosen a different direction, that could only be temporary as far as he was concerned as the love of the land remained strongly within him and he wished nothing more than to obey the call.

Jane confided that it was her immediate intention to travel on to Mokoia and her own little family and mother Maraea whom she had not seen for some months and who were anxiously awaiting her return. She frankly admitted that her fighting days were now over and that she no longer wished to take an active part in the war against the Hauhau. She had been proud to uphold the Christian tradition and to support the resolute stand taken by Te Arawa against the insidious scourge of Hauhauism and was glad that it had now been driven from the region. It was time to lay down the weapons of war and take up the implements of peace, progress and the ultimate prosperity of the new colony. In that respect, she had decided to join The Reverend Thomas Chapman at TeNgae and take up teaching again at the school he had built and at which she had herself once attended as a little girl.

So they sat together as the evening drew on, two adult and self-assured people engaged in intelligent conversation but neither would have glimpsed at that early stage the glowing spark of romance that had kindled and was soon to flare into courtship, then to settle to a sublime period of dedicated and devoted faith in each other.

Early next morning, they left the Travellers' Rest together on a cross country ride to Rotorua. Denis had insisted on accompanying her all the way to her home on Mokoia and he had already saddled up two fine horses and had them waiting and ready to go well before Jane had come down to breakfast. The track between Maketu and Taheke, on the North-western end of Lake Rotoiti, although clearly defined and in regular use, was quite steep and winding in places with several streams and gullies to negotiate and, for its entire length, masked in virgin bush. The horses were willing enough and made light work of the first few miles but as the day drew on and the going got harder, they were content to settle to a steady walk and, like their riders, became quite weary by the time they reached Taheke in the late afternoon. An overnight stay in the village and, at daylight next day they left by canoe up the lake to Mourea, through the Ohau Channel and out into Lake Rotorua where they were greeted by the imposing sight of Mokoia looming large before them.

Warm and intimate was the welcome given them by her little family as Jane and her special guest stepped ashore. To the children, their mother had at last come home and to Maraea and the ageing Mango, their *atua* had again delivered their favourite daughter safely to them. Jane stepped out in front of the welcoming party and looked searchingly and anxiously across the fields towards a certain *hinau* tree, and soon her eyes lit up in delight and she cried out in ecstasy as she beheld two little *tirairaka* gaily swooping and cavorting towards them and as they came to circle above before leading the way up the path to the village, she knew that her attraction towards this man was real and that her special *atua* had bestowed their blessing upon them both.

Denis returned to Maketu the next day but not before making it known to Jane that he would become a regular visitor to Mokoia Island for as long as it would take to convince her that he was truly in earnest.

Jane's Story Chapter 29
A New Door Opens

It was on Easter Morning 1866 that Jane and her family from Mokoia crossed to Te Ngae to attend the divine service conducted by the Reverend Thomas Chapman in the rather unpretentious but picturesque and scrupulously maintained and cared for chapel on the hill opposite the mission house and where, in the afternoon, all were entertained to an extended family dinner prepared by Mrs Chapman and a host of willing helpers in the spacious grounds of the mission house where flowers and fruit trees flourished in profusion. And it was in this idyllic setting that Jane, in the quiet of the fading afternoon walked with Mr Chapman and confided in him all that was on her troubled mind, just as she would have done with her own dear father had his wise counsel been there for her.

Firstly there was the proposal of marriage from Denis who, since those first days of their chance acquaintance, had been quite unremitting in the pursuit of his courtship. She could feel the glow of emotion rising within her and she would gladly respond to him in kind but she knew that she was not at all free to do so. She was already the mother of four young children and was also responsible for her own mother Maraea and her ageing great-aunt Mango. There was also the settlement of ownership of the family land at Hauanu on Mokoia upon which she had built a home for herself, Maraea, Mango and the children and the rights to which, she had been able to prove, descended directly from their ancestor Whakatauihu. There was so much to be done before she could feel free to contemplate marriage to Denis and, even more pointedly, she wondered what the attitude of the Church would be towards such a relationship? Denis a Roman Catholic and she an Anglican who had been left the casualty of an ill-advised and failed previous marriage.

As she poured out her troubles to the good Reverend that afternoon, he listened intently to what she had to say. Then placing a comforting arm around her, he spoke: "My dear you are barely twenty-nine years old, a young woman with the greater part of your life still to open before you. You have already devoted so much of your life to others and served your people and your country well. You must now put aside your inhibitions and follow your heart. You are not one to neglect your responsibilities nor forsake your present family but rather share with them your new found happiness. As for the attitude of the Church, this is a fresh and flourishing new country where men and women of all nationalities and religious denominations have been thrown together in a mass of commonality and whose paths have become inseparably intertwined. Who are we to split them asunder? For you and Denis therefore my dear Jane, I should be glad to officiate on the chosen day". And as he drew his arm away from her shoulder, she felt that he was drawing away the burden of all her doubts and misgivings also and she was at last given to see clearly the path that she must take.

Denis had already expressed his wish that she come to live with him at Maketu after their marriage and that she would be welcome to bring the children with her. However, since Jane had come to live on Mokoia, she was aware that the day would come when TeKiri Karamu, the father of her children would come forward and claim them in the name of the hapu of Ngati Rangiteaorere. This would be especially true of her eldest son Rangiteaorere who would assume the title of "first-born son" (*matamua*) to succeed his father's chiefly rank and power (*mana ariki*). Of course she would never agree to part with any of her children but, in due deference to tribal tradition, she would always respect the *mana* and *tapu* associated with it and do nothing to interrupt the unbroken line of descent (*whakapapa*) which had perpetuated for generation after generation. She would therefore not deny her children access to their extended family (*whanau*) and would leave the way open for them to make their own decisions as they grew older.

Security of tenure of lands inherited through her mother's ancestry including not only that which they had already occupied on Mokoia but also on the Eastern mainland, required to be registered with the newly inaugurated Native Land Court to ensure that it would always remain in the family. This would take time as, by necessity, sittings of the Court were circuitous and shared among several other centres and all evidence had to be presented orally often at gatherings of many dozens of people.

And so it was that Jane, although she became resigned to sharing her first little family with their father Te Kirikaramu and her mother Maraea who, after all had practically reared them as her own from birth, was never to lose contact with them nor lose their affection towards her as their loving and fiercely protective mother no matter the vastly changed circumstances that would eventuate in the formative years that followed.

Great was the joy among the small gathering of people at the little chapel at TeNgae as family and friends celebrated the marriage of Jane and Denis in the autumn of 1867. The Reverend Chapman, true to his word, was happy to call down the blessing of the Lord onto the handsome young couple as they exchanged their vows in the presence of that delightful congregation. Again, it was in the magnificent grounds of the mission house that the wedding breakfast was served and when the time came for the newlyweds to depart, two fine saddle horses were brought up and Denis lifted his bride up onto one and mounted the other whilst all of the guests lined up along the pathway to wave and wish them well as they rode off into the distance. Thus was the beginning of a deep and devoted partnership that was to build upon a mutual respect for the aims and aspirations of each other. It would take a lot of hard work and sacrifice to achieve the ends they were seeking but each was unswerving in their resolve that together they would triumph.

The immediate call was to raise the standard of service and extend the facilities of the Travellers' Rest Hotel at Maketu. With the increase in trade between Auckland and the Bay of Plenty resulting from the cessation of hostilities between the Government and the Eastern tribes and also the improvements to the access road to Rotorua and the thermal attractions, there developed a considerable influx of visitors to the region with most of them choosing to stop-over at Maketu. There was therefore a much improved class of accommodation and service required and it became a labour of love to be shared between Jane and Denis to provide it and, in so doing, the air of enthusiasm generated from their efforts was quickly to be recognised amongst the travelling public. The business flourished and in a short time, came their just rewards.

Of course all this was to take some time, nearly three years in fact, during which Jane was to give birth to two sons, James Denis (Jimmy) in 1868 and John William in 1869. To both Jane and Denis those first three years of sharing devotion, working hard and looking towards the future with absolute faith in each other would prove to be the most gratifying of their newly found lives together.

They had both agreed however, that although it would likely take some time to accomplish, their long term goal was to raise sufficient capital from the sale of the business to allow them to ultimately purchase a block of land upon which they could settle and become farmers. It was quite by accident therefore that Jane should one day receive a visit from Colonel St. John a distinguished British Officer who had recognised her as the redoubtable Heeni Te Kirikaramu of Gate Pa fame and wished to thank her on behalf of the family of his dear friend Colonel Booth who was mortally wounded during the battle and to whom she had carried water in complete disregard of her own safety under heavy fire.

In the course of conversation the Colonel mentioned that the

Government had been charitably lenient towards the Ngai te Rangi people in recognition of the peace pact signed by Hori Ngatai before Colonel Greer at Te Papa and the laying down of their arms. There was also a deep respect held by the British of the chivalry shown by Rawiri Puhirake and his fighters in the battles of Gate Pa and Te Ranga. The extent of land confiscation for white settlement had therefore been greatly reduced and indeed several hapu of Ngai te Rangi had their lands returned to them totally un-alienated. There were also several blocks of highly productive land along the coast North-west of Tauranga in the KatiKati area which remained available to Ngai te Rangi for re-distribution. Upon learning from Jane and Denis the extent of their desire to take up land in the region for farming, Colonel St. John resolved to recommend them both to the authorities on his return to Tauranga and he was confident that when it became known who it was that was making the application, their success should well be assured.

And so within a few short weeks, Jane and Denis received an invitation to come to Tauranga to accompany the Government Land Settlement Officer on a tour of inspection of land blocks available for settlement in the KatiKati area. The block that they chose (and were duly granted) was part of a Government projected township and farm settlement at Kauri Point on the Tauranga Harbour about twenty-five miles along the coastline to the North-west of the township.

A broad strip of land extending North-west from Tauranga had already been cut up to provide free sections for discharged war veterans and, at its extremity on the bank of one of the many streams which flowed down from the Kaimai Ranges to the harbour, stood an old blockhouse still complete with rifle loopholes and perimeter trenches around its base, a grim reminder that the East Coast war had only lately ended and that there was still some territory closed to Europeans. At the uppermost end of the harbour was the small settlement of Bowentown which boasted a thriving trading post run by a man named Alf Faulkner and his Maori wife. There were other families, mostly Maori, domiciled along the shore of the inner harbour in the shelter of Matakana Island but, to the little group of pioneer settlers to which Denis and Jane had become attached, there appeared only a broad and windy expanse of fern, scrub and tutu with taller trees in the gullies stretching away to the more heavily bush-clad hills to the South. There were neither roads nor bridges or crossings over the many swiftly flowing streams and the only access was by boat from Tauranga some twenty-five miles away. All their household goods would have to be dragged up through the tidal estuaries to higher ground where hastily built raupo huts (***whare***) would have to be thrown up for protection against the rolling fog from the sea or wind-lashed rain and there they would have to stay for a year or more until the first acres were cleared and planted and a more substantial house of sawn timber could be erected.

"Denis, is this what you really want?" Jane asked of her keen-eyed, exuberant husband. "Ah yes, it might be a trackless wilderness now but the time will come when these narrow lands between the mountains and the sea will be covered in green fields, sturdy homesteads and happy contented people." was his prophetical reply.

Such was the faith that Jane placed in this man that she would commit herself and her babies to whatever unknown hardship and privation lay ahead, for better or for worse to share with him the realisation of his dream and, on that day as she stood beside him and looked out over the brooding wilderness that was to be her future home, she reflected on the role of pioneering women everywhere who had been moved to uproot from their homelands and follow their menfolk into the daunting new worlds that had beckoned them. Across the prairies of the Americas, the veldts and jungles of Africa, the bushland and red plains of Australia to the lush green forest and pasture land of New Zealand. New frontiers to be conquered in the ultimate but not without heartbreak and sacrifice in the fulfilment.

Jane Foley
Circa 1870 (33 years old and living at KatiKati)

Jane's Story Chapter 30

Shamrock Amongst the Fern

Christmas Day in the year 1870, in the small village of Kauri Point was the first to be solemnised in the Christian tradition in that small sector of the Western Bay of Plenty that had been recently approved for European settlement. The few Pakeha families that had ventured to settle along the coastline from Tauranga as far West as Bowentown, had joined with several Christian Maori families whose adjacent lands had been handed back to them after confiscation, to attend an open air service conducted by **Father Borjon** from the Roman Catholic Mission at Maketu who had come to visit Denis and Jane to see how they had fared since they left the Travellers' Rest Hotel to seek "a more rewarding munificence on the land".

That his visit happened to coincide with the festive season, prompted the good Father to celebrate Christmas Mass with as many of the inhabitants of the upper harbour as wished to rejoice on that holy day and, though his pulpit and chancel was none but an outside washing table and his cathedral a grove of crimson flowering *Pohutukawa*, the sermon he preached on that pristine headland rising up from the sea, to the mixed congregation sitting around him in the morning sunlight, was to remain in the memories of the old and the very young for as long as they were to live. Here was the beginning of a new chapter in the storybook of life for all who had assembled there; the farmers, the fishermen and the prospectors all poised to move through the land to confront whatever the future would hold in store for them.

To Denis and Jane by this time a regular daily routine had already developed and was being shared between them. Up early in the morning, the cow to be milked, breakfast to be prepared, babies to be fed, household chores to be done, lunches to be packed and then everybody out to the fringe of the scrub and fern, armed with axes, spades and slashers to slowly but surely push back the frontier wilderness and win over fresh acres of land upon which to increase their prospect. There were fences to erect, wetlands to be drained, crops to be planted, weeded, harvested according to the season, animals to be introduced as grazing land was prepared and last but not least a more permanent and comfortable house to be built and furnished. And so it was that in the immediate years that followed, they were both totally immersed in their work and there was little time to think of anything else. Contact with the outside world was extremely difficult as the only access to Tauranga was by Alf Faulkner's steamer which served as the only means of transportation for livestock, farm supplies and produce, mail and passengers, even as a hospital ship or funeral bier as and when called upon, however reliable or otherwise it might be.

At first the results of their harvest was phenomenal and far exceeded all expectations. The ground from which the fern was cleared proved to be so highly productive that from only two bags of seed, tons of potatoes were harvested, cabbages grew in profusion with some weighing up to 14 pounds (6 kg). Peas could be sown for a third time off the same seed; that is, in the one season they could be sown, ripened, sown again, ripened and then sown for the third time all in the space of six months. Such was the bounteous potential of soil and climate. A ready market for the products of their labours was available to them in Tauranga and the proceeds from sales enabled them to extend and improve their holding and look towards a prosperous future.

The promise of that first season was unfortunately not maintained. In the second year they noted with concern that the crops were by no means as prolific as those of the previous summer and, the deterioration was to continue in subsequent years until the yield would stabilise at a much lower level. This turned out to be a quite common occurrence throughout all of the newly settled country where the fern, after decaying over a period of many years had produced a rich deposit of potash which could be quickly worked out leaving the land to rapidly lose quality. A later generation was to discover that the remedy was the application of fertilisers and the sowing of more suitable crops and grasses. However, the early pioneers like Denis and Jane were not well informed on such matters and in many cases were dismayed to watch their farms deteriorate before their eyes. Fortunately for Denis and Jane as it happened, their holding comprised a better than average soil quality and fertility and although its productivity was observed to have dropped off considerably from the first year, the yield remained reasonably constant and they were still able to maintain a comfortable existence.

In those initial years, occasions when Jane was able to visit her family on Mokoia Island were rare indeed yet visit them she did whenever it was possible. Taking her babies with her, she would catch the steamer to Tauranga and then ride on horseback over the direct route through the Kaimai forest to the Awahou on the Western shore of Lake Rotorua in Ngati Rangiwewehi territory and thence by canoe across to the Island where she would stay for only a pitifully short time before having to make the same exhausting return journey back to Denis and the farm again. But to her credit and commendation, in all that time she never lost contact with her extended family nor neglected her responsibilities towards them. She would however be first to acknowledge the patience and understanding extended by Denis during those difficult days.

In 1870, the most powerful figure in New Zealand politics was *Sir Julius Vogel* a clever, erratic visionary who, through his efforts as Colonial Treasurer and later Prime Minister, enjoys to this day a measure of immortality as the author of a bold development policy. It was he who proposed to borrow 10,000,000 pounds (that sum later to be doubled) to be used in the building of roads, railways and bridges and assistance to immigration. He claimed that in ten years he would treble the population and resources of the country and, in response the young colony, glowing with self confidence, embraced his proposals with enthusiasm. Although the merits of his policy were somewhat obscured by the worldwide depression that followed in the 1880's, much of what he prophesied actually came to pass. Between 1873 and 1877, the mileage of railways increased from 145 to over 1000 and the population rose from 256,000 to 490,000 by 1881. Unfortunately, the state debt showed the same facility for expansion by rising almost fourfold in the same period.

On the other side of the world in faraway Northern Ireland, *George Vesey Stewart* the young son of Captain Mervyn Stewart of Martray, County Tyrone, Ulster, in the year 1856 graduated with honours in Classics from the venerable foundation of Trinity College. On his return to his family seat, he married and settled down as a farmer, estate agent and country gentleman but it was from a German gentleman, Baron von Steiglitz to whom he had made his first property sale, that he first learned of the opportunities that emigration to the colonies of Australia and New Zealand were offering to young people of ambition. "Young man" he would say, "there is nothing for you in Ireland. You will do much better in the colonies." By 1870 by chance he remembered the words of Baron von Steiglitz and his thoughts again turned to emigration. He was then in his 40th year and had already developed a reaching and fertile imagination and the driving power to carry his schemes through and, for a man who habitually took a broad view, he had an extraordinary grasp of detail. Tenacious as a bulldog, he cared nothing for opposition and dearly loved a battle. Ambition was the keynote of his character and he burned to write his name indelibly in history and this gave him an unusual turn of plan for emigration. If he was to seek his fortune in a new land, it would not be as one of "your huddled masses yearning to breathe free" but as the leader of a party that would arrive with adventure in their hearts and the resolve to succeed.

Gradually he evolved the conception of a special settlement of Ulstermen in New Zealand where he would rule in the patriarchal fashion of a Highland chief. He would draw his settlers from two sources, the country gentlemen of his own class and the tenant farmers of Ulster. The first to contribute the capital and provide the desired social atmosphere, the other to do the farming. The time was opportune for such a scheme and Vesey Stewart, confident of finding encouragement from the New Zealand authorities, made his first advances early in 1873. He contacted *Dr Isaac Earl Featherston* the New Zealand Agent-General in London, seeking terms the Government would be prepared to offer for the introduction of an initial party of 30 or 40 families.

Dr Featherston however, was strangely sceptical about the whole scheme and had come to the conclusion that immigration agents were a costly luxury but after further representation he agreed that Vesey Stewart should at the invitation of the New Zealand Government, himself proceed to the colony and select a block of suitable land. He sailed on the "Mongol" the first steamship to visit New Zealand direct, and reached Dunedin in January 1874 after a passage of 49 days. During the next three months he travelled the length and breadth of the colony exploring Otago, Canterbury, Nelson and the Hokianga but nothing he was shown appeared to fulfil the requirements he held firmly fixed in his mind. At last he came to Tauranga and fell in love with that delightful spot immediately. The Survey Office placed at his disposal a young guide called Sam Middlebrook who would later become one of his best settlers. One morning they rode out towards the Northern end of the harbour when, after twenty miles of hard riding they reached the Aongatete River which was the Southern boundary of the KatiKati block, part of the area confiscated from the Maori after the Bay of

Plenty war. As Vesey Stewart looked across the rolling stretches of fern country watered by six rivers, with forested mountains on his left and glimpses of the blue sea on his right, he knew that his search was over and, after a careful inspection over the next three days, he returned to Auckland to make official application for 10,000 acres of the KatiKati block.

If he expected his application to pass unchallenged however, he was soon undeceived as during the next few months he was to learn something of the perversity of colonial politics. The Provincial Government informed him that the lands concerned had passed to the Central Government which body had in turn referred him back to the Provincial Council and, but for his resolute insistence, he might have been jockeyed out of his scheme altogether. At length the Provincial Council agreed to set up a select committee to consider the question and it finally reported in Vesey Stewart's favour and recommended that the Government consent to the reservation of 10,000 acres at KatiKati and an agreement was duly concluded on 24 June 1874 and named the "*Charter of KatiKati.*"

The chief terms of the agreement were briefly as follows:

1. Vesey Stewart and his party would be allocated a block of 10,000 acres comprising lands between the Aongatete and Tuapiro rivers but excluding several small native reserves including Kauri Point which was the projected site of a Government township (Denis and Jane's farm was there), and also a large flat area adjacent to the Te Ririatukahia River. In addition, the Government agreed to survey and road the block and divide it into allotments.

2. Vesey Stewart to organise a party of Irish farmers having adequate capital and comprising not less than forty families.

3. The Government to provide a vessel from Ireland to Auckland or Tauranga, the fare for steerage passengers to be five pounds ($20). Single women between 15 and 35 years whose parents had assisted passages, to travel free.

4. Vesey Stewart as leader of the party to reserve 500 acres with 40 acres on account of his wife and each of his children. Each member of the party over 18 years to receive 40 acres with an additional 20 acres in respect of each child between 12 and 18 provided that no household should occupy more than 300 acres.

5. Each draughtee provided he had resided continuously for three years and had at least one-fifth of his holding under cultivation, to receive a Crown grant of his property. Alternatively, the term might be less than three years provided he had cultivated and fenced the entire property and erected a dwelling house thereon.

6. The date fixed for termination was 1 January 1876. If by that date Vesey Stewart and at least 30 families should not have arrived at Auckland or Tauranga in one ship, the agreement would be null and void.

Well satisfied with the terms of the agreement, Vesey Stewart returned to Ireland to assemble his party but, in London he still encountered difficulties with the New Zealand Agent-General over the interpretation of the agreement and it was only by the timely intervention of Sir Julius Vogel, having arrived in England at that time, that matters were taken personally in hand and settled at a single interview whereupon Vesey Stewart was freed to proceed with the formation of his party.

The assembly of the party proceeded with rapidity and by May 1875, the compliment of 30 families was more than filled. On 5 June, two fine ships provided by the New Zealand Government, the "Carisbrooke Castle" and the "Dover Castle" appeared in Belfast Lough. These were vessels of 1400 and 1000 tons respectively and were capable of doing over 300 miles a day in favourable circumstances. The "Dover Castle" sailed on the day after her arrival with a body of free emigrants and, the "Carisbrooke Castle" was reserved for the members of the special party together with a few miscellaneous emigrants. The departure of the settlers created no small stir in Belfast for this was the first time Ulstermen had been organised to emigrate to New Zealand and so, on 8 June 1875, the last farewells were said and the "Carisbrooke Castle" was towed slowly down the harbour carrying 238 KatiKati settlers and 125 Government immigrants and within a few hours the coast of Ireland had disappeared from view. "Then," recalled Vesey Stewart, "for the first time I came to realise in my own mind, the responsibility that rested on my shoulders at having induced so many souls to leave their homes, their friends, their native land."

On the 8th day of September they arrived in Auckland Harbour and no more delightful introduction to New Zealand could have been imagined. As they dropped anchor in the stream and beheld the snug bays and pohutukawa-fringed cliffs glowing in the warm sunshine of a spring morning, they could hardly contain their expressions of delight. In a few days they were transferred to two Government steamers, the "Rowena" and the "Pretty Jane" and taken to Tauranga where an equally hearty welcome awaited them and, as they steamed up the harbour, the guns at the Armed Constabulary Station at Te Papa thundered out a salute. The settlers crowded eagerly onto the deck and Vesey Stewart pointed out the blue hills to the North-west which would be their future home.

It was Alf Faulkner who brought the news to Denis and Jane of the impending deluge of Irish settlers poised to pour into the KatKati district. He had just returned from a delivery run to Tauranga and had witnessed the arrival of the "Rowena" and the "Pretty Jane" and the resounding welcome given them as they reached up the harbour. Denis and Jane were not altogether surprised however as they had already met Vesey Stewart during his visit in the previous year and had entertained him in their Kauri Point home during the three days that he and Sam Middlebrook explored the KatiKati block. There was never any doubt in their minds that Vesey Stewart would return with his band of Irish settlers after observing the intense enthusiasm he had shown for what he declared was this very special place.

The sudden influx of so many people to the area would create unimaginable changes to not only the landscape now mainly of un-depthed wilderness but also to the very existence of the few scattered residents who had become accustomed to living in almost exclusive isolation. There would be new roads and bridges over the streams, great tracts of land cleared, fenced and cultivated, colourful houses and gardens adorning the countryside, schools, shops and places of meeting and worship, and everywhere new people, their faces to acquaint to and recognise by name and all speaking in the lilting brogue of their mother country. Truly the shamrock amongst the fern.

Jane's Story Chapter 31

Of Good Times and Bad

As the spring of 1875 was already well advanced, the settlers were anxious to get onto their farms as quickly as possible. Some had elected to hire scrub-cutters in Tauranga and proceed to Kati Kati independently whilst the others decided to remain with the main party and proceed as directed by the appointed leaders. There were three main landing places one each at the mouths of the *Aongatete*, *Uretara* and *Tuapiro* rivers at which rough dwelling huts had already been erected to house the families as they waited to be shown their allotted sections. So anxious were they to sow their crops that the surveys were only hastily completed and in some cases the surveyors merely stepped out the distances with many errors being found later as the lots were checked over. Following Vesey Stewart's advice, they cleared the land by burning from ten to thirty acres at a time and then roughly ploughed or harrowed it over before surface-sowing in grass. Horses and ploughs however were hard to come by and some enterprising settlers undertook the work for their neighbours by contract   Rough tracks ran down through the scrub to the river landings and for some time communications with Tauranga remained chiefly by water. While they waited for their crops to ripen, the settlers attended to the building of their houses and whilst the more affluent like Vesey Stewart planned substantial homes like those they had known in Ireland, the majority were content with a four-roomed gable and lean-to cottage with a chimney of corrugated iron.

For Denis and Jane all the bustle and activity that had come amongst them marked the end of an era of blissful but rather lonely existence. Together they had come to this isolated place on the very edge of civilisation to wrest their own private living from the land and, in doing so they learned to work together to respect the ever changing moods of nature and also to feel and appreciate the moral strength, spirit and unwavering devotion they held towards each other and their little family in the sharing of a common ideal. By now they had four children the last two of whom, Sophia Bertha (Sophie) and Robert Henry (Harry) had been born here at Kauri Point. There was another child born after Harry, a beautiful little girl in 1874 whom they named Isobella after Denis' mother in Ireland but tragedy was to strike just two years later when a mysterious fever overcame her and, by the time a frantic Jane was able to get her to the hospital in Tauranga, she had passed beyond any medical help and there was nothing that could be done to save her. She was brought home to be buried at Kauri Point.

For the sake of the children however, the time had now come for Denis and Jane to take their places among this vibrant new society that had visited upon their remote little world offering hitherto unimaginable expectations and it was not long before they became fully integrated into that thriving and industrious community.

A close and lasting friendship soon developed between Vesey Stewart and Denis whose knowledge and experience in the development of the land, the selection of the most suitable crops and their cultivation, the most successful farming methods, relations with the inhabitant Maori population etc., was called upon more and more as the settlement became established. As their leader, they were happy days for Vesey Stewart for he warmed to popularity and was greeted on all sides with admiration and respect. He remained in close touch with the Provincial Government and represented his people at every opportunity, pressing for the development of roading access from Tauranga and the establishment of public schools for the increasing numbers of children. On May 11, 1876, he called the settlers together to elect trustees for a School Board and a Highway Board and, upon being elected to the chair, he read the Provincial Government Gazette convening the meeting and then called for nominations.

It is interesting to note that of the total of 41 settlers attending the meeting, five including Denis were not of the new arrivals but were of the original independent families who had taken up land some years before the advent of the Vesey Stewart party. Interesting because neither that five nor most of the other independent settlers who made up a total of twenty before the close of 1878 and were recognised as being amongst the original 77 foundation members of KatiKati, were true Ulstermen but had come mostly from the Roman Catholic South. However, if any great animosity existed between them back in the old country, it was discreetly put aside in the new. By tradition, colonising was in the blood of the Irish particularly among those of Ulster whose homeland was only theirs by adoption. In the days of James 1, the North of Ireland after seven years of furious civil war, was cleared of its native inhabitants and planted with settlers of Scottish and English origin. This was the celebrated "Plantation of Ulster" and it was from these people and those who followed in later generations that most of the KatiKati settlers were descended. Vesey Stewart however, by his sagacity was always at great pains to ensure that no seed of sectarian discontent between Protestant and Catholic that still persisted in the homeland, should be permitted to blight this new and unspoiled land and, it never was.

On that day when Vesey Stewart called for nominations to the School Board, five members including two resident ministers of the church, two of the more prominent farmers and himself as chairman were elected. A discussion on the sites of schools followed and the chairman thought that at least three would be necessary, one at the proposed Government site at Kauri Point, one at Tahawai and the third at Te Ririatukahia. He calculated that about ninety children were likely to attend. The gathering then proceeded to elect a Highway Board and another five members including Vesey Stewart were duly elected as foundation members of what soon became the representative body of the district. The meeting was not unduly prolonged for, in the tradition of their forebears in the mother country, a substantial lunch awaited the visitors as there existed among them a strong belief that "food was an aid to thought" and, after having done justice to the good things, they entered upon their favourite pastime of working systematically through a long and exhaustive toast list and, when they had drunk the health of everybody they could think of, they finished up by drinking their own. So they talked on, the listeners solemnly pulling at their pipes and gravely applauding each outburst of oratory until at length the shades of evening drew in and milking time, that relentless curfew of the dairy farmer, called them home.

It was strange that for three years the settlement remained without a definite township site. The Government had proposed to establish the township on Crown land at Kauri Point (where Denis and Jane had their farm), but had taken no further action to have it subdivided for sale. In any case that locality was seen as not being central enough and besides, the sea approach to it through the KatiKati Heads had proved to be more difficult to work than was expected. So the "Village of Te Kauri" was never to proceed beyond an impressive appearance on the map. Interest shifted more towards the Uretara Landing where the advantages were too obvious to be ignored. It was located more towards the middle of the block but still accessible from the harbour by navigable river, it had already become the centre for several dwellings and was a popular meeting place. It had also become further enhanced with the establishment of Joseph Wylie's Pioneer Store to be followed later by an accommodation house run by the widow Mrs Bell and her son.

Beyond the store and the hotel (which was later granted a licence), there was little other evidence of civic development by the end of the year 1878. A post office had been opened in Wylie's Store but the telegraph was still installed at Bowentown. Though three schools were projected, only one had been thus far built and that at a lonely spot on Kauri Point Road. There were no churches though both Anglicans and Presbyterians worshipped regularly in private homes. The spring of 1878 witnessed the arrival in Auckland of the "Lady Jocelyn" from Belfast on 17 August with a second party organised by Vesey Stewart and that event may be regarded as marking the end of the first stage of the Kati Kati settlement and, notwithstanding several early disappointments, progress had been steady and positive. The triennial census taken in March 1878 showed a population of 238. None of the special settlers who had definitely taken up their allotments had broken with the settlement whilst there had been several new recruits, some being Ulstermen who came independently from Ireland and others like the two arrivals from Germany, Bernard McDonnell and Louis Konig (King), who had been encouraged to emigrate by their Irish employer Thomas Mulvaney who owned coal mines near Dusseldorf and who himself decided to join Vesey Stewart's second party. Progress after the first three years was adequately summed up in a report by the Crown Lands Officer in November 1878: "Many settlers have done a great deal of work and have farms that would do credit to a district of much longer standing. The roads are good and a carriage and pair could be driven over them without difficulty. There are 35 allotments under cultivation with averages of 50 acres in pasture although several had as much as 150 acres in grass or crop. All had substantial weatherboard houses with improvements in seven cases being valued at 7000 pounds".

The main portion of the area totalling 10,000 acres allotted to the second party, was a block about six miles in length and two in width lying directly behind the land of the first party and extending from the Tuapiro River to the Te Aroha Track. Much of it was swamp and upland and was on the whole inferior in quality to the first grant. Its area was about 7500 acres and the remainder was made up of three parcels: about 1200 acres between Tuapiro and Athenree, about 700 acres on the Kauri Point peninsular which had been forfeited by the first party, and 600 acres near the Waitekohe River (part of which was to be purchased by Jane later to increase the Foley holding). At the end of 1879, the settlement was in a healthy condition. The population had increased by 200 with the arrival of the second party, a further 38 weatherboard houses had been erected and the improvements over the whole block were valued at over 25,000 pounds.

It was in 1879 also that Jane and Denis became somewhat perplexed to learn that they were about to be blessed with an addition to the family. Quite totally unexpected, for they had long since been given to believe that their reproductory days had long since ended. However, in October of that year along came baby Margaretha May, a perfect little girl who quickly dispelled any lingering misgivings for, as foretold by her mother Maraea when Jane confided in her, she arrived bringing her own special love and everyone adored her. All was well in the land and the family continued to prosper. But alas they were not to know that this fair prospect was soon to be over-clouded.

In the early 1880's, New Zealand became engulfed in devastating worldwide depression so severe that its causes and no less its effects were to change the face of history. Twenty years of intermittent warfare in Europe, the ruinous Civil War in America, the sudden fall in the price of gold and silver, the over-production of wheat and other farm products, all had their repercussions throughout the civilised world. Prices and wages fell and unemployment became widespread and in New Zealand the position was further aggravated by internal conditions. The heavy expenditure of the Maori wars still weighed upon the country and the brief boom created by the Vogel borrowing had already collapsed. Men tramped the country looking for work and in three years, over 5000 working men emigrated to Australia.

In Kati Kati, local conditions made the situation particularly acute. The two chief exports of New Zealand in those days were wool and gold, and KatiKati produced neither. For other produce there was no market; Auckland was too far away, Tauranga was too small and Waihi was practically non-existent until about 1886. Among the poorer settlers who had no private income, there was much real hardship. There was not as a rule any shortage of food although bread and dripping was ever present on the daily menu. But there was little real money and, since the farms became self-supporting, a system of barter was developed where a bag of chaff, a crate of eggs or half a dozen pigs whilst bringing no return of money, could be used to reduce the store-keeper's bill. There was no entertainment for the women and children beyond the annual school (or church) picnic, an occasional dance or a trip to Tauranga once in two or three years. On many farms there was no horse fit to ride and no conveyance except a sledge. Wood had to be cut and water had to be carried from deep gullies by the women who bore the hardships uncomplainingly and shared in much of the farm work, milking a dozen cows twice a day, shelling maize by candlelight or following the plough through a hot afternoon to plant potatoes in the furrow.

Jane and her young family, were to endure all of this privation as they witnessed their own little world seemingly to collapse around them. Yet steadfastly they suffered their adversity together and patiently waited for better times to return as they surely must. Jimmy, the eldest son was now a strapping youth and with his younger brother John had become more and more helpful around the farm and also made themselves available for work on neighbouring farms or on the fishing and delivery boats that plied the Tauranga Harbour. Sometimes they would be paid in money but mostly it would be in material form such as food for the table, tools and implements for the farm, even livestock. Right from boyhood, Jimmy had shown a natural affinity towards horses and their handling. He became an accomplished and masterly horse-breaker and his services soon became in popular demand throughout the whole settlement and beyond as his reputation grew. Their sister Sophie was not to be left out of the action either and she went looking for work among the families of the settlement, minding babies, helping with the housekeeping, washing and ironing, sometimes stacking the shelves in Wylie's store, anything she could do to help her family to survive.

Jane herself was kept very busy as her day was not only occupied with the work around the farm, but also included teaching at the little school at Kauri Point. It was there that the children of the settlement received their early education and although at first the attendance was small and facilities for teaching were crude and quite rudimentary, it was at least a beginning and would soon develop as full-time teachers became available and proper teaching aids and materials were procured. Although she had always been responsible for the education of her own children, it was to Jane's credit that she should be willing to devote her time to others as well. But for her solicitude those first children of the settlement would have been denied an education altogether.

And so in spite of the difficult times, Jane was left with good reason to be content with the efforts of herself and her little family in making life somewhat easier not only for themselves but also others of the settlement whose fortitude was now being so sorely tried. But however, how could she know that a crisis was looming large for her as she fought to suppress a nagging thought that had begun to torment her every waking moment and had now thrust itself inescapably to the fore?

Jane's Story Chapter 32

Another Time, Another Crisis

It seemed to be quite harmless when it first started, just getting together around a drink or two with the boys after a hard day's work. Jane, who never touched an alcoholic drink in her life, had nevertheless always been tolerant with those of her acquaintance who did imbibe; certainly her husband Denis, who after all had been a purveyor of liquor for many years. Perhaps it was just the flood of opportunities that presented themselves and the mateship that developed during the breaking-in of the settlement that allowed things, in many cases, to get out of hand.

Jane had already made the observation that the Irish were very much like the Maori in their social inclination. They were happiest together in communal groups, they liked to sing their family praises, they loved the land and living close to nature, they would always stick together in times of hardship and strife yet they would fight at the drop of a hat. She noticed also however, that the slightest excuse was all that was needed to bring the men striding down from their farms to gather at their favourite meeting place, which happened to be Barney McDonnell's pub, to resolve any problem great or small though the solution might evade them until late into the night.

The real centre of old KatiKati was the hotel. It will be remembered that a temporary licence only was granted the widow Mrs Bell, but the Tauranga Licensing Board had let it be known that no objection would be raised if a strong land-lord could be found. Throughout history, it has been proven over and again that the "hour of crisis will always produce the man" and so it was that with the air of a conjuror, the thirsty men of KatiKati produced Bernard (Barney) McDonnell. No better choice would have been imagined and if ever a man was fitted to deal out rough-handed justice, it was he. A jovial, deep voiced, big-bearded Irishman, he stood six feet two, weighed twenty stone and had a most compelling personality which found him at ease in every class of society and allowed him to lead as a matter of course in any situation. He made the Uretara Hotel an institution and he himself became a legend. He would have no fights and no blasphemy in his house and, as he was always ready to enforce his decrees with a shillelagh, people with a reputation of lawlessness would respectfully keep their heads down. If a dispute flared, it had to be settled outside and, on Saturday nights, Barney was often to be seen superintending fights in the hotel paddock, holding two candles above his head and shouting unheeded advice as the combatants settled their differences.

Barney was, in the best sense of the term, a man of the world, for he had seen life in many countries and had acquired a wealth of wisdom and experience. His advice was sought by all and sundry, it was freely given and seldom at fault. Even omniscient District Councillors, on their way to monthly meetings in Tauranga would habitually call at the Uretara Hotel to seek Barney's mental as well as liquid inspiration. Though a good Catholic, he was no bigot and often displayed his diplomacy. Ministers of all denominations passing through KatiKati were given free lodging at the Uretara and a room in which to hold their services. Once when a scrupulous member of the Orange Lodge protested against the iniquity of buying liquor for the annual celebrations from a Roman Catholic, Barney promptly sent the Lodge half a dozen bottles of whisky as a present. There were no further objections.

Much of the day to day business of the settlement was connected with the Uretara Hotel which had the homely atmosphere of an English Inn. Often farmers would meet there to discuss market prices of their produce, buy, sell or exchange livestock, compare notes on land and stock management, even discuss more personal subjects such as the pending marriages of their offspring. And all the time enjoying the hospitality of Barney McDonnell. It possessed of course the usual fraternity of seasoned drinkers who could be found at all hours of the day quarrelling in the billiard room, sitting out on the verandah in the throes of alcoholic remorse, or enjoying the hospitality of some kind benefactor in the bar. Many was the tale told of those old KatiKati inebriates who had completely succumbed to a life of absolute abandon. One of them was the holder of a bush section close to the township to which he would wend his weary way homeward at the end of a strenuous day's drinking. Halfway home he would often stop and carry on a vigorous conversation with a wayside tree. At first he would address it patronisingly but as his one-sided argument became more heated, he would launch into a furious tirade and strike out at his unresponsive adversary until he flopped exhausted at its foot and there he would remain until he had either slept off his preoccupation or had wakened some hours later feeling chilled whereupon he would shuffle away home.

This was a classic example of delirium tremens (the D.T.'s or "dingbats" as known to Australians) which was defined as a condition of violent delirium accompanied by convulsive trembling resulting from excessive alcoholism. In such state, men were known to become quite mentally deranged sometimes showing fear of imaginary reptiles, rodents or other vermin running up walls or rushing forward to attack them or, at other times imagining themselves as monsters of murderous intent that would display such prodigious strength that it would take a team of strong men to hold them down.

The boisterous, somewhat wayward traditions of the Irish were imported into the settlement in their full flavour and, regretfully there was heavy drinking to a degree that was far in excess of that normally tolerated in other colonising communities. Festivities were often prolonged far into the night till one by one the guests would sink beneath the table or be carried up to bed mildly protesting in the early hours of the morning. Regretfully also these became fertile grounds in which the seeds of chronic alcoholism would settle amongst the more easily influenced of the male population of the district.

Although chronic alcoholism was to become a problem amongst the characteristically hard working, heavy drinking Irishmen of KatiKati, it was already arousing wide concern throughout the entire colony wherever men were to gather. The miner up from his shift, the axeman and the sawyer in from the bush, the shearer off the board, the farmer in town for the sale, the soldier back in his barracks, the sailor in from the sea. The liquor strong and in plentiful supply, the fellowship and camaraderie all persuasive. Of the settlers on the land like the commoners of the KatiKati selection, those who suffered most were the women and children. As their menfolk spent more and more time in the pub, so the responsibilities of the farm befell the mothers and the eldest children. The cows still had to be milked twice a day, crops had to be planted, tended and harvested, the children had to be fed, clothed and educated. Life had to go on but how much harder it was to manage in the absence of the chief breadwinner, the so called man about the house? Were these the original "grass widows" of New Zealand society?

Unfortunately for Jane and her family as well, despite their being earlier established in the district and therefore not so involved in the day to day community affairs of the more recent arrivals, they were not to escape this sorry decline in moral integrity that had descended upon the menfolk. Jane had become aware for some time that what started as an occasional civic duty attendance by Denis at the various gatherings of settlers on regional and community business, had become more and more frequent as time went by until a couple of hours between milkings became a whole afternoon, then of late it was the evening as well. She was lucky that her boys were now old enough to run the farm without their father and that Sophie, her daughter was there to help around the house. She feared however for the outcome. How much worse would the situation become? Was this to be the end of a long and loving partnership together with the man in whom she had placed all her trust? Was this to be the end of a promising new world which they and their little family had wrested from the wilderness? Was it now all to burst like a bubble about them leaving nothing but despair and desolation? And should all of this be so, would she ever find the strength to start again?

It was in a state of delirium tremens that Denis arrived home late that night in November 1884 and confronted Jane in her bedroom. Upon lighting a candle and holding it up to him, she caught the terrifying glint of madness in his eyes. He was shaking wildly all over and in his hands he held up a reaper's billhook. There was no coherent speech, just an enraged roar as he swung the weapon down upon her. She had hurriedly raised her arms to ward off the blow and felt the stunning sensation of her arm being slashed to the bone and her head receiving the remaining force of the impact. She felt herself slipping into unconsciousness as she heard the screams of her children Sophie and Harry as they were awakened in the adjoining bedroom.

What made Denis desist when he did and not carry on to end her life, Jane would never know but when she finally fought her way back to consciousness it was to find the thirteen-year old Sophie bending over her, bathing and staunching the wounds to her arms and head and wrapping them in bandages that she had torn into strips from sheeting. She had already despatched Harry to ride to Bowentown to fetch Jimmy and John who were working there for Alf Faulkner. She carried on quite calmly with her work and reassured her mother that Jimmy would be arriving soon and that he would know what to do.

It was then but a short time before Jimmy arrived with his brothers to carry their mother down to the landing and accompany her in the boat to the Te Papa military hospital where it was the doctors Armitage and Campbell who immediately attended to the relief of the poor suffering Jane. Jimmy was later ordered to accompany a detachment of constabulary back to KatiKati to find his father and assist with his arrest and indictment. Denis was duly placed under arrest and escorted to Te Papa where he was brought before two Justices of the Peace before whom he pleaded guilty of the assault. His submitted reason was that his wife had been bewitching him and it was better therefore that she should die. Acting on the evidence of a medical certificate of insanity however, the Court ordered that he be committed to the mental hospital in Auckland for further assessment. As a matter of interest, it had become the recognised practice of the time to commit all serious and otherwise incurable cases of delirium tremens to that same institution for a "drying out period" which in some cases would last for many months.

Under professional care and attention at Te Papa and being constantly remembered in the prayers of her loving and devoted extended family and friends, Jane made a full and rapid recovery and although she was to carry the dreadful scars to her arms and shoulder for the rest of her life, her distinctive facial features remained mercifully unblemished and she was able to hold her head high again and brave the world undaunted as always she had.

During the absence of their mother in the hospital, the little family under the leadership of Jimmy who was all of sixteen years old by then, worked as a closely knit unit and managed the running of the farm every bit as efficiently as when both parents were there. Jimmy and John were still able to earn a little extra money by doing outside work and Sophie too somehow found the time to work for the neighbours as well as keep house for her siblings. They received no word of their father after he was taken away but they were able to keep in constant touch with their mother with at least one of them being offered a ride in the boat to Te Papa on most days. To Jane there was never any question that she would return to the farm and carry on with its development. What better future could she offer her sons than what the land could provide? The market for farm produce was slowly improving and the signs were that KatiKati was turning the corner from the years of depression earlier than most other districts . This was due to the impending rise of the Waihi gold-mining operations which, it was popularly predicted, would create a town of several thousand inhabitants at a distance of only sixteen miles to the North.

How magnificent also was her compassion that in spite of the terrible wounds that were inflicted upon her by her husband, Jane should still find it within her to forgive. How could it be, she wondered, that the unshaken resolve of her champion of those early years of hardship and deprivation, when they stood together alone in the world to build their home upon the rock of hope and faith in each other, should now fall into such despair and abandonment? She could not accept that such extreme reversal of personality was at all intentional, but rather that Denis had become possessed of some cruel, debilitating sickness that had totally alienated his mind and that now, he was in desperate need of help. She would go to Auckland and bring him home.

On that golden, sunny day when the boat pulled into the landing at Kauri Point, and Jane stepped ashore to be greeted by her overjoyed little family, she could not help but notice the changes that had taken place to the landscape since she and Denis first landed there those fifteen years before. The fern had given way to lush grassland, the bush was now embellished with laden fruit trees, and the old raupo-clad whare was now transformed into a fine weatherboard house with gardens gaily flourishing their wild splash of colour. There were tears of sheer delight as she observed the pathway up from the landing had been strewn with flowers of welcome from her exalted little family, thankful that their mother had at last come home.

That evening, she gathered them all together to explain what she had in mind, that she would shortly be going to Auckland to bring their father home, that he would still not be completely well but together they would care for him and help him back to full health and happiness. And, as she stood in their midst, her arms spread protectively about them, she looked up to the heavens and spoke: "From this day onward, no man shall presume ascendancy over me or my family ever again!" And she meant every word that she spoke.

Jane's Story Chapter 33

A Spiritual Healing Process

Was it to be just a straw in the wind after all? Could she really go back in time and pick up only the good things that happened, bringing them forward to be built upon and leaving the bad behind to remain forever buried in the past? Could her faith alone work such wonderment?

Jane had already made up her mind to try in any case and once deciding on a plan of action, she dismissed any lingering doubt or inhibition and caught the boat to Auckland to find Denis and bring him home. She was rather shocked to see him as he looked so thin and haggard and she despaired that he was but the shadow of the confident, self-assured young man she had married. Her arms reached out to him in anguish and she looked searchingly into his eyes for some glimmer of recognition and she praised God that it was there, faint and imploring but still alive. Her long and dedicated task of rehabilitation had thus begun.

When families pull together, mountains can be moved, miracles can happen and a stricken member who has fallen by the wayside can be uplifted and given the strength to try again. And so it was with Denis who was welcomed back into the fold, weakened after his frightening ordeal and needing all the love and support of his family to help him on the long and arduous journey back to health. Without the children to break down the barriers of guilt and direful memories, Jane might not have succeeded in her task but as the months drew onward, the clouds of past misgivings slowly cleared away and the prospect of a complete recovery became more than a forlorn hope. She decided to take him to see her people in Rotorua. To visit her old home on Mokoia Island and return to the places they had known when they were younger and their life together was just beginning. Could they recapture the cherished moods of the past and carry them forward into a new future?

The road up to the village of *Te Wairoa* on the edge of the bush overlooking *Lake Tarawera* had been vastly improved since Jane and Denis first visited the place in those earlier years. It was only a rough bridle track then but now, it had been transformed into a scenic coach road over which visitors from all around the world would be carried and set down at one or other of the two new establishments erected there for their convenience. There was the fully licensed Rotomahana Hotel run by Joseph McRae and the nearby Terrace Boarding House managed by Mr and Mrs Humphreys. The main tourist attraction being of course the celebrated Pink and White Terraces and the hot lakes of *Rotomahana*, acclaimed by the newly established Government Tourist Agency as being among the great natural wonders of the world.

The preferred access to the famous attractions was by canoe from Te Wairoa, across Lake Tarawera which in itself was an enjoyable excursion as it began with a short but steep walk down a bush-clad track from the hotel to a narrow inlet of the lake where the canoes would be waiting to carry the visitors out from the foreshore to skirt along in front of several secluded little clusters of native huts (*whare*) set snugly in against a backdrop of dense bush and towering cliffs. These were the villages of *Moura* and *Waituharuru* which were home to people of the local *Tuhourangi* subtribe (*hapu*) of *Rotokakahi* and *Whakarewarewa*. The flotilla, the size of which dependent on the number of visitors, would then head out across the deep green waters of the lake to the other side where the villages of the *Ngati Rangitihi* hapu, the old fighting pa called *Te Rua-a-Umukaria* {now **Kariri** (Galilee)}, *Waitangi* and *Tapahoro* were strung out along the bush-fringed Eastern shores, totally overshadowed by the fearsome, frowning presence of *Tarawera* the mountain with its three steep and bare-topped peaks, *Wahanga, Ruawahia* and *Tarawera* thrusting their sacred heads up to the sky.

It was at Tapahoro that Jane, with Denis decided to leave the tourist party as she wished to pay her respects to the highly venerated chief *Arama Karaka* who, in 1865, with a considerable force of his Rangitihi, joined Major William Mair's Te Arawa expedition and marched down the Tarawera River to *Te Awa-a-te Atua*, to engage and defeat the Hauhau at Matata and Te Teko. By her own elevated (*Rangatira*) standing, there was no way that Jane could pass through the domain of a chief of such high tapu and mana without receiving his traditional welcome (*Haeremai te mana, haeremai te tapu, haeremai te wehi*) and to be sent on her way with his blessing and that of *Tahoto* the high priest (*tohunga*) who was the tribal guardian (*Kaitiaki*) of Tarawera the lake and Tarawera the mountain. Such were the sacraments (*tikanga maori*) of her ancestral heritage that she would be bound to observe them for as long as she should live.

So it was not until three days later that Jane and Denis were escorted by a party of Rangitihi guides to view the famous Pink and White Terraces at the Southern end of the lake. At the final landing spot, there was a small settlement called *Te Ariki* which, in earlier times had been the home of the American Missionary, Seymour Mills Spencer, a colleague of the Reverend Thomas Chapman of Te Ngae who had established a mission station there in 1845. At that time the place was named *Piripai* (Philippi of the Bible), by the good Reverend and enjoyed a much larger population.

From the landing, there was a walk of about half a mile across a neck of low-lying, scrub-covered wetland to *Rotomahana*, a steaming hot lake which was quite small by comparison, covering not more than 300 acres (120 hectares), irregular in shape and almost completely surrounded with muddy shores. The water was turbid with warm springs and streams bubbling up from the cloudy green depths. The

Eastern shore was the most active with almost every type of thermal activity; geysers, boiling pools, mud cones and hot steam issuing through vents in the rocky sub-surface. There had always been a modest population living at Rotomahana stemming from pre-European times. Ancient cultivations, landmarks, place-names and burial grounds (*urupa*) were to be found over the whole area yet there was strangely little tradition and legend attached to the particular locality and its thermal attractions. There were two small islands in the lake, the biggest being *Puai*, about half a hectare in area and the other, *Pukura,* was even smaller. Both were covered in manuka and fern and several small huts (*whare*) had been built upon them. Near Rotomahana and separated by a low ridge was another smaller lake called *Rotomakariri* (cold lake), quite devoid of any thermal activity but whose shape suggested that it had not always been so.

When Jane and Denis completed the long walk through the scrub and fern from the landing at Te Ariki and caught up with the waiting guides at the edge of Lake Rotomahana, they were held spellbound by the wondrous display that they had suddenly come upon. On their left, rising above the steaming waters of the lake was *Te Tarata*, the White Terraces, their centuries old buttresses cascading down the bush-covered valley to the edge of the lake to spread like a giant fan along the shoreline in a dazzling display of glistening whiteness.

On the opposite side of the lake was *Otukapuarangi* the Pink Terraces, somewhat smaller than Te Tarata but with their delicate shade of salmon pink. They too appeared like a huge beautifully embroidered fan spreading down to the shores of the lake, their exquisitely sculptured basins linked together in a gently tumbling cascade of clear azure blue water.

Many were the descriptions given by people who had visited the terraces in the past but none claimed that their efforts would do them anything like full justice. It was simply that words alone could not fully describe the beauty they had beheld. Jane remembered an attempt made by her old friend Colonel St. John when he tried to describe them to her during his stay at the "Travellers' Rest" at Maketu. He said of *Te Tarata*:

"Imagine a shelving slope descending gradually to the margin of the lake in an uneven series of steps for some 100 metres, bounded on each side by low scrub and bush, and emanating from an open crater at the top from whence rolls out cloud after cloud of white steam. The steps appear from the height to be now white, and now purple, contrasting strongly with the azure hues of the basins, and glistening under the hot sun whose rays dance on the thin film of water constantly trickling down. At irregular intervals on the grades are pools. Pools! – the word is a profanation! – they are sculptured alabaster basins filled with molten silver, blue as the vault of heaven over whose gracefully curved lips pours down with a gentle murmur a never-ceasing flow derived from the boiling contents of the crater above. The more we gazed upon the scene, the more difficult it was to realise it."

There were other distinguished visitors whose descriptions had been recorded; one of whom was the essayist J.A.Froude who most eloquently described *Otukapuarangi* thus: "We could stand on the brim and gaze as through an opening in the earth into an azure infinity beyond. Down and down, and fainter and softer as they receded, the white crystals projected from the rocky walls over the abyss, till they seemed to dissolve not into darkness but into light. The hue of the water was something which I had never seen, and shall never see again on this side of eternity. Not the violet, not the hare-bell, nearest in its tint to heaven of all nature's flowers; not the turquoise, not the sapphire, not the unfathomable aether itself could convey to one who had not looked on it a sense of that supernatural loveliness. Comparison could only soil such inimitable purity."

Ferdinand R. von Hochstetter, the renowned Austrian geologist, was the first man of science to thoroughly report on the terraces and he, like others before and after him, was struck by the beauty of these phenomena. He said of the White Terrace: "The spring has built up a system of sinter terraces on the slope of the hill which, white as if hewn from marble, afford a prospect which no description or illustration has power to produce. It is as if a waterfall plunging over steps had been suddenly transformed to stone   The idea that a picture can give, scarcely reflects the magnificence and peculiarity of this phenomenon in nature. It is necessary to have climbed up the staircase and to have observed the details of the structure in order to receive a complete impression of this wonderful edifice."

"The extensive low toe of the terrace stretches far into Lake Rotomahana. The terraces begin with minor deposits which bear shallow pools of water. The further up one goes, the higher becomes the terraces. They are formed of a number of semi-circular steps or basins no two of which however, are of equal height. Each of these steps has a small elevated margin from which a delicate formation of stalactites hangs down on the step below, and also a platform, narrow or wide, which contains a basin of water shimmering in the most beautiful blue. The basins of water form natural bathtubs such as the most refined luxury would not have produced more splendidly nor comfortably. Basins shallow and deep, great and small, can be selected at will and at a temperature to one's liking".

He then said of the Pink Terraces: "On the West shore, the great terrace fountain of Otukapuarangi forms the counterpart of Te Tarata. Steps reach to the lake and the ascent on high is as on an artificial marble staircase, adorned on both sides with *manuka, manuwai* and *tumingi* scrub. The terraces are certainly not as magnificent as those of Te Tarata but on the other hand, are prettier and finer in their formation. Moreover, a soft rose-red which invests the wonderful formation as if in a glow, giving the whole an especial beauty."

As Jane and Denis walked among the pools of that delicate, slightly mist-shrouded wonderland, exploring each new level of bejewelled beauty, they were intrigued that here was the nexus of two different worlds; the one to be lived in for the present, the other to aspire to when life's work is done. This was a sacred, awe-inspiring place to be recognised and revered. They turned to each other, embraced, and slowly walked hand in hand back to the landing.

Gently the canoe glided over the darkening waters of Tarawera on the return to Te Wairoa and as Jane looked back across to the Western shore she noticed that the rays of the late afternoon sun were lighting up the barren peaks of Tarawera the mountain. High and imposing they were and somehow foreboding as though the gods (*Atua*) who resided there were being disturbed from their slumber. She was glad when they came at last to the landing and began the long uphill walk to the village. There were people she wished to call upon before the day was ended; one of whom was *Guide Sophia* who lived in a little house not far from the hotel and had taken upon herself to welcome all visitors to the region on behalf of the Tuhourangi and Rangitihi people and to acquaint them with the history and legend of the many mystifying features of Tarawera. Sophia was another who had accompanied the Te Arawa expedition to Te Awa a te Atua in 1865.

In the freshly cleared area at the head of the valley where the new coach road from Rororua ended and the two hotels had been erected, there was also a store, a school and schoolmasters house and already there appeared to be a thriving European population established at Te Wairoa. Lower down the valley, overlooking the lake and backed in against the range of steep cliffs, was the original Maori settlement (*Papakainga*) with its neatly laid out cultivations and groves of fruit trees, its dwelling houses (*whare*) grouped around a central *marae* dominated by *Hinemihi* the carved meeting house (*wharewhakairo*) with its steeply pitched roof and its intricately carved fascia boards (*maihi*) standing proudly to the fore.

As Jane and Denis sat with Guide Sophia in front of her little home and gazed out over the lake to observe the last rays of the setting sun striking the highest peaks of the mountain, Sophia spoke of eternity and of the generations of the past who had made their last spiritual voyage in a phantom canoe with high stern post and projecting prow, paddled by a band of warriors (***wakataua***) across the lake to the sacred burial grounds among the crags and crevices of Ruawahia, the tallest of the three peaks. She related to her captivated little audience the deeply held tradition among the people of Tarawera that whenever grave disaster or death was about to strike, there would appear through the mists arising from the lake, a phantom canoe travelling towards the mountain. No-one could tell from whence it had come, nor where it would make its landfall as it would always disappear into the mist as mysteriously as it had appeared. It would be recognised only as an omen (*aitua*) that some great disaster was about to visit upon the people.

Early next morning Denis and Jane said goodbye to their newly found friends and left in the coach for Rotorua. The road wound down through the bush-clad slopes to pass by the Green Lake (***Rotokakahi***) then the Blue Lake (*Tikitapu*) until it emerged at ***Owhata*** on the South-eastern shore of Lake Rotorua. It was from there at Owhata, Jane was reminded, that the legendary ***Hinemoa*** entered the lake to swim across to Mokoia Island and her waiting lover ***Tutanekai*** . Jane and Denis were about to make the same journey but by a much less fatiguing mode of propulsion.

And so it was that their canoe pulled into the familiar landing place on the Island and there to greet them was Jane's beloved ***tirairaka***, darting and coveting excitedly overhead and leading them up the path to the home that had always been there for her. It was good to receive the reassurance that her little *aria* by their appearance, had given her. She had embarked on her own healing process for Denis to soothe his poor tormented mind, back to total recovery and she knew that it would be by faith alone that she would succeed. Soon they would return to KatiKati, the farm and the children and all would be well again.

Jane's Story Chapter 34

Eruption

The healing therapy which Jane prescribed for her husband was now complete. He had been transported back through time to recapture the romantic moods of his adventurous past, his ambitions reawakened with the revelation of a spiritual presence holding ascendancy over all. A last few days rest in the peace and tranquillity of her island home and they were ready to return to KatiKati. The everyday work routine of a busy, productive mixed farm such as theirs left little time in which to reflect upon things of the past best forgotten, so that gradually Denis was left to regain his strength, and with that came his confidence, and it was only a matter of time before he was again master of his own destiny. Fully restored to health, much to the delight of his devoted family whose loving, dedicated care and support had at length been rewarded.

So easily had their lives slipped back to normal that Jane was again finding the time to renew her interest in the affairs of her extended family and to resume her work with the Native Land Court. In the words of one witness before the Court: "I would sometimes see her at Mokoia but only for a time after which she would return to KatiKati which was her permanent home (*kainga*)." It was on one such excursion that, early in June 1886, Jane had prevailed upon her now eighteen years old son Jimmy to drive her and the other children in the family carriage and pair to Rotorua for a brief reunion with their extended family. It was to remain a feature of her inherent matriarchy that she would insist that the children of her two marriages, Te Kirikaramu and Foley, should always be recognised as one family and that never should any distinction arise between them. And so it was that though most of them were to live to ripe old ages, they continued to honour their mother's behest, knowing each other as brothers and sisters to the end.

The first indication that all was not well on the island of Mokoia and that the normal peace and tranquillity of the place had been disturbed, came to Jane when the canoe bringing the family from Hamurana on the mainland, pulled in to the landing place at Atuahu. She noticed that the lake level was unusually high and that the little jetty was almost submerged and, just as she stepped ashore, she felt the earth suddenly move under her feet and an ominous tremor that rumbled up into the hills beyond the village. The children cried out in fear and people were seen to grasp each other for support. In a few seconds it was over and when her mother Maraea hurried to greet her, she announced that such frightening experiences had been going on for several days. Maraea also spoke of a warning (*aitua*) she had received through their **aria,** the ***tirairaka,*** that some terrible disaster was about to befall the people of Te Arawa.

Was it just coincidence that Jane was to immediately think of Guide Sophia and that mindful evening when they sat on her doorstep and looked out across the lake to the three sunlit tips of Tarawera the mountain? The legend of the phantom canoe, portent of disaster; had it appeared to Sophia after all? There was no time to lose; the safety of her family and loved ones was paramount in her mind; she would despatch Jimmy by canoe across to Te Ngae to gather all of the family that lived there and bring them to Mokoia where they would await their destiny together.

Earthquakes and other unusual thermal phenomena were nothing new to the people of Rotorua who had experienced many such surprise interludes in the past, but one quite recent incident aroused rather more consternation than usual when the Green Lake (**Rotokakahi**) gradually turned a most peculiar, more intense, green colour with the temperature suddenly rising by about 30 degrees centigrade and its surface level increasing by almost a metre. The natural outlet, a small creek generally clear as crystal, which ran through the village of Te Wairoa and down over the Wairoa Falls into Lake Tarawera had also changed to green with the discolouration extending far out into the lake and, seemingly thousands of dead and dying fish were being swept down to be cast upon the shore. All of this was looked upon as a very bad omen (*aitua*) by the local Maori inhabitants who feared that there would be far worse to come. More frequent earthquakes of heavier than usual intensity were being felt particularly at Rotomahana and were causing concern not only in the immediate area but also in villages further afield where houses were being severely shaken and articles dislodged from shelves.

By early June 1886, there was nothing to suggest that parts of Rotorua were about to be devastated. It was a normal winter month with people going about their business as usual, and it was only amongst the Maori people of Tarawera that there had been positive signs of impending danger. They had become convinced that something was about to take place and many among those who lived along the Eastern and Southern shores of the lake had already begun to evacuate their villages and remove to Matata for safety.

In the early hours of 10th June, people in many parts of the North Island were disturbed by a series of muffled explosions. There was no immediate explanation and many thought that the oft-revived Russian threat might finally have materialised. This must surely be the sound of salvoes from the cruiser **"Vestnik"** reported to have been sighted off the West Coast. The residents of Tauranga, Whakatane and Rotorua however, were under no such delusion as their hours of sleep had turned into a nightmare. It was Roger D. Dansey, the postmaster at Rotorua who broke the news to the rest of the world at 8.30 next morning when his telegraph to Auckland conveyed clearly the terror of the night before:

"We have all passed a fearful night here" he began; " The earth has been in continuous quake since midnight. At 2.30 a.m. there was a heavy quake, then a fearful roar which made everyone run out of their houses and a grand yet terrible sight for those so near as we were, presented itself. Mount Tarawera, close to Rotomahana, suddenly became active, the volcano belching out fire and lava to a grand height. The eruption appears to have extended itself to several places Southward. A dense mass of ash came pouring down here at 4.00 a.m. accompanied by a suffocating smell from the lower regions. An immense black cloud extending from Taheke to Paeroa Mountain, was one continual mass of electricity all night and is still the same. The roar of the thunder from three or four craters, the stench and continuous quaking of the earth made everyone alarmed and several families left their homes in their night dresses with whatever they could gather in their hurry and made for Tauranga or Tirau. Judging from the quantity of ash and dust here, I fear serious results to the people of Te Wairoa and the natives around Lake Tarawera".

Of those who were at Te Wairoa at the time, William Bird, the brother-in-law of Joe McRae, the owner of the Rotomahana Hotel, recounted the following experiences: "The night of June 9th was blusterly and chilly. The wind had turned to the West and, blowing as it did away from Te Wairoa, and towards the mountain, probably explains why, with the village being but nine miles in a straight line from the mountain, most of the inhabitants should manage to escape with their lives. The first few tremors which preceded the cataclysm were scarcely sufficient to waken the villagers but, with shock following shock with increasing violence and frequency, the now anxious people began to realise that something above the ordinary was beginning".

"The vibrations and jolting now accompanied by an ominous rumbling and increasing in intensity, I dressed and made for the open, taking my wife and eight months old boy with me and, just as we reached the door, a roar and shock as of a violent explosion came out of the darkness from the direction of the mountain and, as we instinctively turned towards the sound, a greater darkness, an inky black pall, visible against the paleness of the Eastern horizon, spread upwards and outwards into the heavens. Truly a terrible sight, spreading fanwise with dreadful rapidity, blotting out the stars and lurching towards us with incredible swiftness – a black murk shot through with globes of fire and flashing sparks as its lightning split the darkness".

Detonation after detonation developed and swelled to a mighty continuous roar till it seemed that nerves must surely crack under the violence wrought with the darkness, the uproar, the crazy swaying of the earth, the uncertainty as to what the next moment might bring. Yet in spite of the holocaust, our feelings were more of awe than fear of the majesty of the spectacle that held us in witness, spellbound. Tarawera the mountain had split from end to end and its three great summits were just a single mound of fire. Tarawera the lake was a copper mirror, reflecting the mountain from base to summit in a lurid glare and, dominating over all, there hung a great cloud-curtain, gloomy and dark above, saffron and orange on its underside, and showering out from it all, great balls of flaming rock descending to vanish in a steaming flash beneath the waters of the lake. Then came a shower of mud and rock fragments falling as thick as hail, blanketing everything in sight and sending us in haste to the village to seek shelter in the hotel. There as we gathered waiting around one small lamp giving only feeble illumination in the smoking-room, the rock particles began to fall more heavily and, any glamour of interest attached to the occasion quickly faded. There was nothing we could do but wait. What was happening to the rest of the village and my wife and baby son who had become separated from me after we left our cottage? A couple of hours passed and there was little talk, no panic, no noticeable excitement. All were resigned to whatever the future might hold".

An ominous sound near at hand drew our attention to the ceiling joists of our refuge and we saw that they were sagging dangerously. Weakened by the weight of mud and the continuous earth tremors, they were on the verge of collapse. Obviously it was time to move to a safer place, so we made our way along the verandah to a room which had only recently been completed. A disadvantage here however was that the door had jammed and the strong wind made the use of the small lamp impossible. The only light now came from the intermittent flashes of vivid lightning. Again we waited. Just a few people cut off from the rest of the world, waiting for whatever was to come but waiting most of all for daylight. Suddenly someone noticed that the house of the schoolmaster Haszard, which stood but a small distance from the hotel, was on fire. Some of us moved to the verandah to see what could be done but there was really nothing. We could ourselves only crouch in the darkness, deafened by the uproar, wondering how long the roof would hold up under its increasing burden. To make matters worse, pungent sulphur fumes added menace to the already choking atmosphere and, though the ceiling beams sagged downwards more and more alarmingly, yet we could imagine what fate awaited us should we leave the shelter. There was nothing we could do but remain where we were and hope for the best".

"Now and again there would come a merciful reduction in the scale of sound but, just as we hoped that the eruption was diminishing, the outburst would rage up again as the very earth continued to tear itself asunder. At 6.00 a.m. we decided to abandon our shelter and, that decision both saved our lives and took us unwittingly to safety. The roof over our heads had stood all it could and would not have lasted another five minutes and so, if we were to die we decided, it would be better that it happen in the open. We crawled out over the debris and onto the road and there, astoundingly, as we peered through the murk, we saw a light. It was truly a welcome sight as it suggested that we were not the only ones left alive on that awful night. We struggled towards the spot to discover that the light was shining from Guide Sophia's hut, a little *wharepuni* with strongly reinforced rafters supported from below with props, and it was crammed full of people including, to my profound joy and relief, my wife and baby son William Junior. When we had become separated outside our own cottage, she had made her way to Sophia's whare and had taken refuge there along with several others. A roll call inside however revealed that Mr and Mrs Humphreys, who ran the now wrecked Terrace Hotel, were not accounted for but fortunately they were later located together with several other survivors in the *Hinemihi* meeting house further down the valley".

"Sophia's hut stood on a rise and commanded a good view of the rest of the valley and, at 10.00 a.m., when daylight at last arrived with a marked decrease in the activity of the mountain, groups of people ventured out into the foggy twilight. There a scene of incredible desolation lay spread below us. A grey waste too hideous even for a ghost village, as time itself usually deals kindly with such abandoned places. That smiling valley which we knew so well was now just a dirty, crumpled blanket of grey, sticky mud.

We thrust our way up to Haszard's house which was still smouldering and there also, unexpectedly enough, we discovered other survivors. When the house caught fire, two surveyors, J.C. Blythe and Harry Lundius, who were staying with the Haszards at the time, and Haszard's two older girls, Clara and Ina, took refuge in the fowl house and there miraculously they were preserved. There was no trace however of Haszard, his wife and four younger children, two girls and two boys, and it was not until later that day that a search party discovered that all with the exception of Mrs Haszard, who was seriously injured, had perished.

Back with Jane and her family on Mokoia Island, all the people had gathered on the ancient *Tamatekapua* marae in the centre of the village and there, when the sound of the first explosions rumbled down from the hills in the East, they were held spellbound by the terrifyingly spectacular display that was building before them. Fiery burst after burst flaring up to the heavens, each one seemingly climbing higher than the last and a great swirling black cloud canopy prevailing over all, striving to contain them, and all the while the mighty earth-shaking roar of the explosions as they thrust their way up from earth's seething cauldrons below. Hour after hour the action continued until there arrived overhead a great grey cloud that appeared as if sandwiched between the towering black canopy above and the fiery orange glow of the explosions below. Then came an ever-expanding mud shower, spreading down from the hills and out over the lake, completely engulfing the island in its path and sweeping onward over the land beyond, spreading a bluish-grey mantle over everything for as far as the eye could see. The substance falling mostly as rounded pellets like large hailstones, intermingled with finer particles as moistened dust. So spectacular were these showers that against the fiery orange backdrop of sky fuelled by the exploding mountain, the teeming pellets plunging and splashing into the lake gave the impression that the water itself was boiling and also, although it was not realised at the time, small fragments of sinter from the Pink and White Terraces that had been caught up in the cloud, became reflected in the light, falling as myriads of sparks dancing in the wind to finally weave their way down into oblivion.

The fears expressed by Roger Dansey had certainly been real enough for the people of Rotorua but morning revealed that little damage, if any, had actually occurred in the township or in the outlying shoreline settlements. There was a light deposit of volcanic mud over most things but not much else was changed. As morning dawned however, fears for the situation of those at Te Wairoa and the other lakeside villages became very real.

Jane, who had shared close vigil over her family all through the night, was thankful that daylight had arrived at last and the worst of the holocaust was over. Frequent earth tremors remained as a constant reminder that the underground forces were still restive and capable of renewing their violence at any time whilst great plumes of clouded black ash could be seen rising sporadically above the Eastern horizon to be followed by the rumble of thunder in the distance. All such aftershock activity, Jane realised, would likely go on for some time. The landscape in the East, right up to the mountain was now strangely transformed. The ground was evenly spread as if it had been rolled out and, hill and dale, land, shrub and tree were all draped in the same sombre blue-grey garb. It was just as though there had been a snowstorm, only instead of snow, mud had fallen which no summer sun could melt. Jane's thoughts however returned inevitably to the people of Tarawera. Guide Sophia, the Tuhourangi and Rangitihi villagers. How had they fared? Had anyone survived at all? Jimmy was already preparing to join the rescue parties and she would hasten him on his way.

Jane's Story Chapter 35

Aftermath and Afterthoughts

As morning dawned in Rotorua, a steady stream of volunteer rescue workers began to assemble outside the Police Station which was in the charge of Chief-Constable Moroney. Captain Gilbert Mair (younger brother of Major William Mair), the officer commanding the Te Arawa military establishment at Kaiteriria, near Lake Rotokakahi, had also joined the scene early. Mr Edwin Robertson, the coaching proprietor, harnessed two of his coaches and, with Ned Douglas, his other driver, set out at 6.00 a.m. with a mounted escort for Te Wairoa. After a difficult trip through the increasingly deepening and clinging mud, they reached the edge of the devastated Tikitapu Bush where they came up against an impassable barrier. The great weight of the deposit, and the force with which it had been driven, had borne down the vegetation, stripping the trees of their foliage and leaving their great trunks laying flat along the ground, their roots an earthy disc in some cases three metres in diameter attesting to the mighty force of the wind that had brought them down. The road here was just a total tangle of fallen trees making further progress with the coaches and teams impossible so that all they could do was stop and wait. It was not long however before the first group of struggling refugees came into view, trudging down through the morass, wet through, muddied and exhausted and so thankful to take the helping hands of those who rushed forward to meet them. Once the women and children were safely aboard the coaches and headed back to Rotorua, the men from Te Wairoa and those who had come to join them turned and walked back to the village to search wider for other possible survivors.

Over the first hill, they came to Lake Rotokakahi, once the Green Lake but now just muddy water. The stream conveying its outflow was completely choked up and the lake level was rising alarmingly. The entrance to Te Wairoa presented a bizarre spectacle with only the tops of the whare peeping out of the accumulated debris and, on the roof of one could be seen the body of its owner only just dug out of the ruins. Three rooms of the Terrace Hotel were still standing but the back part and the balcony had collapsed into the mire   The Rotomahana Hotel was just a shattered, twisted wreck and the roof of the store next door had yielded under the weight of mud. Sophia's whare, which had so strongly resisted the storm, stood out with its now heavily mud-plastered eaves starkly defiant amidst a scene of complete devastation.   Although the average depth of mud was probably not more than a foot (300mm) at Te Wairoa, there were drifts in some places to a depth of over a metre and many of the whare that had collapsed gave the appearance of being buried up to their eaves.   The ruins of the Haszard house were still smouldering although the injured Mrs Haszard and the bodies of those who had died there had long since been located and taken away.

Jimmy Foley, who had brought his two horses around the lake from Hamurana and joined the rescue party at Rotorua, was despatched with a troop of horsemen made up mostly of men from the armed constabulary but with some other local volunteers under Captain Gilbert Mair, to try to reach Te Wairoa by an alternative route via a place which was aptly named "Earthquake Flat", a few miles South of Rotorua on the main Taupo Road, and then Eastward by the old constabulary track to *Kaiteriria*, Captain Mair's old headquarters on the Southern shore of Lake Rotokakahi.   At Kaiteriria, they were joined by *Alf Warbrick*, a well known identity of the district, and *Harry Lundius*, one of the survivors of the Haszard family tragedy of the night before, who had offered his services as a guide. The party had now swelled to about fifteen men, some mounted and leading pack-horses laden with provisions and medical supplies, thrusting their way through the sometime flank-deep mud and ash, and others armed with shovels and slashers following behind on foot to clear and widen the track for easier future access. The going was heavy and difficult and they were forced to make camp for the night in the bush at *Parehuru*.

In the morning, they thrust through to the top of the hill known as *Te Hape-o-Toroa* from which point they could look across to Rotomahana and from there it became so very obvious that a tremendous transformation had taken place. Where there had been a shallow, warm lake separating the Pink and White Terraces on either side, there was now a gigantic basin, its floor and thermal vents many hundreds of metres below and from which rocks and mud were still being ejected midst clouds of steam. Of the magnificent terraces that had adorned the area, no sign remained save for fragments of sinter flung far and wide over the mud-covered hills. The two lakes Rotomahana and Rotomakariri, had completely disappeared as their beds had split open allowing their waters to pour onto the molten magma below, where it instantly turned to superheated steam in a tremendous explosion. This, in simplistic terms, would explain the presence of so much liquid mud which had spread so far and wide. Where two lakes had been, there was now a single giant crater that would ultimately fill and form a new lake Rotomahana at least twenty times larger and ten times deeper than the old one.

Although here and there could be seen the tracks of some human being or animal on the freshly coated surface, and a few gulls had come in from the coast to wheel and cry overhead, there was no other sign of life and the whole place appeared eerily deserted as though this great grey blanket had descended over the land and smothered all earthly subsistence beneath it. The mountain however continued its activity albeit in a much less frightening mood and the frequent earthquake shocks served as constant reminder that all was not yet over. A heavy mist hung over Lake Tarawera, shutting out the view and creating an impenetrable mystic gloom from which all of this great evil had suddenly sprung.

By this time, all thoughts had turned to the plight of the people who had lived at Moura and Te Ariki, the main settlements on the same side of the lake as Te Wairoa, and an expedition would be organised by Alf Warbrick and Captain Mair to investigate by boat, two of which, with considerable difficulty, were being brought up from Rotorua. Early on the morning of 14th June, the party set out from Te Wairoa to row to the villages. They were constantly troubled by waves caused by great avalanches of mud, triggered by the seismic activity, sliding down the steep hillsides and into the lake. Black ash was still issuing from the craters and the entire area remained very much alive. At Moura, there was no sign that there had ever been anything there at all. The village and its entire population had disappeared beneath the mud. The situation at Te Ariki was found to be the same except perhaps that the mud was very much deeper. Some figures could be seen moving around the slopes of the mountain and after signalling them to come down to the edge of the water, they were taken off in the boats. They had come up from the South looking for relatives at Te Ariki but had themselves become distressed trying to wade through the deep mud and ash and, without food and water they were on the point of exhaustion. The searchers were to find no sign of life on the Eastern side of the lake either where the villages of Kariri, Waitangi, Tapahoro and Owhana once stood but it was thought that most of the inhabitants had heeded an early warning and evacuated down river to Matata before the mountain exploded.

At a conference held at Te Wairoa after all rescue parties had reported in, it was announced that some 150 people had lost their lives including six Europeans one of whom was a young English tourist, Edwin Bainbridge who was found crushed to death in the ruins of the Rotomahana Hotel.

The pack-horse train organised for the transport of supplies between Rotorua and Te Wairoa during the days following the eruption, was placed under the control of Jimmy Foley who worked his team tirelessly to bring relief to the bereft and destitute survivors and to support the search and rescue teams with the upkeep of food, medical and material supplies. A close companion of Jimmy on that assignment, was a young man of about the same age called Jack Wallace (not Jack's real name), who was also an excellent horseman. Together they shared many dare-devil adventures as they negotiated the deep and treacherous mud drifts that filled the gullies and concealed unknown perils to horse and man that often lay hidden below. Such was the close friendship that was forged between them during that time, that they were to become life-long comrades both in peacetime and in two future overseas wars.

On the nights that they were obliged to spend at Te Wairoa, they were most grateful for the shelter provided them in the large meeting house (*wharenui*) "*Hinemihi*" which had miraculously survived the raging onslaught of the eruption and was left standing despite the enormous weight of mud that was piled up over its thatched roof. It was quite confounding that Hinemihi, together with Sophia's hut and the Haszard fowl-house should be the only structures to not only withstand the crushing deluge that ravaged the area, but also provide refuge to an otherwise doomed few survivors.

Hinemihi, named after a Tuhourangi ancestor of that name, *Ngati Hinemihi-o-te-Ao Tawhito*, was erected six years beforehand to commemorate the opening up of the Tarawera district to Government- sponsored tourism and the worldwide attraction of the Pink and White Terraces. None but the stoutest of *totara* materials were to be used in its construction and the roof was to be double thatched in specially selected totara bark. All of its traditional wall panelling (*tukutuku*), interior scroll painting (*kokowai*), carved figures on the ridge posts (*pou tuarongo* and *pou tahu*), ridge pole (*tahuhu*), wall posts (*pou*), door and window frames (*tatau* and *matapihi*), front porch (*mahau*), barge boards and uprights (*maihi* and *amo*), the carved head (*koruru*) and the long threshold (*paepae*), were all to be crafted by the most accomplished Maori artisans. As a further embellishment to this unique but rather extravagant edifice, was the substitution of the traditional *paua* shell eye inserts to all the carved ancestral effigies, with *gold sovereigns* in a show of superiority over other hapu of the tribe who did not have access to this new-found wealth brought by tourism. It is however significant to record that strong exception was voiced at the time by *Tuhoto* the high priest (*tohunga*) of Tarawera who warned that such a display of alien wealth would bring grave misfortune to the area.

On the first night that they took shelter in the now deserted Hinemihi which, despite appearing more like a cave backed into the mountainside with its almost total coverage of piled up mud and ash, offered the only available place of refuge remaining in an otherwise desolate landscape, Jack, more than any of the others in the party was held fascinated with the plethora of shiny golden eyes of the carvings around the walls as they appeared glinting in the failing evening light. Prior instruction issued by Constable Moroney in the first place, and re-echoed by Jimmy at the time, that all property belonging to the victims should be recognised as such and respected notwithstanding, Jack found himself quite unable to resist the temptation and, while the others were sleeping, he drew his sheath knife and moved amongst the silent figures prising out their golden eyes. In the morning, Jimmy was first to notice the empty eye sockets and suspected at once who the culprit might be. When he approached his friend Jack, he found him furtively loading a rather bulky saddle bag onto his horse. "Yes I have taken them Jimmy" he said, "but this place is doomed in any case and soon it will all sink beneath the lake". "Be that as it may" Jimmy responded, "but all of Tarawera has been placed under strict *tapu* and any violation could bring disaster down upon the whole party".

It started to rain as the pack-train left on its return errand to Rotorua and, as if to hasten it on its way, a particularly severe earthquake tremor rippled across the valley. Jimmy wondered whether it really was a bad omen (*aitua*) as he noticed also that across the lake the mountain had suddenly spewed out a billowing black cloud of ash. The going became increasingly difficult as the rain turned the mud and ash underfoot into a slippery and treacherous quagmire and just as they were filing around the head of an old inlet arm of the lake, the lead horse, ridden by Jack, suddenly shied to one side and, scrambling to regain its footing, slid relentlessly into the deep muddy morass and disappeared from sight leaving its rider sprawled out on the surface, thrashing wildly to remain afloat. Jimmy rushed down to his aid and thrusting the branch of a fallen tree out to his friend, he called to him to take hold while he hauled back with all his strength to finally bring him to firmer ground. There he lay safe now but a badly shaken Jack; lucky to be alive but now without his horse, saddle, bridle and of course, that saddle bag filled with its golden hoard of piercing eyes; lost forever beneath the fathomless waters of Tarawera the lake. Jimmy reached down to his friend, smilingly shook his head and hauled him to his feet; "Well at least they didn't want you as well, Jack".

In the week following the initial explosions, the mountain continued to belch plumes of billowing black ash high into the air to be carried on the wind over an estimated 6000 square miles of forest and farmland with some of it drifting far out over the sea to sprinkle the decks of passing ships. Earthquakes, some quite severe also carried on for several days and although gradually decreasing in intensity, remained sufficiently taxing to strike anxiety into the minds of the rescue parties and keep the more timid away.

Some of the collapsed and buried dwellings were not unearthed and searched for several days after the eruption and it was in one of those ruins that old *Tuhoto* the *tohunga,* reputed to be 100 years old, was found alive. His *whare* had collapsed on top of him under the weight of almost two metres of mud and had held him captive without food or water, in total darkness and only the air that was trapped along with him, for five days. That he was able to survive for so long, miraculous as it was, there were those among his own people who would have preferred that he had been left there to die as he was as much hated as feared and they were inclined to attribute the present disaster to his evil manipulations. His rescue from a grave largely of his own making was therefore regarded as insensate folly on the part of his well intentioned Pakeha deliverers.

It befell Jimmy and his team to lay the old man out on a litter and carry him down to the road-head at Tikitapu where they were to load him onto a wagon and take him to the hospital in Rotorua. Upon their arrival, the examining officer ordered that, because as the result of his terrible ordeal he had become badly befouled and malodorous, the victim be thoroughly scrubbed and de-loused before being admitted to the ward but, when the message was conveyed to him in Maori, the old man became agitated and alarmed and pleaded with Jimmy not to let them cut his hair whatever else they might do to him. "If they cut my hair, I shall die" he declared. The medical officer however remained unconvinced and insisted that the waist length hair had become so contaminated and infested with lice that there could be no alternative but to get rid of the lot. So it was that **Tuhoto** the *tohunga* and *kaitiaki* of Tarawera, he who had survived the eruption of the mountain and for five days had lain entombed in a muddy grave, should quietly succumb in only a matter of hours after he became deprived of his hair. So ended a long and epoch-making career and perhaps with it, the last totally immersed and constituted high priesthood (*tohunga ahurewa*) in accordance with ancient Maori ritual and custom.

Jimmy was saddened by the demise of the old man as, to him, it spelt the end of an era as though, with the eruption of Tarawera, the ancient world of the Maori had been swept clean of its obsolescence and the way had now been cleared for a new generation of people and values. "***ka pu te ruha, ka hao te rangatahi***" ("the worn out net is cast aside, the new net goes a'fishing"). It was time, he thought, to rejoin his mother and family on Mokoia and prepare to make their return to KatiKati.

Jane's Story Chapter 36

A Family Re-established

At Rotorua, the effects of the eruption on the township itself, after the initial panic of that first night and the day following had subsided, were in reality only slight. Minor earthquakes were to continue throughout the week just to remind everybody that they were after all, living in a highly volatile thermal region. The general appearance of the town had altered little with only a light coating of mud everywhere and some of the regular thermal activity at Whakarewarewa and Ohinemutu somewhat more lively than usual; the level of the lake had risen marginally but that may only have been the result of recent heavy rain; shops had begun to re-open from the following day and schools, which initially served as refuge centres, were slowly being cleared and made ready to resume their normal function.

At Ohinemutu however, a much more dramatic episode was unfolding with the steady influx of refugees from the devastated lands. It was to the *Papaiouru Marae* they came to seek the spiritual security of their eponymous ancestor *Tamatekapua* and begin their deferential *tangi* for the dead, those whose bodies had already been recovered from Te Wairoa and the countless others destined to remain forever beneath the mud of Tarawera and Rotomahana. It was a time of grave uncertainty for these people as a return to Tarawera and its environs was out of the question. It was not simply that mud and debris now covered everything, but also that the deaths there had rendered the whole area *tapu* and nothing would induce its violation.

As it transpired however, help was soon forthcoming from the Government under Sir Robert Stout who had arranged with *Ngati Whakaue* for those (mostly Tuhourangi) who wished to remain in

Rotorua to be given land at Ngapuna and Whakarewarewa, whilst some 500 hectares were made available in the Thames-Waihi district under a similar agreement with *Ngati Maru* for those who wished to rehabilitate themselves there. For six months, none of the original Maori inhabitants would go near Tarawera until finally, on the last day of the year 1886, they returned in a large pilgrimage (*hikoi*) accompanied also by people from Maketu and Matata (mostly Ngati Rangitihi) and with them, the Tohunga, *Himiona* who lived on *Motiti Island,* who conducted the solemn and ancient ritual of lifting the tapu that had been in force since the disaster had struck. The raising of the tapu over Tarawera and rendering the lands free for resettlement notwithstanding however, none of the people showed any eagerness to return to live there preferring instead to leave it entirely up to the Government Tourist Agency to represent their interests.

Even the meeting house, *Hinemihi* was left abandoned and falling into ruin until, in 1892, it was purchased for fifty pounds ($100) by the then Governor-General of New Zealand, the fourth Earl of Onslow, who had it carefully dismantled and shipped to England to be re-erected in the grounds of Clandon Park, Guildford, sixty kilometres South of London. Lord Onslow not only wanted it as a souvenir of his New Zealand sojourn but also to serve as a novel boathouse next to his ornamental lake and so, there it stands to this day, the only carved meeting house (*whare whakairo*) in Britain. There are other Maori meeting houses in European museums but Hinemihi, now owned by the National Trust, is amongst the oldest and the only one standing in open air. It was fully restored in 1970 and presented with new carvings by Maori craftsmen to replace the missing ones. Over the years there has been pressure from members of the Ngati Hinemihi hapu of Rotorua, for the building's return to New Zealand as it is believed that ancestral spirits still exist within its body and in the carvings but, the Trust has no intention of letting it go.

One can only imagine how Lord Onslow reacted to finding so many myopic carvings being unwrapped upon arrival at Clandon Park. In his chagrin would he have, replaced the golden eyes with sovereigns of his own?, reverted to conventional paua shell substitutes?, or resigned himself to leaving those aggrieved ancestral effigies to remain forever in optical oblivion?

At KatiKati, on the night of 9-10 June 1886, Denis, who was at home with only his son John since Jane and the others had gone to Rotorua with Jimmy, was awakened from his sleep by a series of dull explosions from the South. The morning dawned bright and clear but the sky soon clouded over and a light grey ash began to fall. By noon it was pitch dark with the sun appearing through the murk as a faintly glowing ember. As the afternoon drew on, and there seemed to be no end to the darkness, many of the settlers became terrified believing that the end of the world had come. But then, just as slowly as it had appeared, the great cloud moved out over the sea leaving behind its deposit of ash to blanket and eventually destroy much of the vegetation. It was not until two days later that the mysterious visitation was explained with news coming through of the devastating eruption of Mount Tarawera. Villages with their entire populations had been buried and more than a hundred people had lost their lives. The glorious Pink and White Terraces had been destroyed. The rumble of the explosions had been heard 300 miles away in Wellington whilst in the North, some timid citizens had feared that it was the sound of the Russians hammering at the gates of Auckland.

To Denis however, the days that followed were choked with anxiety for his wife and family. He could visualise the absolute chaos amongst those who found themselves right at the forefront of that fiery maelstrom as he was sure Jane and the family would have on Mokoia Island. His worries however were at last dispelled when John arrived back from a hurried ride to Tauranga where he had been reassured that the damage to Rotorua had been only slight after all and there had been no serious casualties there. During the following week, thousands of cattle from Rotorua and the Eastern hill country passed through KatiKati on the way to green pastures in the Thames-Coromandel region and, it was behind one of those herds that Jimmy and the family arrived home after a quite uneventful journey.

The whole family was at home now and soon life on the farm would slip back into its simple routine. Denis and John between them had managed to keep things running smoothly in the absence of the others though their tasks had been greatly reduced at that time of the year when the cows were out for the season and the fields were lying in winter fallow. Jane's first concern was for Denis whom she had deliberately left to manage on his own for the first time since his breakdown. How had he coped with his reintegration into the KatiKati community? Had he been able to re-establish his standing amongst them and, more importantly, did he now possess the self discipline to moderate his drinking and stay within the bounds of accountable conduct? She worried that it would be so easy for him to return to the free and easy, rollicking ways of his Irish compatriots and, therein would lie his greatest challenge. She would still need to watch him closely and intervene if necessary to prevent any possible recurrence of that dreadful episode of the past.

Although the Tarawera eruption had not affected KatiKati directly, it remained a most vivid memory in the minds of most residents as the day the sun disappeared and darkness descended upon the land. To Jane and her family however, it contained a far greater depth of remembrance and despair. But just as the sun returned to shine over KatiKati on that day, so life in that little community returned to normal and the progress of the settlement continued. The matriarchal Jane, always a believer in diligence being the mother of good intention, and idleness, the opposite, decided that as her sons were growing into manhood, and there was the need to keep them and their father fully occupied, their original holdings in KatiKati should be extended. She learned of a 30 acre (12ha) block that had become available for sale at Te Mania due to the defection of the original grantee, Mr Cecil Gledstanes and, although it was still undeveloped, it was highly productive land and would be ideal for mixed farming. She decided to buy it.

So it was that the family, as an industrious, well disposed farming unit resumed their place among the community of KatiKati making their contribution towards the growth of its prosperity and the arrest of the decline which had characterised the eighteen-eighties during the great depression. A new generation was beginning to make its presence felt with the introduction of new and better farming methods, improved grass and grain varieties to replace the straggling English types of old, and the more generous use of artificial fertilisers. Thus presaging the harvest years of which the original leaders of the settlement had dreamed. After some years of disagreement among members of the Tauranga County Council, it was finally resolved that despite the earlier preference for the main highway to be built from Aongatete, over the Kaimai Range to Te Aroha and thence across the Waikato Plain, and also that some of the construction work had already been completed, the best route to Auckland would be through KatiKati, Waihi and the Thames after all. This change of direction was to result in considerable benefit to the farmers of KatiKati as, with the expansion of gold mining operations at Waihi with the resulting increase in that town's population, a highly profitable market for their produce was provided only sixteen miles (25km) away.

As with any close-knit community, tragic happenings which affect everybody sometimes occur and KatiKati in those days was no exception. A heavy blow came to Barney McDonnell, the genial, highly venerated proprietor of the Uretara Hotel, when his little son Bobby was drowned in a big flood that swept through the township.

The boy had climbed through the fence to play and was caught up on the current and carried so far down the river, that his body was not found until the next morning. As the result of that tragedy, it was decided that the hotel be removed to its present site on higher ground. The loss of the little boy brought all of the settlers together for the traditional wake which was to carry on for several days.

It would not be entirely correct to blame that particular occasion for bringing Denis back among his old drinking fraternity as he had often dropped in on Barney since his return to KatiKati without causing any undue concern. He had always held his composure and drank only in moderation. This time however, the lamentation and speech-making was to extend well into the night and through into the next day so that quite by chance it became the supreme test of his will power and resolution. In that eventuality however he was not to fail as, in the end, he was ultimately to find his way home in more or less sober frame of mind. This then became his normal habit and, to his credit, although there would still be occasions when he strayed beyond the bounds of his own self-appointed constraint, he never again allowed himself to become totally addicted to alcohol. Testimony indeed to Jane's influence and perseverance in her efforts to rescue her husband from the depths of degeneration by reminding him of the true principle of life itself (*mauri ora*), its spiritual values and goals to be strived for and, finally, setting him on the road to full recovery and rehabilitation.

Throughout her incredibly active and adventurous life, Jane had often found cause to ponder the fate of the women of this emerging nation of New Zealand. Perhaps it was because they were too widely scattered and busy with the first stages of home-making and management and also with the rearing and, under great disadvantages, the education of their children that, in the early years they were seldom to look far beyond their own doors. The problems that they had to face were therefore mainly domestic. As pioneer women in a new and often inhospitable land, they were forced to accept and endure the most insufferable and debasing privation. Opportunities for many of them to meet together and discuss common problems affecting family life were rare indeed and, in the more isolated settlements, almost impossible. The general attitude towards their women by the male sector, especially those in positions of power, was disrespectful and negative. *"God made men and women differently so they could fulfil different roles. The man is the breadwinner and the woman the home-maker. The man is the head of the house, so he is entitled to the say in the government of his country. It is not fitting that a woman should want a part of these things".* Humiliating as that utterance was, particularly to Jane who would never under any circumstances entertain or accede to it, such chauvinistic attitudes were an abomination. She had already identified the greatest threat to the welfare and security of the women of the country and the future of their families and that was the scourge of alcohol which had blighted the betterment of New Zealand from the first days of settlement. Drunkenness was so common and many families suffered terribly as the result. From her own experience with Denis, she had come to recognise that alcohol addiction was not properly understood and alcoholics were seen as irresponsible and weak. She had long seen the need for responsible women of New Zealand to unite in a body and organise to combat this malevolent, debilitating disease.

It was during one of her terms of residency on Mokoia Island that Jane was given the opportunity to at last do something positive to bring about worthwhile change. She had received an invitation from a group of like-minded ladies in Rotorua to attend a reception to a special visitor, Mrs Mary Leavitt who was an evangelist delegate and foundation member of the Women's Christian Temperance Union (WCTU) of the United States of America and, at that meeting, so ready was the response to her representation as to the work that women could perform in the community, it was resolved that a national body of the WCTU would be formed in New Zealand.

That was in 1885 and by the end of that year, nine branches of the WCTU had been formed throughout New Zealand and that number had grown to fifteen with a total membership of 530 women by the time of their first annual meeting.

Though temperance was the union's first priority, it was also active in many other areas. Night shelters were run for the homeless and soup kitchens were set up for the hungry. Help was given to prisoners and prostitutes, day care and kindergartens were set up. Much attention was given to the unfair ways in which the law treated women and the right to vote soon became the union's most important concern. Adult men were given the right to vote in 1879 but women were denied it. The WCTU resolved to have that law altered and, under the determined leadership of Mrs K.W. (Kate) Sheppard, Superintendent of the Union's franchise department, began its struggle to win the vote for women. Articles were written for newspapers, public meetings and petitions were organised and churchmen and politicians were enlisted to lobby on their behalf although many men remained totally against the idea and voiced their opposition in noisy and often insulting ways. In 1891 the Liberal Government under John Balance was in power and in theory, that government supported the idea of votes for women but there was also a group within that party who were against any change. The suffragists petitioned Parliament on several occasions and in spite of the hard work on the part of the WCTU franchise branches, little progress was made until finally, a petition bearing 31,872 signatures representing a quarter of the New Zealand population of adult women, convinced the government that public opinion was in favour of a change and a new Bill allowing women the vote was introduced and passed by a majority of two. Thus on 19 September 1893, New Zealand became the first country in the world where all adult women had the right to vote.

The opportunity to work towards the formation of a nation-wide organisation such as WCTU, her own personal efforts for the recruitment of members and the setting up of a strong Rotorua branch and the ultimate success of the Women's Franchise Movement in winning the right to vote for all adult women, was to Jane on review, a whole new and satisfying experience as she came to realise for the first time, how far the country and its mix of peoples had progressed towards its own unique nationhood. And so as the final years of the nineteenth century counted down to their close, Jane looked forward to the beginning of a whole new chapter in her absorbing, adventure-filled yet richly rewarding life.

Jane's Story Chapter 37

Death and the Dream Sequence

In the final decade of the nineteenth century, Jane found herself spending more and more of her time at Mokoia. By that time, her Te Kirikaramu family had become almost fully integrated into their father's Ngati Rangiteaorere hapu and had gone to live amongst them permanently. Her eldest son, Rangiteaorere had succeeded his father in chieftainship (*aho ariki*) of that hapu and had taken up residence at the *Mataikotare Marae* at *Waiohewa, Te Ngae* where he had initiated the building of the meeting house, *Rangiwhakaekeau.* His brothers *Atutahi* and *Te Ngahoa* had both married and produced children of their own. Atutahi married *Ani Kopapa* and they had a daughter and two sons: *Meri, TeKirikaramu* and *Tamaitinana.* Te Ngahoa married *Mariana* and they had three sons, *Korokaihau* (Wi Martin), *Hohepa te Rake* (Joe TeKiri) and *Aperahama Riko* (Pera TeKiri), and a daughter, *Atareta.* They all lived on family land at TeNgae, Whakapoungakau and Rotokawa. Rangitauninihi, the surviving TeKirikaramu daughter, never married and went to live at Maketu.

At KatiKati, Jimmy and Harry continued to work on the farm with their father but only when times were busy and the workload demanded the extra manpower. There was however plenty of opportunity for Jimmy to pursue his preferred metier of horse-breaking and training. Harry, who grew into a big strong lad, found plenty of casual work to his liking in the goldfields of Waihi. It was also rumoured that, for the extra money to be made there, he was soon to gain a reputation in the prize-ring as an amateur bare-knuckle exponent. John turned out to be the scholar of the family and showed so much aptitude that his mother arranged to have him further his education in Auckland. Their sister Sophie, seemed happy enough to stay at home with her father and only ventured out occasionally to Tauranga and Rotorua to take up short term work when she needed the extra money.

However dispersed her two families had become in the pursuit of their personal preferences, it took but one signal, unexceptionable circumstance to bring them all together in sorrowful tribulation and that was the death of their beloved grandmother Maraea. She had herself been attending a tangi at the Mataikotare Marae when it would appear she had caught a chill but, true to her sweet and utterly selfless nature, she chose to remain to the end of the formalities before bothering to attend to her own welfare. Tragically though, it was to be too late. She suddenly became stricken with high fever and was almost immediately confined to bed where she was forced to remain. It was considered far too perilous to try to get her to the Rotorua Hospital and it was decided instead to send for a doctor. Jane, who had just arrived at Mokoia from KatiKati, was summoned urgently and made frantic haste to her mother's bedside. Maraea had by then become delirious and was sliding in and out of consciousness and, just as the doctor arrived, she lay back, still and motionless. Her time had come.

And so it was as fate destined, the beautiful Maraea passed through the portal of darkness (*Te Tatau o te Pō*) and entered **Rarohenga** the realm of the great lady of the underworld (***Hinenuitepo***) .

As she knelt at the bedside, her hands grasping those of her mother, passionately willing her own life force to flow through and give her strength to fight off the suffocating darkness and turn again to the light, Jane came at length to experience the very moment that Maraea had passed through the portal and entered the spiritual world beyond. She lifted her eyes to the now darkening sky as though seeking the attention of the Heavenly Father that she might commit her beloved mother into His care, and as she allowed her gaze to linger unseeingly across the divide which separates life and death, there came the tears, welling up from the depths of her despair, flooding pure and clear, unashamedly true and gentle as the softly falling rain. At no other time in her highly dramatic, venturesome life, where death was no stranger among her closest contemporaries in times of crisis and of war and held an ever-ominous presence, had she experienced such heart-rending grief.

Long into the night she held vigil over the frail figure of her mother as she lay in silent repose. She allowed her mind to drift back in time and pictured the beautiful, tall and proud young woman standing protectively over her daughter as they awaited their fate at Kororareka. She recalled her mother's wistful and unwavering faith silently held for the gallant Captain who sailed out of Taitokarau those many years ago that he would someday return and claim her as his bride. She of the absolute dedication to the Anglican Church, its doctrine and its teachings. Her commitment to the Maori King movement and the philosophy of Wiremu Tamihana for peaceful union between the races where the mana of chieftainship and the mana of the Crown might both find a place together; such that she followed her daughter into battle and endured the hardship and suffering that it brought upon them. And lastly, her undying devotion to her grandchildren (**mokopuna**) whom she treated as her very own and for whom she would willingly have died.

Once more Jane looks lovingly down upon that sculpted smooth and waxen face, the once deep and limpid brown eyes now closed in eternal sleep, the raven black hair now tinged in silvery white, softly sprinkled pure as the driven snow. A great shudder surges up from within her and again the tears begin to flow. Her head lowers until it rests on the bed-clothes beside her mother and then, overcome with sheer enervation, she allows herself to slip into a world of darkness.

She awakens as a little girl holding the hand of her mother as they walk together along a sandy beach. She hears the boom of the waves as they crash against the shore and the cries of the seabirds as they wheel and circle overhead. Her mother is dressed in a soft and flowing cloak (*korowai*) and she wears a single white albatross (*toroa*) feather in a woven (*taniko*) headband from which flows her sleek and shining black, waist-length hair. In her hand she carries a sprig of the *hinau* tree which she has brought from the land of Te Arawa.

After walking for what seems to a little girl, a very long time, they come to the end of the sandy beach where they see a lone hill named *Te Arai* at the top of which her mother places her sprig of *hinau*. Then they ascend a long ridge to reach the summit of *Taumataihaumu*, the highest hill around. Her mother now turns to wave farewell to the land which will soon be lost from view forever as they descend the other side. Their path now crosses a small stream named *Te Wai o raropo* (The water of the underworld). Here her mother kneels to drink of the waters but, as Jane also stoops down to join her, she is quickly pulled away; "Not for you my darling" smiles her mother as they continue on their way. Jane was not to know that a spirit may cross the stream and yet return to its body if it does not drink of its waters but, if it does partake, there is then no return and the spirit must pass on into eternity.

They walk on down to the beach named *Te Oneirehia* which may be freely interpreted as the "Twilight Sands" - a short stretch of sand which is quickly traversed, and then the path rises to cross another stream which, from its course makes a gurgling sound amid its rocks and rills and which by its setting, is given the name *Te Waingunguru* (the waters of lamentation). Down the opposite slope, the path leads out to the final promontory jutting out into the waters of *Te Moananui a Kiwa* (the Great ocean of Kiwa). Before coming to the end however, they will have to cross yet another stream called *Te Wai o rata,* said to have reddish rusty coloured water, hence its analogous reference to the rata from its red flowers Crossing that stream, they will come to the edge of a steep cliff, upon the rim of which there grows a sacred *pohutukawa* tree with an exposed root extending down to a rocky platform below. This whole promontory is the renowned *Te Rerengawairua* (The Spirits' Leap) to which the spirits of the dead of all the tribes of *Aotearoa* come as the spiritual point of departure on their last sea voyage. Spirits did not leap off the cliff as the name Rerengawairua might imply, but passed down the exposed root of the pohutukawa which is named *Aka kite reinga* (root of the underworld) and, upon descending the root they would arrive at a rocky platform on the edge of the breaking sea. In the sea, a deep whirlpool would appear, fringed with swirling long tentacles of floating seaweed referred to as *rimui o motau* (seaweed of motau) and, as the waves flowed in, the seaweed would be swept over the hole and, as they receded, the cover would be temporarily swept aside to expose the crystal clear water into which the spirit was impelled to dive and proceed on its homeward journey through *Rarohenga* to the original spirit land of their remote ancestors.

As they arrive hand in hand at the top of the cliff, after crossing the stream named *Te Waiorata*, Jane and her mother come upon a group of people busily preparing a feast which is being laid out on a beautifully crafted mat (*takapau*) with brightly coloured borders. To little Jane, the people appear vaguely familiar, one of whom she instantly recognises and runs forward to greet. It is her beloved great-aunt Mango who looks up and smiles then takes her in her arms and hugs her for a brief moment but, strangely then, gently pushes her away. Maraea who is following behind comes up to the people and accepts the food that they are holding out for her, but again, as Jane holds out her hands for food, her mother pulls her away and, smiling soothingly she says: "No my darling, not for you."

Maraea now rises to take her daughter in her arms and hugs her to her breast, then gently puts her down, turns and descends the exposed root of the pohutukawa (*Aka kite reinga*) to the rocky platform below. She stands for a brief moment on the edge overlooking the great welling pool in the sea, tall and slender, her arms upraised as she lifts her eyes to the heavens and, without looking back to the world from which she is about to depart, she hurls herself into the surging waters. High up on the cliff Jane is standing watching, horrified yet strangely detached. She sees the figure of her mother disappear beneath the waves then rise again to be held suspended in the centre of the heaving stream, her long black hair swirling about her in concert with the motion of the surrounding, floating seaweed of motau. Swirling! seaweed! swirling! black hair! swirling! Jane feels now a gentle hand upon her shoulder. She blinks her eyes open and looks up to see her brother Neri standing there. "Come along big sister" he smiles, "time to go now".

Jane's Story Chapter 38

Tangi

The communal life on the island of Mokoia had experienced many quite drastic changes over the years since the first missionaries settled there and the population had built up to its peak. None more so than the decision by Ngati Whakaue to remove the ancient meeting house, Tamatekapua to the Papaiouru Marae at Ohinemutu. This marked a steady decline in the number of families who chose to live on the island and, by the end of the century only a few families remained in residence. The cultivations on the fertile flats on the Eastern side of the island however remained in full production although many of the owners chose to live on the mainland and only return to the island to tend their crops as called upon. Many of the old dwelling houses had been left abandoned and allowed to lapse into disrepair and, regretfully, some of those that were still being occupied, were showing signs of chronic dilapidation and a limited remaining life. Such was the situation when the time came for the *tangi* for Maraea. There could be no question that she would be buried in the cemetery (***urupa***) named ***Tokanui*** with her mother and father who died in the battle of Mokoia when Maraea was only four years old, but as there was no longer a traditional marae on the island, the tangi would have to be held on the mainland. It would therefore be left to the related subtribes (***hapu***) to state their respective claims to the honour.

Often when the deceased belonged to more than one hapu, a heated argument would arise as to which sub-tribal urupa had the greatest claim to burial but, unless the argument to the contrary was very strong, the decision would usually go to the paternal side though the losers would always put up a vigorous fight to indicate their affection to the deceased. In Maraea's case, the paternal sub-tribe was Ngati

Rangiteaorere through her father, Te Ngahoa whilst that of her mother, Rangitauninihi, was Ngati Uenukukopako. These were the two sub-tribes that held the strongest claim but, due however to her direct lines of succession extending back far beyond both of those ancestors to Toroa of the Mataatua Canoe and Tamatekapua and Ngatoroirangi of the Te Arawa Canoe, other hapu including Tuhoe, Ngati Awa, Whakatohea of the Eastern Bay of Plenty; Tuwharetoa of Taupo; Ngati Whakaue, Tuhourangi, Rangiwewehe, Pikiao and Rangitihi of Rotorua were all able to advance legitimate ancestral claims. After many hours of heated debate therefore, it fell to her own grandson, Rangiteaorere Te Kirikaramu to win the day on behalf of the Ngati Rangiteaorere hapu and it was agreed that the tangi would be celebrated before Rangiwhakaekeau on the Mataikotare Marae at Waiohewa (TeNgae).

Throughout Maoridom, a death imposed a death *tapu* which would remain until removed by the appropriate ceremony and, in the olden days, unlike various other forms of tapu, the death tapu had something sinister and lingering about it and no-one would dare overstep its specific bounds. Because of the death tapu, people feared to sleep on the same spot where someone had died and it was due, incidentally, to this strong aversion that European hospitals were not immediately accepted among the Maori when it was realised that the beds in which patients had died, were continued in use. When placed over a building in which the death occurred, the proper treatment for the removal of a death tapu was the same as for the house of childbirth, namely to burn the building down. An ordinary house could be burned down or abandoned without much loss but meeting houses were too valuable to be destroyed. The only possible way of saving valuable houses was therefore by not allowing anyone to die in them. Thus when patients became seriously ill, they would be quickly moved out of the building to a temporary shelter or, in later times, a tent. Should the patient be someone of note, the temporary shelter would be erected near the meeting house and facing out onto the marae so that if they were to die there, no additional arrangements would be necessary for the next stage of the proceedings.

Wherever the death occurred, whether elsewhere in the village or away in some remote area, the body would be conveyed immediately to a temporary death house on the marae. This was necessary because all public demonstrations of grief by visiting tribes had to take place on the marae. Under certain circumstances however, it was apparently acceptable to have the body placed in the front porch (*mahau*) of the meeting house which, although remaining intensely tapu for as long as the body remained there, did not create such a virulent tapu as it would had it been placed right inside the house and therefore such tapu could be removed without requiring the whole house to be burned down. It has become more popular in recent times however for the coffin to be placed inside the meeting house with visitors and family sharing the space around it for assembly and sleeping.

So the open casket containing the beloved Maraea, her body covered to the neck in a fine tag cloak (*korowai*), was laid out on woven sleeping mats (*takapau, porera*) in the porch of **Rangiwhakaekeau,** her head raised slightly so that she could be viewed from the centre of the courtyard (*marae*) from whence the numerous groups of tribal mourners would seek to address her. The green leaves of the **kawakawa** are the recognised symbol of death but nowadays it is more often the weeping willow woven into head-wreathes for the women, the principal mourners of whom with Jane as chief would be seated in attendance around the deceased to keep up an almost continuous wailing, interspersed with vocal lamentations and the singing of dirges (*apakura*) some of which were composed for the occasion. These women often fasted during the period of attendance on the deceased and could only be persuaded to take nourishment under cover of night.

The first to pay their respects were the local villagers who came in family groups with their women who raised the long wailing cry for the dead. An elder (*kaumatua*) would march at the head, uttering words of farewell such as: *"Haere e whaia! Haere ki te po atu!"* ("Farewell o mother! Depart to the other world, never to return"). The party would stand before the house of the dead and weep loudly with tears (*roimata*) running down their cheeks, and mucus (*hupe*) dripping from their noses. This correct etiquette being accompanied by the following typical utterance:

Te roimata I heke	The tears which fall
Te hupe I whiua	The mucus which is
Ki te marae	cast on the marae
Ke ea Aitua.	Avenge death.

Whilst death cannot be avenged, the physiological secretions stimulated by deep emotion, give physical relief to the pain that grows within. The relatives of the deceased would then join in the weeping and wailing and it would always appear as if the women on both sides were indulging in a competition as to who could contribute the greatest protestation of their grief. The men being much less emotional, would wait for the wailing to lessen before delivering a short speech of farewell to the deceased. The visiting party would then file past the line of chief mourners to press noses (*hongi*) which process could sometimes take protracted time as relatives would express the depth of their grief by the length of time their noses remained in contact. The villagers would then be free to make preparations for the feeding of the visiting tribes who would arrive later to pay their respects.

Visitors would come in tribal groups, massed together and led by their chiefs to advance onto the marae. All would be wearing the green symbols of mourning. Upon sighting them, the home people would assemble on the marae and, if they were not quite ready, a messenger would be sent to hold back the party until the reception line was formed. When all was ready, the home women would raise the shrill cry of welcome (*karanga*) tinged with sadness: *"Haeremai ki o tatau mate e....."* ("Come to our dead"). The succeeding ceremony (*tangi*) would then be a repetition of the earlier village procedure but on a larger scale. The visiting chiefs would repeat their short farewell phrases and the visiting women would seek to at least equal the shrill wailing of their welcoming contemporaries. The younger men, after a perfunctory stand, would withdraw to the back and sit on the ground or on forms provided and leave the older men and women to comply with the necessary etiquette. The home speaker would welcome the visitors by their tribal name and prominent chiefs, in person. He would thank them for coming to weep for their dead and refer to tribal and family affinities, eulogise (*poroporoake*) the deceased and quote from myth and tradition. He might brighten his speech by leading a family lament (*waiata*) and then conclude with the orthodox welcoming phrase *"Haeremai, Haeremai, Haeremai!"* ("Welcome, Welcome, Welcome"). Other local dignitaries who wished to speak would be given their say and then it would be announced "This side is finished!"

The visiting chiefs would then rise to reply but the pattern of speech would differ in that the first remarks would be addressed directly to the deceased in farewell:
>*"Haere! Haere ki te po!"*
>(Go! Go to the other world!)
>*"Haere ki to tupuna!"*
>(Go to your ancestors!)
>*"Haere ki te Iwi!"*
>(Go to your tribe!)

Quotations from myths, traditions and laments concerning death would then be given such as the following example:

"Haere i te ara takimano," (Proceed along the path of thousands)
"Haere i te ara takitini," (Proceed along the path of the myriads)
"Haere i te ara" (Proceed along the path)
"Karere kore ki muri!" (From whence no messenger returns!)

After eulogising the deceased, the speaker would turn his attention to the living with the introductory words *"Karanga, Karanga, Karanga"* in acknowledgement of the *Haeremai* call of welcome by the home people. He would offer his condolences to the family and tribe, refer to tribal affinities, pledge his everlasting friendship and conclude with an appropriate *waiata* accompanied by his retinue of followers.

The third and last stage of the reception of visitors would then begin with the nose-pressing (*hongi*) ceremony with the visitors falling into single file to commence at the outer end of the home line and work slowly along until coming upon the chief mourners whereupon, a little extra pressure and time would be expended out of respect to their nearness in relationship to the deceased.

The length of time the body was kept before burial was indefinite because it could never be known for sure when the last party of mourners would arrive. Time after time a burial has been postponed after a messenger has arrived to announce that another party from distant parts is on its way. Every postponement caused extra expense to the home people who would have to keep feeding the other guests who could not, in courtesy, leave until the burial had taken place. The tangi for Maraea was similarly prolonged due to the number of distant tribes wishing to be represented. Parties came from far and wide and, apart from the genealogically affiliated tribes as earlier mentioned, there came those from Ngapuhi in the North, Ngati Whatua, Ngati Paoa and Koheriki from Tamaki Makaurau and

Hauraki; Waikato, Maniapoto and Ngati Haua from the Maori King Confederation; Te AtiAwa and Ngati Ruanui from Taranaki; Ngati Porou and Kahungunu from the North Island East Coast and Ngai te Rangi and Ngati Maru from the Western Bay of Plenty. It would be true to say however, that those parties who were representing tribes (*Iwi*) of the other canoes, would chiefly have come out of reverence for Jane herself.

During the period that the body lay in state, the visitors, who sometimes ran into the hundreds, would have to be lodged, fed and entertained by the home tribe. Each meal was in the nature of a feast (*hakari*), for tribal honour required that the standard of living should be raised above normal for the occasion. Visiting tribes would be fully aware of the great strain on the local food resources and often they would bring contributions of food with them. In more modern times the custom of *koha* was introduced whereby the visiting tribe would make a financial (usually cash) donation. This stemmed from the ancient practice termed *kopaki* (wrapping shroud) where an appropriate gift such as a jade or whalebone club accompanied by a fine dress cloak would be ceremoniously presented. The etiquette of presentation was for the visiting chief to advance towards the marae reciting in high key, the solo part of an appropriate chant. His followers would take up the chorus, with a shout which would bring everyone running. The local people who by then would have taken up station in front of the meeting house, with their women to the fore would raise a long drawn out cry of *"Haeremai"*. The leader would continue on his stately advance and finally lay his gift on the ground before his hosts and then, after stepping back, his whole party would break into a rousing haka in grand finale. The local chief would then rise to accept the contribution (*koha*) with an appropriate speech of acknowledgement and approbation.

And so at length the tangi for Maraea came towards the end. Most of the visiting tribal groups had arrived and paid their respects in speech and ceremony with each following the other in succession and, after the shedding of tears, farewelling the dead and pressing noses with the near of kin and local hosts, had discharged their obligations and become free to move among and associate with the living. The corpse in its casket and the house of mourning however would be held detached from the social happenings with the chief mourners remaining in attendance and maintaining an atmosphere of sorrow in which to receive any new arrivals with a fresh outpouring of grief. But after the first few days, the tension began to slacken with the wailing and chanting of dirges becoming less continuous until, early in the morning of the seventh day, a piercing wail from the attendant women interrupted the morning silence signalling to the waking assembly that the casket was about to be finally closed.

Again, in the olden days, the body, especially that of a high-born person or chief would be removed from the marae in secrecy at night to prevent enemies from stealing the bones to make fish hooks or other commodities, a procedure intended to degrade the family of the deceased. With the arrival of the Christian missionaries however, there came a much less barbaric attitude towards cohabitation amongst rival tribes and the earth burial (*nehu*) or inhumation of the dead became a more widely publicised and deeply sacred observance.

So it was that the funeral of Maraea was led out from the Mataikotare Marae by a young half-caste Maori priest named **Frederick Augustus Bennett** (later to become the first Bishop of Aotearoa), reciting the funeral obsequies. Heading the cortege was **Rangiteaorere,** resplendent in his fine feather cloak (**kahu huruhuru**), huia feather headband (**pare huia**) and flourishing his historic, ancestral long club (*taiaha*) named *Tiritiri Matangi*. Close behind came the coffin, borne on the shoulders of grandsons Atutahi, Te Ngahoa and Jane's brother Neri on the right, and the three Foley grandsons, Jimmy, John and Harry on the left. Behind the coffin walked Jane and other chief and close family mourners, then a seemingly endless serpentine throng of people young and old. They moved down to the landing on the edge of the lake where the great war canoe *Te Iroiro* with its company of thirty-two warriors was waiting to escort the funeral procession made up of a flotilla of canoes, row-boats and even a steam-driven launch, across the lake to Mokoia Island.

There, waiting at the ancient landing place marked by the totara tree named *Atuahu*, was a welcoming party made up of island residents and their extended families (*whanau*) who had gathered together early to prepare for the burial and the feast (*hakari*) that would follow.

At first sighting of the approaching *Te Iroiro* with its chanting warriors dipping their white-tipped paddles in perfect unison, the women with the best voices moved forward and gave the shrill *karanga* of welcome and of everlasting love (*arohanui*) for the enshrouded one who was being brought home to lay among her ancestors who had gone before:

"*Kaore te aroha ngau kino*	("Alas the bitter pain
I roto ra	which gnaws within
Ki te whaea ka riro"	for the mother who has gone")

When all the people had landed and come ashore, the funeral cortege was again assembled and, with the Reverend Bennett delivering the Christian funeral rites, moved up from the landing to the burial ground (*urupa*) named *Tokanui*. Jane, now a frail figure herself and looking pale and drawn after her long fasting vigil, dressed all in black as was the custom, took her place at the head of the chief mourners and stoically, holding back her tears, marched behind her sons whilst all the while the women kept up their constant wailing interspersed with vocal lamentations and incantations (*karakia*). At the graveside, more words were spoken by the higher chiefs as they delivered their last farewells and exhortations to pass through, unafraid to the spiritual world beyond: (*"Haere, Haere, Haere! E haere atu ra!"*) Then the priest led the congregation in the singing of the traditional (Christian) Maori hymn "*Arohaina mai*" and finally, the Benediction. Immediately after the last amen, the men moved forward to backfill the grave. This was and still remains a peculiar custom with Maori burials intended, it is believed, to deter mourners from lingering at the graveside, weeping and possibly attempting, in their profound grief, to throw themselves in with the deceased. The sound of the earth thudding onto the casket can have a portentous effect on the mind and will quickly shift all but the most pedestrian bystander.

Jane was one who cared not to linger. She felt that she needed to be alone for a time so she bade her family, however reluctant they were to leave her, to return with the others and partake of the *hakari* whilst she remained alone with her thoughts. She wandered up through the rows of cultivations until she came to the fringe of the bush and there she sought out and found a certain *hinau* tree and, in its shade she sat and rested. The two little *tirairaka* whose sanctuary she had entered came down from the boughs above and quite reassuringly settled in the low-hanging foliage about her head. There they twittered and cavorted about as only the excitably restless tirairaka can do whilst Jane remained still and silent, deep in abstract reverie, aware of her intimate company yet preferring not to break the spell. At length she looked up to them and smiled in salutation. "As long as you the *tirairaka* remain on this earth, our female line shall flourish and there shall be no fear of death for, as one of us passes through the portal of the underworld and descends to *Rarohenga*, so another shall rise to take her place".

Jane's Story Chapter 39

Death and a Defining Moment

Her return to the orderly habitual routine of farm life at KatiKati, after the highly emotional and distressful ordeal of her mother's tangi, was to Jane a very welcome relief. She had come perilously close to total exhaustion and needed time to regain her strength and self confidence.

Life in the settlement had continued to prosper and from time to time there would be a flutter of excitement with the arrival of some distinguished visitor or other. Governor-General Lord Ranfurly was entertained in the Talisman Hotel and was delighted to meet some of his old acquaintances from the mother country. An earlier Governor, Lord Onslow also spent a night in KatiKati but his stay was quite involuntary as, while crossing the ranges to TeAroha, he got lost in the bush and was forced to seek lodgement in the settlement. R.J.Seddon was also a frequent visitor during his premiership and his well known partiality for banquets and public speeches was prudently indulged.

More picturesque perhaps but equally as dignified were two earlier tours through the district by the Maori King Tawhiao, and a few months later, TeKooti, both of whom had but recently made their peace with the New Zealand Government   In 1881, Tawhiao had come out of the King Country and laid down his guns before Major William Mair at Alexandra (now Pirongia) and in 1883, TeKooti was granted a pardon and was permitted to leave his place of refuge (also in the King Country) to return to his tribe (*Iwi*) at Whakatane. Although the mellowing years had by now presented them both as kindly old gentlemen, their sojourn however brief, did serve to remind the settlers of KatiKati that the days of conflict between

British colonial and indigenous native could not yet be forgotten and confined altogether to history. To Jane of course those two particular gentlemen held very special significance though, on each occasion, she preferred not to make herself known but remain strictly as an interested bystander.

The years of relative prosperity had also brought a higher order of society among some of the more affluent settlers and this was most evident by the number of fine houses that had begun to appear on the landscape. Mervyn Stewart at Martray, Mrs Gledstanes at Larkspur, General Stoddard at Claremont, all built homes of grand elegance. The leader's house at Mount Stewart, comprising fourteen rooms, was built on a high cliff-top within the sound of the breaking sea and surrounded by tall gums and pine trees. Castle Grace, the home of Fitzgibbon Louch, was distinguished by a lofty tower rising above a copse of trees and visible to ships far out at sea. Stables were as carefully finished as ordinary houses and grounds complete with tennis courts were all laid out in excellent routine. Perhaps the finest of them all was the home of Captain Hugh Stewart at Athenree. Built in old colonial style with wide, low verandahs trailing with wisteria and jasmine. The dining room had a gallery running along one side and crossed swords hung above the mantelpiece. The drawing room was spacious and dignified with a large bay window opening out onto a glorious view of Matakana Island and the blue Pacific Ocean. The grounds were no less attractive with trim lawns and white shelled paths, trees of every description, a vineyard in the front and an orange grove at the back.

Thus after twenty-five years, the high hopes which Vesey Stewart had held before his settlers came to fulfilment and he was able to live on contentedly enjoying the Indian summer of a calm old age. Those who remembered the wilderness into which they were thrown as pioneers in a strange and untamed land, were now at last able to reap the rich harvest of their labours and savour their just rewards. With the growth of prosperity came a halt in the decline and a natural increase in population figures which remained remarkably stable by the turn of the century.

When any group of people find themselves bonded together in kinship to face a common foe whether it be on the battlefield in war, or on some wild and unfriendly frontier in a strange and far flung land, the fellowship and camaraderie that builds amongst them grows stronger with the length of time and the magnitude of the tasks that confront them. Such was the case with the KatiKati settlers and more-so because they had almost all hailed from the same mother country. Moreover, having all "kissed the blarney stone", or its Northern equivalent, and become blessed with the flattering persuasive eloquence of the Irish, their tendency to clan together to enjoy their own mutual conviviality and entertainment, was quite endemic.

Denis Foley, who was strictly not a member of the original "Ulster Plantation" because he was already in residence when they arrived and, like Barney McDonnell and a few other non-Ulstermen, was Southern Ireland Catholic, was nevertheless gratuitously welcomed into the fold to play his part in the development of the settlement. To his credit, Denis made his full contribution towards the progress of the district and willingly enough took time out from his own busy farming operations to serve on the various community boards and committees that were all so important to the development of a progressive society. Apart from his one sorry lapse into ignominy when, in the throes of chronic alcoholism, he almost ended the lives of his wife and family as well as his own, he had since been able to moderate his heavy drinking and fraternise freely among his confreres though there were still times when the revelry would extend well into the night.

It was on one such extended evening in May 1900 that Denis, who had ostensibly left his home that afternoon to attend a meeting of the KatiKati Highway Board held, as all too conveniently, at the Uretara Hotel, decided to fortify himself against the hostile elements of a cold, wet night with one last drink or two before leaving on his long walk home. Heavy rain had been falling all that day and the Uretara Stream had already, in some places, breached its banks. Barney McDonnell, who of anyone needed no reminder of the treachery of the Uretara in flood, called to Denis as he trudged away into the darkness, to take special care as the bridge could well be under water.

Precisely what or when it happened, no-one would ever know as Denis had left the hotel on his own and it was not a night for anyone else to be out and about to witness such event. Jane and the family were not particularly concerned that he had not turned up that night as he had often slept over at the hotel when the weather was bad or when one of his "meetings" had continued late into the night. It was not until daylight next morning therefore that a fishing party, heading out into the harbour, came upon the body of Denis, bobbing up and down at the mouth of the still swollen Uretara Stream.

Fortuitously for Jane, her sons Jimmy and Harry were home on the farm at the time and were able to relieve her of the task of identifying the body and seeing to the funeral arrangements. Though she was never fully convinced that he had completely recovered from the effects of his illness and mental despondency upon his return from the institution in Auckland and after her own efforts towards his rehabilitation, she was yet painfully shocked and dismayed that he should be taken so suddenly. Despite all that had happened in the past, she had come to forgive and believe in him again and continued to abide him as her true and faithful companion as together they would advance into old age. After all, she had loved him deeply, borne his children in total and implicit faith, and contentedly shared with him the greater part of her adult life. The shock to her was as devastating as that of the passing of her mother and strangely, for the first time in her life she began to feel so very much alone.

Jimmy came to her to announce that he had been in touch with the Foley family in Auckland and that they had asked that the funeral for Denis be held there and that he be interred in the family plot in the Grafton Cemetery. Of course! thought Jane, she had almost forgotten the Foley connection in Auckland. Denis had taken her to meet his brother Thomas and sister Winifred and she was aware that there were others but that was some time ago and Denis had not maintained much contact with his family after he had come to live at KatiKati. In recent years however, Jimmy, John and Harry had all made their acquaintances with members of that branch of the family especially John who was now living in Auckland. Yes, she would agree to the request in deference to them and would cherish the reunion. She already held a sentimental attachment to the Grafton Cemetery as that was where her beloved foster father Richard Russell was laid to rest.

And so it was that at 11.00 a.m. on a chilly, sunless first day of June, the funeral procession led by an immaculately turned out hearse, drawn by two sleek black horses, their driver and his assistant adorned in their finest black livery complete with tall bell-topper hats, and a slow, shuffling column of mourners bringing up the rear, wound its way up Grafton Gully and entered the gates of the cemetery. Again, it befell the three Foley brothers to take their stations among the pall-bearers to convey the body of their father the final few yards to the graveside. There they stood with their mother and sisters sombre in their grief as the priest conducted the funeral obsequies. Noticeable among the large congregation was the number of KatiKati stalwarts who had come to farewell their worthy compatriot. With Denis now lowered into his grave and the mourners moving slowly to disperse, some lingering in kindred and intimate conversation, it was announced that a wake would be held at the residence of his brother Thomas that evening. Another wake was held for Denis at the Uretara Hotel in KatiKati as Barney McDonnell and a host of his contemporaries bade their last farewells to a champion countryman.

There had been several tragic fatalities during the development of the settlement, chiefly in the bush-felling and road construction camps but drownings also took a heavy toll, especially during the time when the only means of access to Tauranga was by sea. The Uretara River claimed many victims, notably little Bobby McDonnell, Cecil Gledstanes (from whom Jane had purchased the extra block of land), a school teacher named Wright and now, Denis Foley.

There came a time soon after the family returned to KatiKati with the loss of their beloved 'pater-familias' still weighing heavily on their minds, when Jane called them together to talk about the future and decide whither now they should go. She drew for them the analogy of a stout *Totara* tree. There was the tall trunk, straight and true, representing the founding years that they had shared together as a close-knit, hard-working pioneering family. The bumps and hollows, scars and blemishes, shades of light and darkness showing out on the way up, serving as a reminder of the good times and the bad but always, by holding fast together, emerging triumphant in the end. Now from the head of the trunk sprout the limbs, strong and healthy, exploring every direction, each capable of forming its own separate entity and preparing to venture out on its own. These are the individual members of the family who will each inevitably go their own way yet remain ever culturally as well as integrally bonded to the parent stock.

Already John and Harry had left home to pursue their personal interests among other people elsewhere and were each contemplating marriage. Sophie also had been spending more of her time away from home and Jimmy, had only just disclosed that he and his friend of kindred spirit, Jack Wallace, had volunteered for service with Her

Majesty's New Zealand Forces in South Africa and were awaiting a call-up with the 7th Contingent known as the "Rough Riders" which was to go into training in Auckland very shortly.

Thus for Jane as volitional head of the family, her defining moment had arrived and she was now compelled to make a crucial and far-reaching decision – one which would affect the future of every one of them.. Without her partner by her side, her children now grown up and some already having "flown the nest", the farm could no longer offer the same security nor KatiKati hold the same fond attachment. However regretful it might be, how many cherished memories she would leave behind, she must therefore accept that the die was now cast and she must arrange to sell up all of her property and return with her one remaining dependent daughter Margaretha-May to live in Rotorua.

Footnote: For 66 years, Denis had lain at rest in the Foley family grave located in the Roman Catholic section of the Grafton Cemetery until one day in June 1966, the family was advised in a letter from the Resident Engineer of the Ministry of Works in Auckland, that it was proposed that the graves in the area of the cemetery affected by the construction of the Auckland Urban Motorway, would be removed and re-interred in a communal site within the present cemetery. It was intended to bury the headstones and to erect, on the new site, a suitable memorial inscribed with the names and dates of decease of the re-interred. It was confirmed that the Foley grave would be one of those to be disturbed and it was suggested that should any alternative to the proposal be desired, or should the family wish to claim the headstones, an early reply would be appreciated to enable arrangements to proceed. No objections were made from Jane's branch of the family and to the best of their knowledge, the original proposals were carried out accordingly.

Jane's Story Chapter 40
The House in Whaka Road

The time has come for Jane and Margaretha-May to sever their last ties with KatiKati. Their farm and all the stock has been sold and their personal possessions and items of sentimental value loaded onto the wagon ready for the move to Rotorua. Holding hands together they stand for one last time in that favourite spot above the landing at Kauri Point, gazing at first out over the gentle blue waters of the harbour with the island of Matakana in the distance and the pohutukawa-fringed shoreline of the bay stretching away below them. Then, turning to look back across the fresh green hills and valleys of the settlement with the sombre blue ranges beyond, they behold the neat farm buildings, smoke curling up from their chimneys, the groves of fruit trees and orderly rows of sheltering plantations and they sense the mixed smells of the living countryside hanging in the morning air. Emotion wells up from within them both and the tears begin to flow. Comes now a parting of the ways. Quo vadis? Whither goest thou? *E haere ana koe keiwhea?*

At first, Jane was content to return to her old home at Hapokai on Mokoia Island. It was she who had it built in the first place for her grand aunt Mango who lived out her last days there after being returned to her people by government decree ordering the release and return to their home tribes of all captives and their descendants after the defeat of Ngapuhi at **Ruapekapeka** in 1846 in what was later known as the Heke Wars. Jane's mother, Maraea had come to join Mango during the Waikato Wars bringing Jane's Te Kirikaramu family with her and, at the end of the war and ever since, Jane had become, as she herself once described, an "itinerant lodger of convenience". However, a great many changes had taken place in more recent years, not the least of which was the perceived decline in the resident population of the island. Since the removal of the meeting house *Tamatekapua* to Ohinemutu, and the total abandonment of the Hapokai Marae as the centre of communal activity, the younger people had begun to slowly drift away to the mainland leaving only the elderly and enfeebled to live out their lives in sublime seclusion among the ghosts of their forbears. Besides, a new and exotic lifestyle had come to the heart of Te Arawa where people now lived in a modern emergent township with churches, schools, hospitals, hotels and houses. Neatly laid out streets with lamp posts, carriageways and footpaths. Employment offered for those who wished to earn a living and opportunity existed for those who wished to travel. For the young therefore, a whole new future beckoned. Living on the island was seen as a form of isolation and a move to the mainland would bring them closer to the action.

There was another reason why Jane was given cause to consider leaving Mokoia and that was the well-being of her baby Margaretha-May. 'Baby' as she would always imagine her to be though in reality she was now twenty-one years old. So fragile had she been from tiny babyhood and throughout her adolescent years that there had been times of crisis when it was only by sheer determination that Jane succeeded in bringing her safely through. Such was her susceptibility to the slightest affliction that she would always require the closest vigilance and attention. Going to live in Rotorua would therefore offer easier access to the best available medical care, even hospitalisation should that become necessary.

Through her tribal connections with Ngati Whakaue, Ngati Rangiwewehi and Ngati Uenukukopako, as owners in common of a block of land lying between the existing Rotorua township and Whakarewarewa in the South, which had been offered to the Crown by those hapu for residential development and inclusion in the town district, Jane was duly granted permission to occupy and erect a residence on a section which was later to be designated Lot 1 of Suburban Section 22 of the Suburbs of Rotorua, a triangular area at the intersection of the Rotorua-Whakarewarewa and the Rotorua-Wairoa-Maketu Roads and extending South to be bounded by a new inter-connecting street which, to her delight, Jane was invited to choose a name. She proposed '**Ti Street**' after the grove of native cabbage trees (*Ti Kouka*) which were growing on the corner.

It was not until early in the year 1902 that Jane was able to take possession of her house in 'Whaka' Road (later Fenton Street) and then to think about what she would like to do with the rest of her life. She was by then 65 years old and far from being a spent force. She still remained heavily involved in the Women's Christian Temperance Union which, since their major achievement of winning the franchise for women in 1893, had not been content to rest on its laurels but rather regarded that victory as only a first essential step in its career and had determined to carry on the fight for the introduction to parliament and the passing of several other important reforms and improvements for women including married women to be financially independent of their husbands, equal pay for equal work, better conditions for working women, the right for women to enter parliament, better treatment for prisoners and many others so that there was still plenty of work to be done. It mattered not to Jane and the many hundreds of similar souls up and down the country that they might not live to savour the ultimate fruits of their labours with the achievement of all of those objectives, they would nevertheless press on regardless, confident that in the end success would come.

In the Rotorua region alone, there were now ten WCTU branches, the largest of which was at Oninemutu which claimed a membership of more than fifty and had an elected executive of the following ladies: Emare Poraumati, president; Tui Temuera, vice-president; Jane Foley, secretary and Terita Ratema, treasurer. At Whakarewarewa a thirty strong group had elected Guide Sophia as president, Herena Taupopoki, vice-president; Guide Isobella Thom, secretary and Ani

Waaka as treasurer. At a recent social gathering in Rotorua, more than 200 members and their supporters which included several notable chiefs who had conferred their full patronage towards the movement, joined to celebrate all that had been accomplished within the Te Arawa region. These ladies came from the most influential Maori families in their respective districts and many of them would be seen to carry on and take their places as leaders in municipal, health, welfare and community affairs benefiting citizens of all races. They were not solely concerned with temperance but were also devoted to the education of the children in Bible class, sewing classes and Sunday school.

A regular visitor to Rotorua was Mrs J.D.Hewitt from Whanganui who was a dedicated promoter of the temperance movement in New Zealand and had been instrumental in setting up the inaugural Rotorua branch in 1885. At the latest function to review progress, she paid tribute to a large number of willing helpers with special mention of Mesdames Mitchell, Taupopoki, Paraumati, Foley, Clayton and Temuera. Also Miriama, Isobella and Sophia, all well-known guides at Whakarewarewa, and Miss Ratema, superintendent of Sunday schools. Jane felt very proud to be part of the team and to be included in such exalted company. Among her closest companions were the two displaced young sisters Raiha and Mereana Ratete whom Jane had taken into her care and brought to Mokoia from Tawhitinui in Ngai te Rangi shortly after the battles of Gate Pa and Te Ranga in 1864. They all lived together on Mokoia until the girls had grown up and left to live in Rotorua where eventually Raiha married Pitts Butts, a prominent businessman, and Mareana married Charles Clayton, a Crown Surveyor who had come to live at Ohinemutu.

It was after all a remarkably multifarious life that had borne Jane on the wings of destiny from a comparatively sheltered existence as school-mistress at the Anglican Mission in Auckland, to woman warrior in a bitter interracial war fraught with dreadful privation, to crusader against anti-Christian fanaticism, to devoted pioneering wife and mother in a new and unfamiliar environment, and throughout it all she gained the highest acclaim for her intimate knowledge of the languages and cultures of the two races and her ability to impart the true sentiment between them whether orally or by written submission and she had often been called upon to act as intermediary in many an important transaction between Maori and Pakeha. So popular had she become in that capacity that the demand on her time was heavy especially for the representation of Maori land owners in the Native Land Court which often required her to travel between court sessions in Rotorua, Auckland and Thames. In the furtherance of that work, she applied for and was granted a first class Maori interpreter's licence and that qualified her to join the law firm of Urquart and Rowe where she was given her own office as native agent. This then became her full time occupation and might have kept her happily engaged for the rest of her days had it not been for the sudden death of Margaretha-May.

There was no specific cause, no particular incident that might have given some warning although Jane did recall later that Margaretha had that afternoon bathed with some of her friends in one of the public hot pools in the nearby Sanatorium Gardens. She had however appeared that night to be a little more listless than usual and took herself off to bed early but in the night she became quite delirious which brought Jane hurrying to her bedside. She complained of severe pains down through her back and limbs and that her head was hurting. Jane worked frantically to abate the fever but to no avail and by morning her youngest child was dead.

Fortuitously it seemed that whenever crisis visited upon the family, Jimmy would be there for the resolution. So it was for this testing moment that he had only days beforehand returned home from the war. Jane was left totally grief-stricken with the loss of her beloved daughter following so soon after the departure of her dear mother and then her husband Denis, and she was left to wonder why God had been so wrathful and whether her faith in Him would be strong enough to carry her through the harrowing days that lay ahead.

In a short time the family began to assemble at the house in Whaka Road. There was Harry down from Frankton with his wife Mary Rebecca and their three children, Jane, Denis and baby May; John on his own as his wife had just given birth to a daughter Margarita, his sister Sophie and her adopted (*whangai*) daughter Iris, all down from Auckland. The three TeKirikaramu brothers had also arrived. Rangiteaorere, Atutahi with his son John, Te Ngahoa and his wife Mariana. It was perhaps typical of the uncompromising nature of their mother even on such a pitiably compassionate occasion, that the only surviving Te Kirikaramu daughter Rangitauninihi, had been forbidden to attend the funeral because she had only recently had a difference with Margaretha May and had slapped her face.

There then developed a lengthy and at times rather heated debate on the procedural form that the funeral for Margaretha-May should take. Rangiteaorere, as the elder brother (*tuakana*) of the family and also senior chieftain (*aho ariki*) of the subtribe (*hapu*) of Ngati Rangiteaorere, was first to lay claim on behalf of the hapu for a traditional tangi to be held at the Mataikotare Marae at Waiohewa, followed by the interment (*nehu*) in the ancestral burial ground (*urupa*) of Tokanui on the island of Mokoia. This naturally, was a very strong claim and would have been acceded to without question had it not been for the unexpected intervention by Jane herself who was to make a quite confounding declaration.

Whether it was the result of her recent involvement with the WCTU and the new order that had come to the nation with the need for its people to adopt a more enlightened, Christian outlook, or simply that the past held too many sad memories for her and that she did not feel up to going through it all again, we shall never know, but after many hours of impassioned argument, she remained adamant that Margaretha-May should have an ordinary European style Christian funeral. She announced that she had reserved a plot in the Anglican section of the Rotorua Cemetery which would now be known as the Foley Family Grave and that henceforth all descendants of Denis Foley should be buried therein.

And so it was that the casket containing the body of Margaretha-May was brought to lay in solemn repose on the front verandah of the house in Whaka Road. Her truly extended family (*whanau*) of Te Kirikaramu and Foley standing in silent vigil over her to acknowledge mourners who came from far and wide to pay their last respects. Some were led by distinguished chiefs and elders who addressed the dead with traditional Maori oratory (*whaikorero*) and lament (*waiata*) whilst others advanced singly or in groups to stand in silence, their heads bowed in sorrow for the innocent young life that had been taken. Then followed a short Anglican church service conducted by the Reverend F.A.Bennett before the hearse was summoned to convey the casket and lead the long funeral procession to the Rotorua Cemetery where the final burial service was consummated and Margaretha-May was to become the first of the family to be laid to rest in the newly acquired Foley family grave.

As the sorely aggrieved Jane stood at the foot of the open grave and gazed with unseeing eyes down upon the polished *rimu* coffin now sprinkled with grains of white pumice sand from the loving hands of those who filed past in silent veneration, for the first time in her life she despaired that the inimitable self-determination upon which she had relied to carry her through the most desperate of times, was now about to fail her. Would she still be able to find the strength to cast aside this latest painful infliction and rise again above the hopelessness and dejection to carry on with life however much lonelier it might be or, perhaps more pointedly, would she really wish to do so?

Jane's Story Chapter 41

March of Time, Grief and War

In the years following the turn of the nineteenth century, there developed a great deal of action in the Native Land Courts with tribes (*hapu*) being forced into registering the ownership of their ancestral lands which, in the past had never been brought into dispute. Tribal land was always looked upon as a living entity, the mythological female deity (*Papatuanuku*) from which the first human life form (*ira tangata*) had sprung. It was not a question of people owning the land but more of the land owning the people. Hapu were there to share and preserve their motherland and where necessary, fight to the death to defend it from invading hapu. *"He kura tangata e kore a rokohanga; he kura whenua he rokohanga"* ("A valorous people may fall away, but the enduring land will remain forever").

With the mounting predominance of the Colonial (pakeha) Government however, a whole new interpretation of land ownership was introduced and imposed upon the Maori perception. Whereas traditional tribal lands were shared equally and in common not only among the members of the local hapu but also any newcomers to the tribe who had come to live through inter-marriage or some mutual alliance, without exception or reservation, there was now to be instituted an entirely new process called private property ownership. The first indications that all was not as it used to be, came when tribal land released to the early European settlers including church missionaries, for the establishment of their dwellings and mission stations, was immediately fenced off and declared out of bounds to the original inhabitants.

That was perhaps the most confusing and alien device ever inflicted upon the Maori, to be made so acutely aware that parts of their ancestral lands would no longer be accessible to them once they were given over to the Pakeha. Then, after the establishment of the Native Land Court, they should be obliged to provide proof to the Court of their rightful ownership which was something that could only be done by evidence of continuous occupation, in order to register title to their lands,. Such was the extent of disruption among the tribes with the introduction of these new laws, that Native Land Courts were set up throughout the country and hearings were being held almost continuously.

Special procedures were developed for the processing of title investigations and land transactions, requiring representation of the highest jurisprudence. Native Land Court judges were especially selected and appointed for their intimate knowledge and appreciation of the Maori language, custom, folklore and tradition (*tikanga Maori*). The number qualified to fulfil that role was understandably few yet they became highly respected among the Maori who acknowledged them as wise men of the most noble pre-eminence (*mana*). There evolved also a fraternity of native advocates, totally bilingual and fully trained in court procedures, to represent the native owners in what would be to them an entirely new and daunting experience. From these humble beginnings, there emerged some very big reputations with names like Sir Apirana Ngata, Sir James Carroll, Sir Maui Pomare – men who went on to become exalted members of the New Zealand Government. In Rotorua there were such men as Kepa Ehau, Raniera Kingi, Kata Thompson, Tai Mitchell and others who came to excel in court presentation by blending their natural gifted oratorical eloquence with a classical adaptation of the English language to serve their people with grand and distinguished application. And, one of the earliest members of this august body of devotees was one very special female personality called Jane Foley or **Heeni Pore.**.

By her work in the courts, Jane was soon to gain a reputation as a strictly no-nonsense pragmatist. She based her philosophy on the principle of truth being the doctrine of practical consequence and she would apply it without prejudice or favour towards friend or opponent alike. As her success as an advocate became more widely known, so more and more people came to her door in search of her wise counsel and attestation. Many of them would be tribal chiefs and men of the highest esteem (*mana*) among their peers yet were now to find themselves confused and befuddled with the new laws and demands that had been thrust upon them however willing they were to respect and abide by them. And whilst they would be regarded as wealthy in respect of the vast tracts of land that they controlled, they often did not possess pecuniary wealth in the form of money in the bank. In truth, for many of them the only means of obtaining such wealth was to sell land to the Pakeha and, to the unconscionable discredit of some sharp operators posing as Government agents, that situation was often shamelessly exploited to the full.

To Jane however, she came to accept that payment for her services would not always be settled in cash but, she had not the slightest doubt, would be honoured in some other way. And sure enough, by the end of her career she was to find herself in possession of several small parcels of land and articles of great value (*taonga*) bestowed upon her in token of gratitude and the huge respect and esteem in which she was held among the people of the land (*tangata whenua*). Among such *taonga* were two ceremonial greenstone clubs one of which was named *tokauea*, an exquisitely crafted *mere* which was steeped in tribal history and had been handed down through many generations. Jane was to treasure this throughout the rest of her life and, upon her death, she had willed it to her eldest son Jimmy and any other surviving member of her (Foley) family "to be kept and enjoyed by them as an heirloom".

And so after a sad beginning marked by the loss of her husband

Denis to be followed so soon after with the untimely departure of her cherished baby daughter, Jane saw the first decade of the new century come to an end with the prospect of the next one being hopefully much brighter and happier than the last. Her eldest son Jimmy had come home from the war to live with her permanently in the house in Whaka Road and had established his own contracting business. Though he was the eldest of her (Foley) family, he was the only one as yet un-married and seemed to be in no hurry to remedy the situation. Jane by now had been blessed with five grandchildren and she was always delighted to have them come to see her. Her work in the courts was keeping her fully occupied and she would always be happy to continue her activities with the WCTU.

Rotorua had become by now a Mecca for tourists from all around the world and a compelling first stop for visiting Royalty and other famous celebrities. A high standard of guest accommodation and hospitality had been encouraged by the town fathers to cater for this most welcome, stimulating and lucrative industry. Other civic amenities had been introduced or improved upon with public buildings, hospitals, nursing homes, and bath buildings all given a facelift, and an ambulance service and fire brigade, up-graded and reformed. The railway station, post office, bath-houses and sanatorium grounds were first to be lit by electricity from a power generation plant installed at Okere Falls near Taheke at the outlet of Lake Rotoiti making Rotorua only the fourth community in New Zealand with Reefton in the South Island, Wellington and Stratford, to be supplied with electricity at the time. Jane was also to see the advent of the motor car when in the year 1902 a Dr. and Mrs Humphrey Haines arrived from Auckland after covering the distance in two days, and by 1904, a group of motorists from the Auckland Automobile Association had organised a run to Rotorua to coincide with the summer carnival. It was not long afterwards that motor coaches were making an appearance on the main passenger routes. She was also privileged to attend the first showing of motion pictures in the town when kinematograph operator A.J. (Archie) MacDermot presented a feature film covering the Royal visit of the Duke and Duchess of York in 1901. The decade also saw the passing of several of Jane's old wartime comrades three of whom were Te Keepa Rangipuawhe, Ieni Tapihana (Tapsell) and, the hero of the siege of Te Teko, Te Pokiha Taranui (Major Fox).

Alas however, the second decade for Jane was to turn out even worse than the first. It began quite uneventfully but in March 1913, her son John, who was married and living in Auckland with his wife and only child, Margarita (Rita), was admitted to hospital with what was diagnosed as terminal cancer of the bowel and, within only a few days he died. How long he had been suffering before seeking professional treatment, no-one would ever know but the shock of his sudden and untimely death was profound and the effect on his immediate family in Auckland proved to be quite devastating. To Jane it was another debilitating blow which left her to wonder just how much more she would be able to withstand. Though she loved all of her family intensely, she had secretly held out a special hope for John that he would carry on to pursue an academic career which was something she herself would like to have done had fate not determined otherwise. The omnipresent Jimmy, once again found himself in the role of family master of the moment as he at once left for Auckland to bring the body of his brother home to Rotorua, there to be laid before his grieving extended family and finally, to be buried in the family grave alongside his little sister Margaretha-May. John was only 44 years old.

The memory of John's funeral and his laying to rest in the Rotorua cemetery amidst the grief and anguish of his bereaved family still fresh in her mind and sparing little of its intensity, Jane was soon to experience such further and much more far-reaching trepidation in the shape of war clouds descending upon all of the people of New Zealand, emanating from the flames of discontent in Europe on the other side of the world and sweeping down over the surface of the oceans to envelop all nations great and small. It was to be known as The Great War, the war to end all wars, World War 1. A conflict that would involve forty percent of the available New Zealand male population amounting to 100,000 men and of these, 17,000 would lose their lives. A call to arms that would shake this young country to its very foundations yet such strains and sacrifices would be met unflinchingly. It was only a matter of time therefore that her descendants from both families, Te Kirikaramu and Foley should answer the call to become again a family at war.

Of her Te Kirikaramu family, the three sons of Te Ngahoa; Wi Martin, Joseph Te Raki and Aperahama Te Kiri, were among the first to enlist with the initial contingent of 500 Maori volunteers who sailed for Egypt on the troopship "Warrimoo" on 19 February 1915 and, in June that year, they landed in Anzac Cove, Gallipoli to join the conflict against Turkey which culminated, after three months of the heaviest fighting, in the battle of Sari Blair when they succeeded in dislodging and destroying the enemy at the point of the bayonet after which they celebrated with a tremendous haka which was enough to send more Turks into retreat. October 1915 and by then gravely depleted in numbers, they were withdrawn from Gallipoli and retired to Egypt to await the arrival of the second and third Maori reinforcements when they were re-organised into the Pioneer Battalion (*Te Hokowhitu a tu*) made up of 'A' and 'B' Companies. Second in command of 'A' Company was Captain Roger Dansey, son of R.D.Dansey the postmaster of Rotorua and who had already acquitted himself with valour in the battle of Sari Blair and, in 'B' Company, there was a well known veteran of the Boer War, H.R.(Te Reiwhati) Vercoe of Ngati Pikiao, now promoted to second lieutenant. It was Te Reiwhati who wrote home to say that Gallipoli had been bad for Te Arawa with all but twelve of his unit killed, wounded or missing. In April 1916, the battalion was sent to France to fight alongside the allied forces in all their major battles including

Messines, Passchendaele, Ypres and the Somme, until at last the conflict came to an end.

Meanwhile Jimmy Foley, who at 48 years of age was by then well over the military age limit for active service, had somehow managed to have himself accepted for the 14th reinforcements of the New Zealand Army Services Corps which embarked from Wellington in June 1916 on the troopship "SS Tahiti", arriving at Devonport, England via Capetown and West Africa in August of that year. He was then transferred to the New Zealand Mounted Rifles and sent to France where his unit was immediately drafted into the Otago Mounted Rifles which regiment had only recently suffered dreadful, almost annihilating losses when they had been ordered to dismount from their horses and advance with the infantry in a bayonet charge against almost impossible odds. In France he was able to meet up with several old friends and acquaintances and also his three nephews who were quite astounded to see him appearing in uniform amongst them as they all thought that he would be much too old. Among those who were also surprised to see him was Reiwhati Vercoe, now a Captain, who recognised him at once from his Boer War days when he (Vercoe) was a very young troop sergeant in charge of a mounted patrol at Klipfontein in the Transvaal when Jimmy was very much his senior in all but rank. "You bloody old fool" he roared as he seized his hand, "What the hell are you doing here? You don't know what you've let yourself in for." But Jimmy was not to be deterred. After all, he reflected, life for him had never exactly been a bed of roses.

Jimmy's sojourn on the Western Front however, ended in December 1917 when he was invalided back to camp in Torquay, England among a batch of walking wounded. There he was able to recover sufficiently to continue with his lifelong vocation of breaking in horses which kept him fully occupied until the end of the war. It was while he was encamped at Salisbury in those final months that, because of his widespread renown as a masterly horse-breaker he was one day summoned before his commanding officer to be introduced to the keeper of the Royal Stables who invited him to come up to London to exercise his special skills in the inducement of the white horse used by King George V on ceremonial occasions, to kneel on command to enable his master to mount and dismount with ease. Although it would never be openly discussed, it was nevertheless intimated that for an ageing person of His Majesty's rather rotund stature and physique, such alleviation of physical effort would be received with the most regal approbation. It might be said therefore that this was to become the "crowning glory" of Jimmy's extraordinarily diversified life as he was not only to succeed in his mission but also to share in the Royal congratulations for a job well done.

As with anxious mothers all over the world, those with sons away at the front looked to each new day with trepidation that the postman might call with that dreaded telegram from the war office, and Jane, in her house in Whaka Road, Rotorua, on the other side of the world in far away New Zealand, was no less exposed to that sinister gnawing agony. The local thrice-weekly newspaper, the *Hot Lakes Chronicle* would always publish the latest list of casualties for the Rotorua region on its front page together with any available photographs and whatever other personal information they could glean from the official records. The post office had also set up a public notice board outside its new premises on the corner of Fenton and Arawa Streets to display the latest bulletins as they came to hand.

Personal contact between sons at the front and anxiously awaiting families at home was always sparse as young men generally were not prolific writers and the very occasional postcard was about all that any family might realistically hope for. Jane received her own meagre and quite irregular allocation of postcards from Jimmy for which she considered herself lucky, but for many other mothers, the Maori ones in particular, written word from their sons (*tamaroa*) was practically non-existent and theirs was but to live in hope and prayer. Jimmy had been gone a year now and, from the ever-lengthening lists of casualties being displayed on the town notice board, there was no sign of the conflict abating. The need for reinforcements was still being regarded as urgent and there was even talk of extending conscription to Maori although most tribal leaders had dismissed the idea as being unnecessary.

As for Jane herself, she was now approaching the age of 80 and, iron willed as she had always been, the anxiety brought on by the war, and her concern for not only her own family but all others of her country in conflict, had taken its toll until she at last had come to feel despair. But as the weight of years pressed ever unrelenting upon her now wearied and waning resolution, her thoughts were tuned to the future generations and the legacy that her time on this earth should leave them and she realised that there remained just one more duty that she must perform.

Jane's Story Chapter 42

Mokoia Heritage

For sure, Jane thought, it would not be long into the twentieth century before the ownership of Mokoia Island would have to be established. The Rotorua region, fast becoming a popular tourist attraction with its pristine, as yet unspoiled lakes district and scenery, its awesome thermal activity and its colourful conglomerate of Maori culture, lifestyle and hospitality, interest in the Island for the establishment of a luxury tourist resort was becoming widespread and already several tribal authorities were being approached by would-be entrepreneurs. Already also there were several motorised launches plying the tourist trade from the waterfront at Rotorua on what was billed as "The Six Lakes Trip" with overnight stays at the various places of special attraction around the region. Having Mokoia as the central dispersal point of all this activity therefore would, for the tourist industry, be of exceptional appeal.

However, to the true descendants of Mokoia, their home was steeped in ancient history and the thought of parting with any of it, especially to the Pakeha who would insist on fencing it off and turning it into private property as was his way, and therefore deprive its original owners of any rights of access forever, would be totally contradictory to their way of life and could not be entertained under any circumstances. Mokoia to them, had from time immemorial been a sanctuary, a refuge in time of danger and a place of common occupation for Te Arawa. Its summit, which is named *Te pari o tama whakaikai* , and had since become the burial ground of high chiefs, was the place where the fabled Te Arawa hero, **Hatupatu** emerged after calling on the earth to open up and swallow him as he fled from **Kurangaituku,** the goddess mother of the birds of the forest when she was alerted by the fantail (*tirairaka*) that Hatupatu had been snaring and eating some of her children. Hatupatu was so relieved to have escaped her wrath that he took a frond of *totara* from his headband and planted it on the highest point of the island where in time it grew into a giant tree.

The lower slopes of Mokoia were also the hiding place of the famous idol, *Uenukukopako,* which had not seen the light of day for many generations. It is hewn from some strange trachytic stone, stands about 1.5 metres high and is modelled on the image of the eponymous ancestor of the Uenukukopako hapu. It was last uncovered during a visit to the island by Governor Sir George Grey in 1866 when *Pango* the resident high priest (*tohunga ahurewa*) was persuaded to unearth it from an ancient temple site (*tuahu*) near the Eastern shore of the lake. An attempt was also made at that time to locate the bones of *Tuhourangi,* son of *Rangitihi* and high chief of the Tuhourangi hapu who lived in about the sixteenth century. It is said that he was a giant of a man standing three metres tall. Although his first resting place was known to the old tohunga and marked by slabs of stone, it was obvious that his remains had long since been shifted from there and also that they were not likely to be found on that day even though the true whereabouts would have been known to more than one of the elders present. It had always been feared by some however, that the bones of Tuhourangi had been removed by *Hongi Hika* and his *Ngapuhi* and taken to *Taitokarau* after his victory in the battle of Mokoia in 1823 although this has never been conceded nor verified and it must therefore be accepted that they remain just where they were intended to be – somewhere on the island.

It was also during the visit of Sir George in 1866 that he was presented with the small stone kumara god (*atua kumara*) named *Matua a tonga* which he took with him on his return to Auckland where it was kept as part of the 'Grey Collection' until some years later when it was transferred to the Auckland Museum before ultimately being returned to Mokoia where it remains to this day. As mentioned earlier in Jane's story, *Matua a tonga* is not its proper name as, according to ancient legend, *Rakeiora* who was the navigating priest of the *Tokomaru* Canoe, settled near the *Mohakatino* River in North-western *Taranaki* where the *Tokomaru* had landed after its voyage from *Hawaiki*. It was there that Rakeiora introduced the sweet potato (*kumara*) to the land and, so prolific was its fertility in the Mohakatino district, that Rakeiora became famous and was deified by his people as a kumara god. His fame soon spread abroad and that led to a raid on Mohakatino by *Tauwhare* and *Patuone* who headed a marauding Te Arawa war party (*amiowhenua*) whose objective it was to steal the material symbol (*aria*) of Rakeiora which was in the form of a little stone idol, and carry it off to Te Arawa where it would bring high fertility to the kumara of that region. They named it *Ṃatua a tonga* meaning "Father after the manner of the South" and housed it in its own little shrine on Mokoia Island.

Then there is the ancient *totara* tree named *Atua ahu* which stands at the edge of the lake and marks the landing place of the great war canoe that brought the body of *Tuhourangi* to its last resting place on the island. Thus the tree to which the canoe was tied after it had landed with its highly venerated (*tapu*) and lamentably mourned cargo of death, was referred to by the high priest (*tohunga ahurewa*) who conducted the burial rites (*nehu*), as the symbolic link between vibrant life as depicted by the ever restless waves of the lake, and ultimate death represented by the tree firmly rooted to the earth that forever lays still. The tree was therefore named *Atua ahu* and thenceforth became enshrined to mark that memorable occasion.

In another time, it was in the thermal pool named *Waikimihia* that *Hinemoa* rested after her epic swim from the mainland at *Owhata* (now Hinemoa's Point), across the lake to Mokoia to join her lover, *Tutanekai* and thus eternalise perhaps the greatest Maori love story ever told. Her father, *Umukaria*, high chief of the Tuhourangi, had refused Tutanekai of Ngati Whakaue the hand of his daughter in marriage and had forbidden them both to see each other. To make sure that Hinemoa would not try to run away and elope with her lover, he ordered all of the canoes to be drawn up high above the shore line and placed under heavy guard day and night. At his home on Mokoia, the heartbroken Tutanekai yearned so much for his loved one that he could not bear to live without her. Each night he would sit on a hilltop overlooking the lake and play his flute (*koauau*) so that the plaintive, lilting melody would float across the waters on the evening breeze with its message of sweet love to Hinemoa lying fretful in her father's house.

One very dark and moonless night, when all was still and the sounds of Tutanekai's flute came drifting over the waters of the lake, Hinemoa stole silently out of the house and down past the sleeping guards to the beach where she quietly entered the water and swam towards the enchanting strains of the flute of Tutanekai. On and on she swam and all the while the music of the flute drew her ever nearer until at last her feet touched the ground and she heard the lapping of the waves on the shore. By then she was completely exhausted and she knew that she would have to rest. It was then also that she found the entrance to the warm pool called *Waikimihia* and she crawled through to lay in its soothing waters. In a short while she looked up to see a man-servant (*mokai wheteke*) holding a calabash (*ipu*) of fresh water that he had collected from a nearby spring. She motioned to him to hand her the ipu and, after drinking from it she smashed it against a rock. The servant left in despair to return a short time later with a new calabash which he filled from the spring, and again Hinemoa took it from him, drank from it and smashed it against the rocks. This time the servant ran to his master Tutanekai and told him of the stranger in the pool that was breaking his water bottles. At once an enraged Tutanekai strode down to the pool to despatch this insolent intruder but, when he arrived there he stood astounded. It was his beloved Hinemoa smiling up at him with the most mischievous look in her eye. Gently he lifted her out of the water and carried her in his arms up to his fine house on the hill and there they lived together happily ever after.

To Jane however, as with all of the living elders whose ancestral heritage was bound infinitively with Mokoia, the much more recent history of the devastating raid by **Hongi Hika** and his **Ngapuhi** and the resulting deaths of so many of their kinsfolk (*whanaunga*) still remained uppermost in her mind. Right from her earliest memories, she had tried to picture the scene of shocking carnage that had descended upon the normally peaceful, pastoral fields of their homeland on that terrible day. Her mortally wounded grandfather, **Te Ngahoa** lying on the battlefield, his life slowly ebbing away, and his proudly, defiant wife, **Rangi tauninihi** standing protectively over him until at last she too fell victim to the relentless, overwhelming Ngapuhi horde. The vast burial grounds (*urupa*), so drastically extended as the result of that action, two on the lower ground and the one high up on the summit where the fighting chiefs now lie. Hallowed ground all. By its proud and illustrious history, both ancient and modern, as handed down and exemplified on the marae, there could be no thought now nor ever, of relinquishing possession of any of the sacred soil of their homeland (*papakainga*).

But to reach consensus among the several hapu whose ancestors came to live on the island, inter-married, took part in the many battles of the period and thereby claimed rights of occupation, there was much work to be done to bring everyone together and prepare a joint submission to the Native Land Court. It thus became the ultimate determination of Jane by virtue of her standing as the oldest living elder (*kaumatua*) and also her wide experience in Court procedures that she should see the matter of registration of ownership of Mokoia Island written into law. This would require a mass meeting (*hui*) of all owners or their advocates where they would put forward hereditary claims based on evidence of ancestral genealogy (*whakapapa*) from one or more of the sub-tribes (*hapu*) having occupational rights.

Several such hui were held around the region at which some very heated argument had evolved as people of one hapu, even close families (*whanau*), would declare superiority over the other. Jane observed that the claim on behalf of the hapu of *Ngati Rangiteaorere* was being confidently represented by her eldest son, *Rangiteaorere* who could claim descent through his father (*Te Kirikaramu*) on the male side and his great grandmother, *Rangitauninihi* on his mother's. Jane could also make strong representation on her own behalf and therefore that of her Foley family, through the hapu of *Ngati Uenukukopako* where a direct line of descent could be established from *Whakatauihu,* who was paramount chief on Mokoia at the end of the sixteenth century, down through her mother, *Maraea*.

So the case for the claimants was duly prepared and the first of several hearings of the Rotorua Court began early in 1915 and proceeded for several months until at last Judge C.E.MacCormick pronounced his final decision on 16 November 1916 (in Jane's 80th year). The full pronouncement was to occupy several closely typed foolscap pages and whilst it cannot be reproduced here in its entirety, some of the salient points made by the Judge have however been selected if only to show the complexity of the case that was put before him, the profound and acute sagacity he displayed in making his judgement, and the outcome that had resulted.

Judge MacCormick began his address as follows: "This is about the most unsatisfactory case in this Court's experience. The evidence is a mass of contradiction, and the parties are so mixed up that it is impossible to deal with them as hapus (sic). The Court finds a mother against her children, brother against brother, uncle against nephew and so on. And all the hapus are broken up amongst the different parties. There should have been four cases set up instead of twenty."

"*Ngati Rangiteaorere* claim the whole island. This claim is so completely disproved by the evidence in former cases that Court can only express its wonder at the party thinking it worthwhile to set it up. They must have a very low opinion of the Court's intelligence. I do not propose to set out in detail all the evidence against this claim as the references are all in the minute book but one or two may be pointed out. There is also the evidence of (the late) Te Kirikaramu himself who declared that his father, *Awekotuku* was a chief of both Ngati Rangiteaorere and Ngati Uenukukopako, and who further stated that Ngati Whakaue's first pa was at *Kaiweka*. He also said *"Ngati Rangiteaorere is my hapu. Ngati Uenukukopako is my tribe. Ngati Hinepare is a hapu of Ngati Whakaue"*. The evidence as to the fights of Putu o Tongara and other battles of the same period shows that the two hapus, Ngati Rangiteaorere and Ngati Uenukukopakao, were always associated and came together from Mokoia on several occasions. Te Umu himself belonged to both hapus. There is not a tittle of proof that the sole right to Mokoia came from Rangiteaorere. My opinion is that these two hapus are practically one and the same people – at all events all the principal members of them are descendants of both ancestors and have been welded together by continuous intermarriages from the time of the children of the ancestors to the present day".

"The claim of the party represented by Wi Karena (Wi Hape) that the whole island belongs to *Ngati Uenukukopako* only must also fail. The sudden change of front by *Heeni Pore* of their party has had no real effect upon the mind of the Court. Quite apart from that there is ample evidence that Ngati Rangiteaorere have a right. It is plain also from former cases that *Ngati Whakaue* have a right. Te Kirikaramu's evidence has been referred to. There is a great body of other testimony. The references given by Raureti may especially be mentioned as showing that some hapus of Ngati Whakaue have a right. The Court is clear that both Ngati Whakaue and Ngati Uenukukopako have rights, but it does not follow that all the members of those large hapus have had occupation. The witness for Ngati Uenukukopako, Mita Tuhuruhuru, admits the right of *Ngati Rangiwewehi* – so do several other witnesses. On the other hand a number strongly deny their claim. There is less support of this claim to be gathered from former cases than there is with respect to the other three main hapus, nevertheless after a careful consideration of the evidence the Court holds that their right is established

"The Court then finds that Mokoia belongs to the four hapus: Ngati Rangiteaorere, Ngati Uenukukopako, Ngati Whakaue and Ngati Rangiwewehi and that all the cases set up come under one or more of those main hapus. A very great many boundaries have been given by the different witnesses. Each disagrees with the other. A glance at the sketch map prepared will show the great variety of the boundaries. There is some evidence of an attempt a number of years ago to settle boundaries by agreement, but it is too inconclusive to act upon. It seems probable that the main occupation of the hapus has been on the part of the island nearest their mainland headquarters, that is, Ngati Whakaue in the South, Ngati Rangiwewehi in the North-west with Ngati Rangiteaorere and Ngati Uenukukopako in the East and North-east, but the Court cannot find any definite boundary line between them. The Court would have liked to have made its award according to hapus but has found that impossible owing to the manner in which the hapus have split up among themselves. So that the award must be according to the separate parties before the Court."

Judge MacCormick then went on to refer briefly to each of the 18 cases of these parties, approving some and reducing or dismissing others completely until he arrived at a total of 16 claims which varied in validity according to the evidence put before him. He created

1002 shares, that is to say three shares to the acre, and after full consideration, divided them among the parties as follows:

Claim		Hapu (Origin)	Shares
1)	Rangiteaorere te Kiri and party	Rangiteaorere	139
2)	Wi Kingi and party	Whakaue	120
3)	Wi Matene and party	Rangiteaorere & Uenukukopako	125
4)	Karaitiana Kowhai and party	Ngati Manawa (Whakaue)	70
5)	Kiwi Te Amohau and party	Whakaue	35
6)	Wi Ereatara and party	Rangiwewehi	90
7)	Arama Karaka and party	Rangiteaorere & Uenukukopako	55
8)	Hohepa te Rake and party	Rangiteaorere & Uenukukopako	90
9)	Mita Tuhuruhuru, Heeni Pore and party	Uenukukopako	139
10)	Maria Hamiora and party	Uenukukopako	100
11)	Whare Hooro and party	Rangiteaorere	6
12)	Mariana te Ohu and party	Whakaue	6
13)	Haki Tamati and party	Whakaue	9
14)	Miri o Raukawa and party	Uenukukopako	6
15	Tiaki Awa and party	Uenukukopako	6
16)	Tonohopu te Teira	Whakaue	6
		Total:	1002 shares

It seems therefore that the allocation of shares to each hapu, through some magic formula known only to Judge MacCormick, had fallen into place almost precisely as he had envisaged and that each received their fair and appropriate proportion. That is to say that Uenukukopako, being the most heavily represented hapu received the largest portion of 386 shares or 38%, followed by Rangiteaorere (28%), Whakaue (25%) and Rangiwewehi (9%), in order of preference. If, as the Judge suggested, the two hapus (Rangiteaorere and Uenukukopako) are "practically one and the same people", and their respective allocations were added together, it would give them 666 shares or 66% of the total which would not be unrealistic considering the weight of evidence presented.

With the establishment of ownership now resolved, Mokoia Island then became Maori Freehold Land by Freehold Order of the Maori Land Court. It was always Jane's wish however that the island would forever remain in the possession of its Maori owners and that the title would be vested in Court- appointed Trustees having as their object the preservation and improvement of the Island and its areas of special significance, and the promotion of tribal interests. And while she was to devote the rest of her days working towards that end, sadly, inasmuch as the wheels of justice oft'times become mired in their own deliberation, she was not to see its fulfilment as such order was not effected until 17 January 1953 - just 20 years after she departed this world to join her tipuna in the land from which no messenger returns (*karere kore ki muri*).

Jane's Story Chapter 43

Journey's End

The year was 1919 and Jimmy had not long been home from the war. He had lost little time in shedding his uniform and literally "converting his swords to plough shares" as he quickly and happily resumed his old occupation as an agricultural contractor with his team of working horses and variety of farm implements. Of course his preferred pursuit would always remain the breaking-in of young horses for which service he was to find no scarcity of demand around the freshly revitalised farming district. He had been happy to move back into the house in Whaka Road with his elderly mother who was glad to have her favourite son safely home again.

However, it was not long before Jane's ever astute powers of observation were to discern a distinct change of character that had come over Jimmy since his return. He would become absent-minded when she was speaking to him and would often respond as though he hadn't heard a word she had said. He would also absent himself for days at a time without telling anybody or offering an explanation. Such odd happenings were to continue for several weeks and, whilst Jane refused to be overly concerned, she could not help wondering just what it was that was causing the change. Then one afternoon, Jimmy drove up in his immaculately turned out buggy and pair with a very special passenger on board. It was Maggie, his sweet young bride. "Yes Mama" he called to Jane, "I am 50 years old, but good things sometimes do take time".

Maggie was the daughter of *Alfred Clayton* (1859 – 1913), a Crown Surveyor who came to New Zealand with his elder brother Charles in 1878, from their family estate of *Longford*, near Launceston in Tasmania which was founded by William and Sarah Clayton of

Lincolnshire, England in 1805. Her mother was *Hikapuhi Poihipi* of *Ngati Rangiunuora*, a subtribe of *Ngati Pikiao* of *Te Arawa*, a gifted spiritualistic medium (*matakite*) and highly revered among her own people. Although opportunities for his children to receive much more than a basic education in the frontier regions in which he was required to work and live would be extremely limited, Alfred Clayton insisted that they take all that was offering and he would also supplement that with valuable special lessons of his own. At nineteen years of age therefore, Maggie was perfectly competent to manage the house in Whaka Road and, however reluctant Jane might have been to relinquish her authority, her advancing years would indicate that the time had come for her to stand aside. It would take time for her to get used to the idea, but secretly she was relieved that again it was Jimmy who had stepped up when the hard decisions were there to be made, just as he had done so many times before, and for that she would be eternally grateful.

Of course it was to be expected that early complications would arise during the initial settling in period with Jane, who had always been very set in her ways, finding it difficult to adjust to any new changes that Maggie wished to introduce. She had however insisted on clinging to her own familiar routines and, as long as she was left alone to indulge in them, she would not interfere. On Maggie's part however, she was to find that her worries would be compounded with the endless stream of humanity that seemed to be attracted to the house in Whaka Road. It was not as simple as only having to look after her elderly mother-in-law and abide by her whims and fancies, but she also found herself having to accommodate at any time, day or night, any number of a wide variety of visitors, mostly arriving unexpected and un-announced and always hungry and looking for a bed. Most were family who had come to visit their old matriarch (*kuia*) and stay a few days, others were casual visitors - journalists, historians, Church dignitaries and old friends - all coming to interview and pay their respects to the grand old lady.

Jimmy didn't help either as he was always arriving home with some social dropout or other whom he would find homeless and jobless, "down and out" as was the term used to describe them, victims of the difficult times that the country was going through. It was just his hugely hospitable nature that compelled him to extend a helping hand to anyone worse off than himself. However, that did not make Maggie's work any easier. Then there came the additional burden of Harry, her disgruntled and brooding brother-in-law with whom she would always feel slightly uncomfortable and hesitant. He had come to stay permanently at his mother's house after his wife Mary, for reasons known only to herself, had run away and left him. Fortunately though, their children were all grown up and capable of looking after themselves. The eldest, Jane, was already married and expecting her first child, and the other two, Denis and May were also making their own way in life although they had elected to come with their father. There was yet one other addition to the household and that was Rita, the daughter of the late John Foley and whom Jimmy had more or less adopted as his own after her father's death.

Maggie, however did not mind having these young people around her in the least. Whilst being married to their uncle Jimmy made her their privileged aunt, they did not incline to see her as such because they were all born of the same generation and were happy to share in and enjoy a youthfully jubilant companionship. And so though life from then on was busy, sometimes chaotic when the numbers of guests outgrew the capacity of the kitchen and the available bed space, Maggie was able to cope although her workload would at times reach almost impossible proportions. Once when the girls asked her how she had chosen to marry such an old man, her cheerful reply was, "Oh, I had heard that a girl could be either an old man's darling or a young man's slave". Ruefully though, as it turned out for Maggie, she was to become both an old man's darling and a slave to his extended family. Yet she remained cheerful and uncomplaining throughout it all and, in the following year, she gave birth to their first child, a gorgeous little girl who they named Winifred Rosaline after her father's favourite aunt.

In the silence of the wayside clearing where the buggy had stopped to rest at the top of the hill, Jimmy could look out over the bush to the North and catch a glimpse of the sea sparkling through the blue haze in the distance. The bush itself was bathed in sunlight, a tableau-vivant of shining leaves and shifting shadows dancing on the morning breeze. How often had he gazed across this familiar vista of vibrant native New Zealand bush with its ever changing pattern of colour, its fragrance sometimes sweet and warm, sometimes sharp and pungent, its birdsong rich and mellow, pealing and resonating through the leafy cathedral halls of nature to blend in harmony with the soughing refrain of the wavering wind. A magnificent and enthralling testimony that had never failed to hold him in absolute wonder and fascination right from the days when he was a boy growing up in KatiKati.

The horses were becoming restless now, stamping the ground impatiently, snorting and tossing their heads up and down, tugging at the reins. They were ready to be on their way and were eagerly awaiting the command from their master. Jimmy was all too aware of their mood as he was himself keen to move on. The sun was quite high in the sky and there were many miles to go before they would reach Maketu. He had not been keen on taking his old mother on such a long journey in the first place but she was so insistent that it was her duty to attend such an important gathering of the tribes (*hui tau*) on the ancient Te Arawa marae of **Kawatapuarangi**, where her esteemed presence and wise counsel had been earnestly requested. He could feel her frail body snuggled up against his side, restful and unmoving, and he could sense that she was still wrapped in deep and all-absorbing thought into which, however reluctant he was to do so, he must now obtrude. He passed an arm around the warm and motionless bundle curled up beside him and gently shook his old mother awake. "Come along Mama" he called, "time for us to move on".

Slowly she stirred into wakefulness as the scene about her returned into focus: the horses stamping and swinging their bodies restlessly, the tall trees reaching up to the sky, the sun shining through the branches throwing light and shadow across the clearing and onto the road, the sweet smell of the rising mist of the morning. "Oh look Mama!" Jimmy cried, "here is one of your little favourites come to see you". Jane looked up to see a fantail (*tirairaka*) flitting and frolicking down towards her from the tree canopy high above. She smiled in recognition and raised her hand in greeting, but then she settled back sensing that something was different. Instead of swooping down to circle excitedly just above her head as was the familiar salutation, the little bird, after arriving overhead, had curiously begun to fly higher. Up and up she climbed, twittering and cavorting, growing ever smaller until at last Jane's failing eyesight was no longer able to follow her and in only a few moments, even the sound of her singing was gone.

Gravely apprehensive now, Jane searched for some further sign (*tohu*) from her guardian deity (*atua kahukahu*) but to no avail. She must therefore acknowledge and take heed of the ill-omen (*aitua*) that had been sent to warn her that she must not proceed on her journey. "Take me home Jimmy, take me home". "But Mama" Jimmy began, but when he looked into his mother's eyes he came to understand and would say no more. In humble acquiescence then, he turned the horses around and started them back down the hill. Was it also in deference to the *tohu* that came to Jane on that fateful day that she should thereafter resign herself never again to venture outside the precincts of her home in Rotorua? True, it could not be denied that her health had of recent years begun to fail her and with it her renowned indefatigable spirit, but it puzzled Jimmy nevertheless that she should decide to go into retreat so meekly and without a murmur.

As the years wound down, life from the house in Whaka Road experienced many changes. Jimmy's contracting work had caused him and his family to move to Raetihi, in the King Country for four years while he was engaged in a Government scheme to salvage timber from the burnt out forests following the devastating bushfires that ravaged that region in the early 1920's. During their time there, Maggie gave birth to three sons, John, Alfred and James, each being born within 18 months of the last. Their sojourn in Raetihi was however to come to an abrupt end when the three little boys became victims of an epidemic of whooping cough, aggravated it was stated by the amount of smoke and soot-laden air that was being inhaled from the bushfires. However true that might have been, it was sufficient argument to induce Jimmy to quit his work there and return to Rotorua with his ailing infant family.

There was no-one more relieved to see the return of her favourite son and his family than Jane who had, in their absence, noticeably become more senile and enfeebled. Maggie observed also that the home had been sadly neglected during her absence even though Harry and his adult family had continued to live there. There was much to be done to restore the level of good housekeeping that had prevailed up until the time that she had left. It was shortly after Maggie had taken charge again that Jane's condition declined to the extent that she was no longer able to rise in the morning and join the family and, as the months passed into years, she became more and more infirm and impotent until finally she was confined to her bed altogether. How could she know that this was to be the beginning of seven years of a slow but inexorable slide towards the ultimate end and the colours of her rainbow were to finally fade unto death (*ki te koma te aniwaniwa, kamate te tangata*)?

Though her frail old body was to grow weaker in that time, not so her mind and her powers of observation. Confined to her bed as she was loathe to defer to, she remained ever alert and ready to intercede in even the slightest of domestic affairs. As three small boys growing up in that environment, we never ceased to wonder at the seemingly magic powers of our Granny Foley. She was known to all of us as the sole occupant of the front bedroom and none was to enter, much less touch anything in there. We could tiptoe past on our way to and from our own bedroom and, if her door was open and we were really quiet, we could take a quick peep inside, but it seemed that no matter how quiet or quick we were, she would somehow spot our presence and demand to know who we were. Then there were the plum trees outside her window in the front court. When the plums were ripe, or near enough to it for most little boys, they became a huge temptation but, it didn't seem to matter how stealthily we sneaked around the side of the house to come up close to them, the moment a hand was extended to pick the first one, there would come the staccato tap, tap, tapping of an angry walking cane on the window and a high-pitched voice saying "Get away from there you naughty little boys, I will tell your father." It never ceased to mystify us how she could have known that we were there at all, but in the end, we all came to believe that it was her birds that told her.

There would be the rare occasion when our dad would gather her up in his arms like a baby and carry her down to the kitchen to sit with us for a while and it was at those times that we noticed how white and wrinkled she was and also how she knew us all by name to speak with each one in turn. Her favourite seemed to be our sister Winifred to whom she gave the ancestral name, *Hinerangi toariari* after the daughter of *Tuhourangi* and *Rongomaipapa* who lived on *Mokoia* in the sixteenth century.

And so at last the time had come for the spirit (*wairua*) of Jane to depart her mortal body and set forth on her journey to the spirit-land (*Reinga*). To cross the *Te Waiorata* and this time partake of the food prepared for her, then to descend the root-to-the-underworld (*Aka kite reinga*) and stand at the edge of the sea to await the parting of the seaweed-of-motau (*rimui motau*) before plunging into the waters-of- lamentation (*te wai o apakura*) to proceed through the underworld of the Great-lady-of-the-night (*Hinenuitepo*). *Haere, haere ki te po!* She died at the age of 96 years on 24th June 1933 at the Rotorua Hospital and, in accordance with her last wishes, a *tangi* was held for her in the *Tamatekapua* meeting house on the *Papaiouru Marae* at *Ohinemutu*, after which a service was held at *St Faith's Anglican Church* before she was taken to the Rotorua Cemetery to be buried in the family grave there to lay with her son John William, daughter Margaretha-May and also, by that time, an infant great-grandchild, Robert Dwyer, the second son of Harry's daughter, May. Only one year later, Harry Foley died from a tetanic viral infection contracted after being kicked by a young horse that he and his brother Jimmy were breaking-in. He too was buried in the family grave.

Then came the fateful year of 1936 by which time Maggie had given birth to two more sons, Charles in 1929 and Robert in 1935, and we had all moved out of the house in Whaka Road and into our newly completed home in Wairoa Road which was in the same neighbourhood. Suddenly it was our sister Winifred who was stricken with a lethal and then unknown virus which was to act with such rapacity that despite the most desperate efforts of the hospital staff, within eight days she would be dead. It was not until many years (and inexplicable deaths) later that the virus was isolated and identified as a deadly amoeba which frequented the natural thermal bathing springs of the region and entered through the nasal passages of its highly susceptible victims. This would possibly account for many of the mysterious and untimely deaths recorded in Rotorua in those early years including that of Margaretha-May and little Robert Dwyer. In hindsight also, it was possible that Jimmy, on coming to accept that this merciless, unrelenting pestilence was about to take the life of his only daughter, should himself succumb to a massive heart attack that would leave him lying stretched out across the garden path on the morning that we found him, fully dressed in his riding clothes, his horse saddled up and ready to take him to the hospital to spend another day in prayer at her bedside.   He died on the first day of November 1936 and, on the fifth day Winifred was to follow. She was but sixteen years old.

Thus, in the course of four short years, there came the end of a virtual dynasty steeped in the early history of the New Zealand wars, its cultural heritage and pioneering achievement.   Tragically however, it was to leave a terribly aggrieved Maggie all alone in the world with five little boys to care for. Whither would she take them?   How were they to fare? Ah but that's another story. This was Jane's.

Maori Prophecy (Matakite)

Kei tua te awe mapara, he tangata ke
(Behind the tattooed face, a stranger stands)
Mana e noho te ao nei – he ma
(He will inherit this world – he is white)

————————————————

Other Works by the Same Author

1) Motiti Adventure

A short story of yesteryear, of a troubled family and a Magic Island as seen through the eyes of a seven-year old boy.

"As for our Motiti adventure, it would remain in our memories forever though it was not that many years later that we grew into adulthood ourselves, the whole world around us changed dramatically and we each went our own separate ways. But the saga set in a bygone era, that which had passed on and could never be lived through again, would continue to hold a very special place in our hearts, a price less gift to be treasured always" (finale).

2) A Sprinbok Tale

The story of the South African high veld, Rotorua and Rugby, and the epic adventures of a very gallant New Zealand soldier.

Grains in the Sands of Time

Not the triumph of man in times of war
Nor the glory that victory may bring
Not the return to the homeland, the job well done
Nor the praises and welcome awaiting
Not the life thereafter in peace to succeed
Nor the labours of love that give joy
But the message that rides on the wings of chance
And crosses the oceans of time
That brings his greatest reward

A.D.Foley

3) Pharzie

The story of a horse who was almost human, and the family he grew up with. (The sequel to **"Jane's Story"** and how Maggie survived her terrible ordeal and found a new life for her five little boys).

"Came the end of the year 1950 and by then the transformation that had beset that bewildered little family of bereft widowed young mother, her five little boys and a very special chestnut pony, all of whom only thirteen years beforehand had found themselves uprooted from the security of their home in Rotorua and transported to a whole new world of different people, different places and different ways of living, was complete. The zenith had been reached, the job well done. Regrettably though, by then Jimmy Wade had died and Maggie was left a widow once again although this time she didn't have the same worries, her sons were grown up and her future was secure".